Neo-Industrial Organising

Much discussion among researchers and academics has focused on the ongoing transition to a new economy and to a new society. Popular terms to describe this transition have been 'post-industrial society', 'information society' and 'late capitalism'. Yet, perhaps the most profound changes have concerned the way in which economic activities are organised in industry as well as elsewhere.

Neo-Industrial Organising explores an emerging area of importance in management and organisation studies, namely the trend towards a projectisation of the economy as a whole and the inter- and intraorganisational relations of renewal projects. By reporting on the experiences of 25 renewal projects from a wide variety of both local and international organisations, the authors develop a theoretical framework based on action and knowledge, in order to answer such key questions as: What is neo-industrial management? What does the future hold for organisations? How will institutions be formed? What effects will neo-organising have on the individual and his or her work situation? Topics covered include:

* industrial renewal, organisation and management
* project management and temporary organisation
* personnel recruitment, selection and training
* the crucial balance: permanent vs. temporary

Distinctive, relevant and accessibly written, this book will interest researchers and students in the field of organisational behaviour.

Eskil Ekstedt is Associate Professor at the University of Uppsala and a Senior Researcher at the National Institute for Working Life, Stockholm. **Rolf A. Lundin** is Professor in Business Administration at Umea University, Sweden. **Anders Söderholm** is Associate Professor at the Royal Institute of Technology, Stockholm. **Hans Wirdenius** is Senior Research Associate at the FA Institute for Research on Business and Work.

Routledge Advances in Management and Business Studies

Neo-Industrial Organising

Renewal by action and knowledge
formation in a project-intensive economy

**Eskil Ekstedt, Rolf A. Lundin,
Anders Söderholm and Hans Wirdenius**

London and New York

First published 1999
by Routledge
11 New Fetter Lane, London EC4P 4EE

Simultaneously published in the USA and Canada
by Routledge
29 West 35th Street, New York, NY 10001

Routledge is an imprint of the Taylor & Francis Group

© 1999 Eskil Ekstedt, Rolf A. Lundin, Anders Söderholm and
Hans Wirdenius

Typeset in Baskerville by
Prepress Projects, Perth, Scotland
Printed and bound in Great Britain by
Biddles Ltd, Guildford and King's Lynn

British Library Cataloguing in Publication Data
A catalogue record for this book is available
from the British Library

Library of Congress Cataloging in Publication Data
Neo-industrial organising : renewal by action and knowledge
    formation in a project-intensive economy / Eskil Ekstedt... [et
    al.]
    p. cm. – (Routledge advances in management and business
    studies : 9)
    Includes bibliographical references and index.
    1. Industrial organization. 2. Project management. 3.
    Knowledge management. I. Ekstedt, Eskil, 1945–. II. Series.
    HD31.N434   1999
    338.9–dc21   98-31605
    CIP

ISBN 0 415 20334 1

Contents

**7 Marrying action and knowledge formation
   in 25 renewal projects** **155**

8 Neo-industrial managing **186**

9 Neo-industrial organising – implications and prospects **209**

Illustrations

Figures

Tables

Preface

The four authors of this book have come to the study of project-oriented businesses from different academic backgrounds (business administration, economic history and psychology) and from a variety of general life experiences. We soon came to realise not only that projects are crucial for the businesses being studied but also that they seem to be poorly understood either as practical phenomena or from a theoretical point of view. Furthermore, after scrutinising the business literature, we quickly concluded that projects have (with a few very important exceptions) rarely been considered in the study of organisations. Since projects appear to be very important to many businesses, and because project professionals across industries have formed themselves into worldwide groups such as the Project Management Institute (PMI) and the International Project Management Association (IPMA, formerly Internet), we decided to study projects as phenomena.

Our original intention was to investigate a wide variety of projects with the aim of determining how they function 'internally' and how they can be described in different settings and without placing too much emphasis on defining a priori what a project might be. At the same time, we examined all the literature we could find on the theoretical and practical aspects of projects. Empirically, from the outset we chose to study pairs of projects that we expected to have something in common but also to exhibit some evident differences. Thus, we have studied a wide variety of projects, including the development of a new opera (*Lolita*, with music by the Russian composer Rodion Schedrin) as well as product development in an industrial setting (the new Volvo 850) and an attempt to renew industrial production (the T50 project of ABB). During analysis of the projects we found this general notion of simultaneously 'maximising' and 'minimising' differences very useful. The variety of projects studied provided an interesting set of inputs for our discussions and our attempts to relate our cases to the literature that we had studied. The variety was also very useful when we expanded the empirical work to other cases at a later stage.

When analysing the data collected and our impressions of the projects, we attempted to make a critical assessment of our conclusions and to evaluate why we came up with those interpretations. Some of the results of this phase of our work have been reported elsewhere (see the references in the bibliography with ourselves as authors). Eventually, however, our reflections and our discussions about the projects we studied led us away from individual cases and towards analysis at a synthetic level. There emerged from the totality of projects that we studied a pattern that we have tentatively labelled *neo-industrial organising*. This emerging pattern led to a reanalysis of projects that we had studied in the past. The projects had one thing in common: they were all related to some aspects of *renewal* ambitions and had a bearing on industry. To be more precise, *action* as demonstrated in the projects and the learning gained through action emerged as a basis for renewal efforts in which *knowledge formation* in relation to the host organisation also played an important role. One important aspect of our work has been to relate what we have seen to recent theoretical developments.

It is the results of these interpretations, deliberations and developments that can be found in the present book, in which we aspire to describe what we mean by neo-industrial organising. We consider how the field has been developing as well as the empirical data upon which we build our conjectures, and we also provide some of the theoretical bases for the statements made. Rather than mimicking the historic–logical structure of this preface, the book places the emphasis on the neo-industrial processes. In our view, projects and temporary organisations play prominent roles in those processes. We believe (on the basis of what we have seen) that temporary organisations will in the future dominate industry and transform it into something that has never been seen before.

Even though the four of us have different backgrounds, we tend to describe ourselves primarily as organisational researchers ambitious to add to that theoretical field. Nevertheless, we must admit that we feel that our main contribution in this book is not on the level of individual organisation but on a meso level, over and above the individual organisation. The main thesis is that projectisation plays an important role on that meso level. Critics might very well suggest that we started out by studying projects and, lo and behold, they were found to be important. To those we say: please read the book and tell us where pragmatic or theoretical arguments went wrong.

Acknowledgements

We are indebted to many organisations and to many individuals for various kinds of support. Access to the projects studied and to the people involved in them has been very easy for us. All actors we have encountered in the field have been extremely constructive to and supportive of our work. We have indeed enjoyed good rapport all along, for which we are very grateful. The Swedish Council for Research in the Humanities and Social Sciences, Bank of Sweden Tercentenary Fund and the Swedish Council for Work Life Research have provided generous financial support for our studies on projects and temporary organisations. The same generosity has been bestowed upon us by our own host organisations. Routledge, and in particular Stuart Hay, has been very supportive in getting this book project into its final form. Four anonymous reviewers working for the publisher provided us with very important inputs for the writing process. And we have had the pleasure of working in very creative settings and of discussing our findings with a wide range of people. Some of them belong to the International Research Network on Organising by Projects (IRNOP) and some of them are colleagues in the various settings where we are involved. To anyone not mentioned, you are not forgotten; to all of you we say 'thank you'.

Now that this particular project has come to its conclusion, there are also reasons to say thank you to each other. It has been an exciting learning process for us. Being a group of four covering an age range of at least three generations and working together for a considerable time has been a thrill. Not only these generation differences but also our different backgrounds have proved useful in our discussions. Together these differences have formed the bases for combinatorics and pluralistic integration to allude to two concepts we will be using in the book. The alderman in the author group is Hans Wirdenius, and we dedicate this book to his wife, Birgit Wirdenius (Hans has no say in this!), to whom we are grateful for providing for us so well at endless meetings in the Wirdenius home.

Eskil Ekstedt, Rolf A. Lundin, Anders Söderholm and Hans Wirdenius

Abbreviations

ABB	Asea Brown Boveri
CSN	Central Study Support Committee
EPQ	efficiency–productivity–quality (in the Västerbotten Medical Care Area renewal project)
ICT	information communication and technology
IPMA	International Project Management Association
IRNOP	International Research Network on Organising by Projects
IT	information technology
JAS 39 Gripen	A combined fighter, fighter–bomber and scouting plane
K-Concept	continuous improvement of quality, capital, cost, communication and knowledge to develop competitive power to win customers (in the Sunds Defibrator renewal project)
NICs	newly industrialised countries
NIM	neo-industrial management
PM	project manager
pmbok guide	Project Management Body of Knowledge Guide (issued by the Project Management Institute)
PMI	Project Management Institute
PO	permanent organisation
STIS 2000	Study Support Information System (in the Central Study Support Committee renewal project)
3T	total time thinking (in the Skanska Construction renewal project)
T50	50 per cent reduction in order-to-delivery times (in the Asea Brown Boveri renewal project)
TO	temporary organisation
TO(d)	regular, recurring product development project
TO(p)	regular, recurring production project
TO(u)	unique temporary organisation
VL	Västerbotten Medical Care Area

1 Neo-industrial organising – issues and challenges

Features of neo-industrial organising

For several decades there has been incessant talk about an ongoing transition to a new economy and a new society. The discussion has covered a wide variety of attempts to spell out a new society, ranging from popularised versions of brainstorming about the future to more serious research efforts. This new society has been labelled differently depending on which tendencies in the development have been emphasised. However, in most descriptions it is the traditional industrial capitalistic order that is losing its dominance. Some writers stress just that and have confined themselves to terming the emerging new situation the post-industrial society (Touraine 1971; Bell 1976). Others who are more specific about the new situation talk about the service society, the knowledge society or the information society (Machlup 1962; Drucker 1969; Helvey 1971; Lewis 1973; Martin and Butler 1981; Gershuny and Miles 1983) to mention just a few of the early and most popular denominations. In the 1980s, some writers seemed to discover another type of trend, denoted a Second Industrial Divide, with expanding industrial districts characterised by flexible, specialised networks (Lorentzoni 1981; Piore and Sabel 1984). The network metaphor has also been used to describe connections between companies as relation oriented as opposed to transaction oriented and the effects that this might have on the functioning of the economic life in society (Johansson and Mattson 1987; Powell 1990; Jarillo 1993). There have also been company-level attempts to describe a new order, with the focus on flexibility of response to customer demands and market changes and in which important economic activities are not necessarily confined to the individual, legal entity – the corporation – but extend to a set of important relationships between different types of entities in the economic sphere. In attempting to characterise such organisational traits the terms virtual organisation (Davidow and Malone 1992) and imaginary organisation (Hedberg *et al.* 1997) have been coined.

We do not repudiate these descriptions. Each one of these trends, extrapolations or methods of description holds a great deal of substance. The service sector has expanded and employs more people than the pure industrial sector in a majority of the so-called industrial nations (Singelman 1978; Forsman 1984). The institutionalised development of knowledge in schools, universities and companies has increased markedly (e.g. Louise database 1996). The same applies to modern information technology (IT), which has spread to all parts of society. And the current search for new, loose organisational forms indicates that the notion of a virtual organisation is in fact very real. In many cases, however, one line of development has been inflated without consideration of the others. In addition, it is often taken for granted that the existing circumstances will in some mysterious manner give way to or be replaced by this new situation. Thus, although there have been a few attempts at integration (Handy 1989; Kanter 1989), there is still a need not only to combine descriptions and analyses of the previous type of situation in order to envisage the totality of developments through synthesis, but also to outline how the transformation or the transition is taking place or is to take place.

We will focus on the transformation, or more precisely on the organisational aspects of this transformation. Dramatic changes at various levels – macro, micro as well as meso – can be observed. An entirely new organisation in business and industry begins to emerge. A new work division is to be seen, and new modes of working in organisations are developing. In addition, economic activities are appearing in new organisational forms. However, these changes, even if revolutionary, are not always easy to discern. In fact, as can be seen throughout economic history, changes seldom develop in definite jumps but rather occur gradually and in small steps. However, they can still be highly dramatic during a human lifetime. One often seems to exaggerate changes in the short term and at the same time underestimate them in the long term. Many individuals have experienced during their lifetime the transition of society from an agrarian to an industrial one. Such a transition could also involve change from tradition-bound work undertaken together with, or in close contact with, other members of the family or village to a hierarchical and rule-directed work organisation with consequent social isolation and alienation. And the transition often necessitated change of domicile, sometimes even native country. Residence and place of work became separated, as did working hours and what is called leisure time. However, despite these fundamental changes, it is important to remember that the agrarian sector still exists as a solid, supporting sediment in the modern economy. Agrarian production has increased rather than decreased in most, if not all, industrialised countries, and even though fewer people are directly employed in agriculture, many are still involved in the handling of its outputs through the trading and catering businesses. Similarly, we can see the development of industrial activities. Industrial production is still expanding in a trend-bound way because, even though the number of people directly employed in traditional industry is declining, many people work in activities that support industry. Detailed statistical evidence in support of these statements is available (Singelman 1978; Aoyama and Castells 1994; Furåker 1995).

The fact that industrial products have become more numerous and have changed and grown more complex during the 200-year history of this epoch is something that we are constantly reminded of as consumers and through the media. The concurrent conversion of the industrial organisation into a new form of organisation, a neo-industrial organisation – or rather into a new form of organising – neo-industrial organising (to stress the becoming rather than the being aspect of industry) – has not received the same attention. This can in part be explained by old ideas having survived within certain spheres of society. In large sections of the educational system, industry is still portrayed as being typified by an old-fashioned factory with massive, fixed capital and assembly-line production controlled by multilevel managerial decisions. This perception – outdated as it is – does not take into consideration the fact that the majority of the well-educated staff of many consulting firms actually work in industry-related projects. In addition, industrial robots and computerised procedures have taken over much of the physical production, which in turn accounts for the trend towards decreased employment but increasing production within industry in most developed countries. Neo-industrial development is associated with another type of capital-intensiveness in industry, and with other forms of knowledge, as well as with other ways of exploiting available resources. In other words, we are not experiencing the end of industry, of industrial production or of capital intensity in industry, but industry is changing and taking on new, alternative forms in which production *per se* is less in focus than previously.

Today's neo-industrial economy thus exhibits many of the features that have been described in the futurological books. It is knowledge as well as service intensive, utilising an information technology that is developing and spreading at a rapid pace. We believe, however, that the most radical change in our daily work is to be found in the way in which economic activities are organised. Old routines, roles and rules are being transformed into or exchanged for new ones. Knowledge and conceptions of work and its organisation are changing. Large production units are being replaced and/or supplemented with flexible organisations. Temporary organisations and projects are becoming more common (Boznak 1996; Dinsmore 1996; Eriksson 1997) as instruments. Rule systems, traditions and other institutions, are becoming obsolete in the same way as in the agrarian society during the traditional industrialism. There are good reasons for asking whether those institutions that handled renewal in traditional industrial societies will also work in a neo-industrial economy. The changes also suggest that the traditional relations between work and leisure of industrialism should be reconsidered. What will happen to permanent terms of employment and spatially stationary places of work? Will the view of work change dramatically? And how will the aspirational lifestyles and inclinations of today's relatively well-educated young people (who have grown up with computer games and Net surfing rather than with fairy tales) fit into the transformation? In short, what are the crucial aspects in the developments of a neo-industrial economy and in what ways can they be understood?

Thus we can visualise an economy in which production of goods still has an important, traditional, influence. But it is becoming more and more complex; products are becoming more sophisticated, and are often supplemented by advanced services. The way of organising economic activities is also becoming increasingly flexible. Large permanent organisations, the industrial enterprises, are supplemented by and combined with smaller, temporary organisations in which Schumpeterian tendencies for revival (Schumpeter 1966) could be said to be built in. Much concrete economic activity is carried out in time-delimited projects, while the overall coordination of activity and planning is still handled by entities of a permanent type: companies, industrial groups and various kinds of authorities. However, it is the relation between the temporary and the permanent activity that is the overall focus of this book. Today's industrial institutions are in many respects relics of the past, when this relation was of less importance. We maintain, supported by evidence from empirical studies, that this relation is fundamental for understanding and dealing with industry as it is now emerging.

We believe that the neo-industrial form already has an important influence on the economy, and that this influence is continuing to grow. The question is whether this trend can be verified empirically. There is no simple answer to this. Most indicators have been constructed to support another view of industrial activities. There are, however, a great number of direct as well as indirect indicators showing that the traditional way of organising is changing. What will come instead is perhaps not quite clear. In addition, such comprehensive conversions are often so slow to develop and long-term that they are seldom captured by general statistics. What is apparent, however, is that traditional industrial work is decreasing, and that service production is increasing – not least the industry-related part of it. There are also indications that industries or businesses that are dominated by project organisation are growing in number, and that the flow process in traditional organisations is being replaced by project organisation, or at least is being supplemented by projects.

In what follows we will base our arguments primarily on trends in organisations, most of which in one way or the other are related to Sweden. The selection of organisations certainly implies a bias like any other selection would. However, these trends are of a general nature. The Swedish structural transformation is at an early stage from an international perspective, and the Swedish economy has very strong international links. Some of the companies we have studied have a multinational character as well, with centres in different countries.

Three observations

We have scrutinised a wide selection of projects (or temporary organisations) from the fields of product development, organisational change, building construction, societal change, theatre activity, etc. Whereas a permanent organisation supposedly has a complicated goal structure that is expected to govern behaviours in the organisation over periods of time, a project is generally defined by a fairly clear-cut task to be fulfilled within an imaginary time limit subject to resource restrictions. Since most projects emanate from permanent organisations, we relate the projects to their host organisation (or to their host organisations in the case of a many-to-one relationship) to understand better the interplay between temporary and permanent economic activity. We do so by reviewing empirical evidence and by applying a wide variety of theoretical approaches. Recently, we have made three general observations that we find very important to keep in mind when analysing the developments in the field.

1   *The prevalence of projects is increasing.* The use of projects and temporary organisations seems to be on the increase in industry as well as in society at large. Project work and project vocabulary play increasingly important and general roles in life for most of us, and at the same time project matters are becoming increasingly important in economic life. There is an abundance of projects in the economy, and projects *per se* as well as project vocabulary are finding new applications.

2   *Relations between permanent and temporary organisations are poorly developed.* Thinking about permanent organisations and about temporary organisations seems to be well developed practically and to some extent also theoretically (although there seems to be more potential for substantially new theoretical development in the field of temporary organisations). However, although this is true for the two fields considered separately, understanding and coping with relationships between what is considered to be permanent and what is considered to be temporary appears to be much less well developed to say the least.

3   *The character of permanent organisations is undergoing transformation.* Even though understanding permanent organisations in terms of theory is in some ways very well developed, the general character of permanent organisations appears to be changing. The recent fashion for outsourcing is only one minor facet of this change. Consequently, permanence in the traditional sense should not be taken for granted in this era when change and renewal are not only lauded but regarded as indispensable. As indicated by some organisation researchers, there is also a need to redefine the permanent (see, for example, Jarillo 1993 and Davidow and Malone 1992).

The transformation dilemma and the renewal paradox

These observations lead us to the main focus of this book: *renewal* or, to be more precise, *organisational renewal*. On the one hand, it appears that the transformation of traditional industrial organisations in the neo-industrial direction requires extraordinary renewal efforts. Certainly, some of the cases we studied exhibited a project-intensive structure. For example, a major tool in the T50 programme of ABB was the introduction of goal-directed groups working in a project fashion. On the other hand, it seems that the invasion of project organisation in itself changes the conditions for renewal. The built-in motor for renewal by technical change that one finds in traditional – and permanent – capital-intensive flow production activities loses much of its power in a projectised economy and has to be supplemented. The interplay between long-term engagements in permanent organisations and the short-term activity of temporary organisations enters the agenda.

In the traditional permanent industrial organisations there exist well-developed systems for education and research which are assigned the task of supporting the renewal of economic activity. In these systems, the focusing on technological development and on exploiting technological advances plays a prominent part. Special roles or even special subunits for renewal work have also developed in companies. They are distinct from those roles concentrating on current, routine operations.

Engineers, in recent decades brought together in separate R&D departments, in the main still work on the technological development of the production process. By improving the real capital assets, and to some extent the products, and through the purchase of new equipment it has been possible to increase the efficiency of operations that have mainly been engaged in large-scale production of goods. The technological conditions to a considerable degree determine the organisational set-up.

In recent years, technological development has to an ever-increasing extent been supplemented by ventures focusing on staff development carried out by individuals with a degree in psychology or professionals in industrial training working directly or on a consultancy basis. Most large permanent organisations have in-company training programmes (Eurich 1985; Ekstedt 1988).

In spite of recent changes, it is not to be expected that the almost automatic renewal power built into the traditional industrial organisation can transform itself and be adopted to the neo-industrial setting. Existing renewal institutions have difficulties in handling a customer-close, knowledge-intensive and flexible economic activity. The modern technology is not imperative but does have many different potential uses. Hence the greater organisational freedom that is afforded by modern technology produces an increased pressure for individual and organisational development. But are current organisations capable of initiating renewal or will they compliantly adapt to the 'whims of the market'? What we see are attempts to come to grips with *a transformation dilemma*; the institutions handling renewal in traditional industry, e.g. education and research institutions, have problems in coping with the transformation to the new organisational order.

The challenges for educational institutions are evident, and the question is whether traditional educational institutions have the capabilities to adapt. It appears that fundamental ontological assumptions for educational efforts have to be questioned and possibly replaced. The double challenge of education is that it has to adapt not only to the systems of today, but also to the future systems. A revival of continuing, lifelong learning can be expected (Lundgren 1998). And the concept of on-the-job training takes on new meanings.

If one maintains that education faces a double challenge, one might well say that research faces a triple challenge. Applied research should be ahead of practice and basic research should be ahead of applied research. Research delving into past practices and education based on a traditional view of the world both function to conserve ancient and outdated practices. Educational institutions (not to say educators) will experience a definite need to rethink education and to switch to other methods using new educational material. Similarly, researchers with emancipatory ambitions will have to take on the scientific establishment (Kuhn 1970).

In organisations that traditionally exhibit neo-industrial characteristics such as projectisation – for example the construction sector – there exist obvious renewal problems, as is often testified by experts or actors in the sector. It can generally be said that this sector is organised in project networks (Bröchner *et al.* 1991). Typically, a circle of mostly familiar actors form a temporary organisation with the aim of carrying through a project conceived by themselves to be more or less recurrent or even repetitive. Through long experience the participating actors have learned their roles, and these can be combined into a stable and foreseeable project process. It could be said that these roles in a way replace the stabilising function of real capital in the industrial process. The roles define how participants should act, and repetition results in stabilisation. However, by comparison with the traditional industry process, there is one important difference. Renewal institutions are almost non-existent in this production. Companies in the construction sector rarely have separate R&D departments. In reality, the permanent parts of construction firms are rather weak organisations in view of the scope of the projects. Nor is it clear how the work division between the permanent and temporary organisation sides of the construction industry is functioning or should function. A problem often discussed is how knowledge gained from one project can be made available to the next, and generally how knowledge gained in the totality of projects can find its way to future projects in the organisation.

Experience in the construction sector leads one to suspect that *a renewal paradox* is lurking in project-organised activities. The high degree of flexibility exhibited in daily activity does not seem to be reflected in long-term renewal. Each new construction project starts from scratch: the building is different, management is changed, the work crew is recruited specially for the new construction site, etc. Such organisations would be expected to be similar to a 'tent' organisation, which has been prescribed as an ideal model for survival in a complex and changing world (Hedberg *et al.* 1976). One might expect the renewal rate to be very high in these circumstances. However, as mentioned previously, that is not the perception among people involved in the business. Rather, the general feeling is that the renewal capacity has not been used to its fullest potential. The paradox is that 'the general situation and the circumstances that surround construction activities should make the companies innovative, but the fact is that they are not' (Ekstedt *et al.* 1992). Experience gained in a project seemingly evaporates when the project ends so that even mistakes are repeated. Phenomena of this type are not confined to the construction business but have also been observed in completely different project settings, e.g. in the form of routinisation in commissioned process research (Ferlie and McNulty 1997). Thus, project-organised activities are not necessarily conducive to renewal, which is a matter of concern to researchers as well as to business people.

This discussion of the transformation dilemma and the renewal paradox leads to the general, conceptual structure of the book. Essentially, industry faces two renewal problems, as described in the grossly simplified, general frame of reference for the book shown in Figure 1.1.

Thus, the argument is that the movement towards neo-industrial organising actualises two renewal problems that are of concern in this

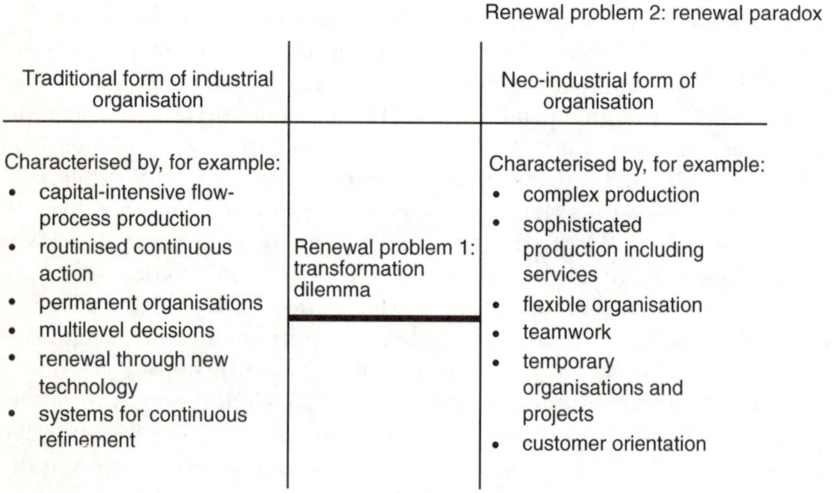

	Renewal problem 2: renewal paradox
Traditional form of industrial organisation	**Neo-industrial form of organisation**
Characterised by, for example: • capital-intensive flow-process production • routinised continuous action • permanent organisations • multilevel decisions • renewal through new technology • systems for continuous refinement	Characterised by, for example: • complex production • sophisticated production including services • flexible organisation • teamwork • temporary organisations and projects • customer orientation

Renewal problem 1: transformation dilemma

Figure 1.1 General frame of reference for the book.

book. Both problems appear to be related to the occurrence of temporary organisations and/or to the interfaces between permanent and temporary ones.

Action and knowledge formation in permanent and temporary organisations

In this book we are concerned with the contrasts between temporary and permanent organisations and the changing relationships between them. How can the connections be conceived and how can our knowledge about how they are functioning be utilised? The phenomenon of *renewal* (which will be discussed more carefully in Chapters 5, 6 and 7) is relevant for permanent as well as for temporary organisations. However, renewal implies a move away from routine and repetitious behaviours, and sometimes behaviours are greatly affected by (read governed by) the rules and the traditions that are prerequisites for the stability that permanent organisations and the surrounding society can provide. Project work that is considered to be repetitious by the project participants is equally predictable because of the strong prototypical thinking among practitioners in the project field. Thus, two main forms of renewal can be described: renewal of an individual organisation and renewal of the organisational field and of its rules and traditions. The renewal of an organisation is, of course, easier to comprehend than renewal of the field, but the latter is of more general importance.

We argue that two conditions for renewal are of more fundamental interest than others, and that they can be captured in two concepts, namely *action* and *knowledge formation*. These concepts will be defined and discussed more fully in the next two chapters. Action is singled out for its more or less inherent relation to projects, i.e. projects signal actions. For now it should be sufficient to point out that action stands for the idea that things have to happen and that action is observable in a direct sense. Essentially, projects belong to an organisational form (or an organisational mode) that distinctly promotes action. Decisions about action in projects are of virtually no interest unless they can be implemented. The action orientation is problematic since the emphasis on action presupposes deliberations about what action to take and why the chosen task is important. There is also a distinct contrast between action and talk, which is particularly important when considering the relations between temporary and permanent organisations. Projects in general are designed for action and for promoting efficiency in carrying through action, which means that effectiveness-oriented deliberation (concerning the appropriateness of action), and talk and decision making have to take place elsewhere.

Knowledge formation is an equally important prerequisite for renewal. In essence, radical renewal increases the demand for fundamentally new knowledge. However, learning and knowledge formation involve more than change or replacement of knowledge. Storing knowledge for future use can be a task for the individual, but it is likely that a permanent organisation will also be involved to provide the stability that is needed for such a task. A temporary organisation may well promote learning by providing the means to gain in experiences and through project results, but the outcome, the knowledge, has to be stored elsewhere. Moreover, individual learning and organisational learning have different characteristics and the differences have to be understood. In any case, experience gained through action and by evaluating the outcomes of action is crucial for knowledge formation, which means that both processes are essential for renewal at the organisational level.

There follows a number of statements that will be discussed in this book. These arguments, general trends and empirical cases will be the basis of our ideas:

1   The industrial society is undergoing a long-term, radical transformation towards a neo-industrial economy, spurred on by increasing demands for production flexibility and customer satisfaction and by opportunities offered by developments in information technology. Action and knowledge formation stand out as crucial factors in renewal, which is necessary for the survival or the development of organisations. Project organising evolves as an effective means of coping with the new situation: both by promoting action in the current operations and by facilitating the necessary organisational renewal (Chapter 2).

2   Both traditional organisation theory and traditional project theory are weak in dealing with renewal: the organisation theory because it does not acknowledge the action parameter (but observes the knowledge formation problem) and the project theory because it does not consider the knowledge formation aspect (but illuminates the importance of action focusing). The relationship between action and knowledge formation is, therefore, a central theme of the book (Chapter 3).

3   A broad selection of organisation renewal projects from various spheres of activity will provide an empirical basis for analysis of the relationship between action and knowledge formation, and will constitute one important foundation for our attempt to develop a neo-industrial organisation theory (Chapter 4).

4   We argue that action takes on different shapes in temporary organisations compared with permanent ones. In permanent organisations, actions generally assume a routine form, whereas temporary organisations tend to foster creative behaviour, i.e. actions of a more unique type. Temporary organisations, therefore, will have to take on the role of 'action formation partners' and in the process

provide a sense of emergency to the more routine-based permanent organisation (Chapter 5).

5 The institutionalised models for knowledge formation in real-capital-intensive permanent organisations (e.g. R&D and training), which are generally geared to incremental change, must be combined with approaches that further renewal. This can be achieved by combinatorics, by providing for diversity of experience when organising project teams and by developing means to utilise the knowledge formed in projects (Chapter 6).

6 As indicated previously, the transformation dilemma is difficult to handle. A 'happy marriage' between action and knowledge formation is a prerequisite for organisational renewal. The spheres of knowledge on which action is focused are therefore of vital importance. Action directed towards the physical and the institutional spheres has a greater impact than action directed towards the individual or the organisation. The comparative advantages of the permanent and the temporary organisations must be utilised in their interplay (Chapter 7).

7 By combining action and knowledge formation, four different organisational and leadership situations can be distinguished: the traditional permanent bureaucratic industrial organisation; the recurring temporary organisation (project) for product, process or knowledge development; the traditional recurring temporary organisation (project) for production to customers; and the temporary organisation (project) for renewal. The four situations demand managerial competence different from the traditional one, and will also introduce new management roles. One important managerial task is to ensure that the renewal paradox is dealt with appropriately (Chapter 8).

8 Some of the changes seem to have problematic consequences for individuals and for society. What are the societal, organisational and individual implications and prospects of neo-industrial organising? Will an increasing number of project-based organisations contribute to a segmented labour market? Will the new work division have detrimental effects on the organisation and the individual? Will personal work satisfaction, identity, influence, training and development be impaired in a projectised organisation? These are some of the questions which have to be dealt with in order to promote a more critical view of the developments (Chapter 9).

The aim of the book

From the traditional, social engineering point of view, the aim of this book is to discuss and analyse the two kinds of renewal problems arising from the emerging neo-industrial society that we have identified (see

Figure 1.1). Firstly, there is the transformation dilemma; institutions involved in traditional industries and faced with renewal often find it difficult to cope with the transformation to the new organisational order. Some of the renewal projects we are referring to in this book are obviously making attempts to deal with this institutional shift. Secondly, there are problems associated with the renewal paradox. The ways in which short-term flexibility of project organisation can be adapted to long-term economic renewal is a theme that will be followed up in this book. This leads us to a theory of neo-industrial organising, which focuses on an idealised division of work between permanent and temporary organisations. A second but considerably less ambitious aim of the book is to provide some critical comments on current developments.

The discussion of this introductory chapter will be followed up in the book by answering the following questions:

- What are the characteristics of neo-industrial organising?
- In what ways does the renewal process in the neo-industrial setting differ from that in traditional industry?
- What is the role of temporary organisations and what are their relations to permanent organisations when it comes to renewal and how do they interact in order to bring about renewal?
- Can the neo-industrial form of organisation be understood by applying organisation theory; what would such a theory look like?
- How should leaders of neo-industrial economic activity combine organisations with different characters?
- How might the developments outlined be problematic?

To sum up, one can say that this book highlights challenges for general managers, project managers, organisation, management and information technology consultants, project consultants and researchers. How should leaders and other actors handle the transformation to a neo-industrial order and how should they initiate and manage renewal processes in neo-industrial organisations? Consequently, it also challenges the present state of research. Presently, far too little knowledge is available about action and knowledge formation in project-intensive parts of the economy and especially about the relation between permanent and temporary parts of economic activity. The renewal aspects of traditional organisational and project management theory are questioned. In this sense, the book is critical of the appropriateness of present theory, but the intention is also to present some indications of critical views on neo-industrial organising *per se*. The neo-industrial situation is not free from problems but should be scrutinised with a critical eye.

Finally, a word about the writing style. Project managers are generally men so, for the sake of simplicity, managers and other actors are generically referred to as 'he'. When describing actual cases, 'she' will be used when appropriate; however, in only two cases were project managers female. It may well be that project management thinking is male thinking. For the time being, we leave aside that critical comment as being less important than our endeavour to describe neo-industrial organising as it seems to be developing at the present time.

2 Towards a project-intensive economy

In this chapter, long-term transformation processes are outlined in an attempt to clarify the economic background against which a project-intensive economy has developed. We will also attempt to describe the processes underlying the development of a project economy. It will be argued that a variety of push and pull factors are involved in the transformation, ranging from changing consumer demand patterns to exploitation of IT. Various aspects of the neo-industrial movement as it is now emerging will be commented upon, and, in particular, we will examine the projectisation phenomenon.

Traditional industrial organisation challenged

The dynamism and success of the traditional industrial–capitalist mode of production depends on a capacity to change. This encompasses, on the one hand, the development of new products and combinations of products, new technology, new types of organisation and new markets, and, on the other, the continuous reorganisation and elimination of any parts of the supply system – including the people in it – that represent an obsolete and inefficient production technology. This system has promoted a continuous renewal of knowledge for a long period. As long as start-ups either match or slightly exceed eliminations, the changes are perceived as predominantly positive, even when the rate of change is very rapid. This was the case during the golden age of the industrialised world in the 1950s and 1960s.

This period was characterised by a high level of economic growth, moderate inflation and low unemployment in the Western world. The increase in industrial production was impressive and, on the whole, very stable. Industrial investments showed much the same trend, although naturally with bigger fluctuations. During the 1950s – and even more so during the 1960s – productivity also increased rapidly. In fact, the increase was so fast that it cannot be explained solely in terms of investment and technological development; it was also due to structural improvements following eliminations and the replacement of obsolete and inefficient organisations and machines.

Since the mid-1960s, however, the balance between start-ups and shut-downs seems to have been disturbed in some countries, e.g. the United States and Sweden. In some other Western European countries, these changes took place somewhat later. The basic industries – notably the textile and clothing industries, mining and the iron and steel industry – which represented the backbone of the golden age successes, were losing ground without being completely counterbalanced by other expanding activities such as the manufacturing and pharmaceutical industries.

Developments in industry changed so fundamentally after the middle of the 1960s that we could speak of a structural shift. A new division of labour in society as a whole was introduced. As in earlier phases in the history of the industrial society, events in the iron and steel industry seem to have played a particularly crucial role in these disruptions. Reconstruction after the Second World War led to a shortage of steel, which lasted until the early 1960s. Capacity for steel production was increased enormously, particularly in the newly industrialised countries (NICs) and Japan. It seems that the golden age of iron and steel coincided with that of the traditional industrial society. And the end of both is becoming increasingly apparent.

The decline in steel production and heavy industry has had major regional effects, not to say repercussions, in Western Europe and in the United States. Economic life in much of the English Midlands, in the American 'rust belt', in Belgium, in northern France and in Bergslagen in Sweden has been dominated by large, specialised companies. The steel companies of the German Ruhr area have sometimes been described as 'cathedrals in the desert' to signify their domination, as whole communities had been built up around them. The rationalisation of steel production and the problems facing the giants of steel thus paralysed the economic life of the area. What remains of Swedish steel production today consists mainly of the manufacture of special steel, which is confined to a small number of mills. In Germany, several of the large steel companies have increased their investments in knowledge-intensive operations, including, for instance, equipment for environmental control (Grabher 1989), but the fact remains that total production of iron and steel has decreased in the 'old' industrial countries. This example from the iron and steel industry serves to illustrate the structural shift phenomenon.

The economic historian Lennart Jörberg maintains that three important structural shifts have occurred in the past hundred years (Jörberg, 1982). The first occurred in the last quarter of the nineteenth century (1873–96) and was most marked during the 1880s; the second took place during the 1920s and early 1930s; and the last one during the 1970s. These structural shifts also define the different stages in the development of the capitalist society: from the developed agrarian phase, through the traditional industrial phase and into what we would prefer to call the neo-industrial era.

Thus, the first of these structural shifts marks the breakthrough of modern industrial society. Industrial development up to 1870 was characterised by the introduction of new techniques into the manufacture of already familiar products such as iron and textiles. However, from that point on, development meant the renewal of both products and processes, and this in turn resulted in a dramatic change in the conditions of human life. New means of communication created opportunities previously undreamed of. The transmission of energy was revolutionised. Towards the end of the nineteenth century electricity began to bring power and light into workplaces and homes. But there was also another side to this transformation: the possibility of earning a living in many old established lines of business or industry vanished. Professional traditions and vocational pride were demolished in one blow. Organisational ideals such as Taylorism were introduced. The development of transoceanic transport and American agricultural machinery left European agriculture open to tough competition, with the result that this hitherto important industry faced a deep and profound crisis. In the iron industry the innovations led to extensive rationalisations and consequent shut-downs, followed by mass unemployment and migration. On the start-up side, however, there were also a number of important innovations during this period. In addition to the electrotechnical industry, the chemical industry and the railways were both growing dramatically. It was also during this period that 'inventor companies', such as Siemens, AEG, L M Ericsson and ASEA (now Ericsson and ABB, respectively, which are discussed in this book), appeared on the scene.

The revolutionary economic changes that occurred after the First World War culminated in the profound crises that hit the world economy in 1921 and 1930. In Sweden, the first of these crises was the deepest. The 1930s depression reached Sweden late, and its effects were, in fact, less devastating than in other parts of the world. Adjustment had been difficult after the First World War, when the overheated economic climate of the war years gave way to more normal conditions. A number of poor investments were exposed and many companies were unable to cope with the increasingly tough competition. The result was massive reconstructions of several businesses and industries. Some companies disappeared and others were reconstructed, particularly as regards their economic status. However, in parallel with financial consolidation there was also a general radical restructuring of operations. Much of industry was given the thorough overhaul that it so badly needed. After this radical cure, Swedish industry coped surprisingly well with the external pressures of the world depression. This structural transformation may also have contributed substantially to the successes of the post-Second World War period.

During the 1970s, investments in machinery, typically 'rationalisation' investments, were more important than investments in buildings ('expansion' investments). By analogy with the two previous structural shifts, it could perhaps be said that the turn of the millennium is experiencing a change from a stagnation period characterised by substantial rationalisation to an innovative expansionist phase, in which computers, other electronic technology and biotechnology are the driving forces, just as the electricity and the communication industries were in an earlier era.

However, the fact that the introduction of a completely new technology creates major organisational problems of adjustment cannot be denied. The economic historian Paul David has claimed that the impact of electrification on the organisation of industry was so strong as to inhibit productivity growth for about 20 years (David 1990). Modern IT constitutes, if possible, an even greater techno-economic paradigm shift that might still be in its infancy. Thus, the economist, Robert Solow, has pointed out that 'you can see computers everywhere but in the productivity statistics' (the so-called Solow paradox; Lundgren and Wirberg 1997). However, computers are not only capable of controlling production, they can also be exploited for administrative tasks. The division of labour between and inside different kinds of organisations can now be fundamentally altered. Virtually, the physical potential of decentralisation knows no bounds.

Modern IT can intervene in a very resolute way in the design of organisations, as illustrated by the example of the Central Study Support Committee (CSN) in Sweden. CSN is an organisation whose role is to distribute grants to university students, and until recently it consisted of 12 local, relatively autonomous, units each allocating grants in its own region. Although interchange of information between units certainly occurred through training and directions, each individual unit essentially operated independently. However, quite recently a computer system capable of handling all operations for the entire CSN was introduced. As a result, the organisation changed drastically. It became possible for everyone in the organisation to access the system and to deal with any case. Managers were now in control of an integrated organisation in which geographic distances were of no importance. It was easy to see how the workload was distributed and, as a result, local imbalances could be avoided (Ekstedt and Wirdenius 1994a).

Thus, by utilising IT, individuals performing the same work tasks can be physically separated, although the roles of coordination and customer contact and the exercise of power by top management are unchanged. Because employees are directly connected to the technology, managers can monitor exactly how they work, and as occurred in CSN, periods of work shortage can be filled with training via the computer screen. Foucault's image of the automatic power of a panopticon seems to have come true. His physical model envisaged a circular prison in which each cell has two windows, one facing away from the circle and one facing the centre of the circle, in which there is a tower with a place for a prison guard, who is able to see everybody through one-way mirrors or screens. Since prisoners believe in his presence he has a disciplining influence on them (Foucault 1987). This serves to illustrate that a technical design can enforce a uniform behaviour and a particular cultural adaptation. Although it is true that exchange via the IT system is characterised by communication between the actors, power relations may also come to be cultivated and changed. Knowledge and power are closely related.

Computerisation and IT

Computerisation thus provides managers with an efficient control tool that frees them from many mundane day-to-day activities. In this way, decentralisation is actually based on an efficiently centralised communication system. Another remarkable feature of the computer is its enormous usefulness in the service activities. The steering of enterprises and other organisations can be rendered more effectively by the ability to combine masses of economic and production information in a clear and distinct way. Innumerable routine tasks can now be automated. The cashier is replaced by plastic cards and the typist by the word processor. Human input can be concentrated to various knowledge-intensive tasks. There can be more direct contact with customers and clients.

At the same time, computerisation involves a dramatic increase in the volume of information. More and more people have to be engaged in advanced auxiliary tasks – sorting, processing and interpreting information, i.e. preparing the ground for various executive functions. These changes in work organisation in industry and the service sector are certainly creating a new and growing need for training – for people already employed as well as for potential newcomers – and for other types of knowledge formation.

The question is whether this most recent transformation is any more fundamental than the changes that occurred at the end of the nineteenth century or during the 1920s and 1930s. There is no doubt that overall division of labour in society is undergoing profound change. Individuals are acquiring new skills and undertaking completely new tasks. The area of services connected to industry expanded noticeably during the 1980s. This subject is also described, from a global perspective, by Castells (1996) in his discussion on the network society. Castells argues that current changes in technology and the associated accelerated rate of innovation will lead to a more flexible work situation and probably a highly segmented social structure in the near future. This also implies a change of work content and work organisation. The almost continuous increase in industrial productivity is also essential to the change. In Sweden, a substantial increase in industrial productivity occurred in the early 1990s at the same time as other spheres of the economy were experiencing major problems. By their very nature, new technology and the revolution in information processing naturally pave the way for substantial renewal. However, we should not be tempted into believing that the evolution of a new form of organising exactly coincides with the introduction of a new technology (Orlikowski 1992). The possibility that this technology would be able to have such a revolutionary impact existed long before the technology itself.

The organisational historian James Beniger has shown that during the past hundred years we have been undergoing a continuous 'control revolution', which has been a prerequisite for our capacity to exploit modern IT (Beniger 1986). The most important technical innovations have always been related to organisational innovations. The evolution of new processes or products in the production apparatus has led to the development of service functions in companies and societies. For example, before railways could function properly it was necessary to expend effort in coordinating and developing logistical systems such as timetables. At the same time questions of general safety became a matter of juridical public concern. Another example is that, before cars could be efficiently mass produced, it was necessary for all the components to be standardised and controlled. Bureaucracies evolved to deal with planning, research, monitoring, the allocation of jobs and the maintenance of contact with other companies and customers. These were supported and controlled in turn by a public bureaucracy in charge of such areas as education, research and legislation. Some technical inventions, such as the punched card, typewriters and calculators, appeared later to rationalise the work of these bureaucracies.

Thus, the traditional production system in permanent organisations, with its specialisation and large-scale operations, presupposes systematisation and standardisation. Time must be metered out and a clear system of logistics introduced. Only when these conditions are fulfilled can modern computer technology carry us on into a new form of production.

Increased knowledge intensity

Thus, we can assign a vast array of service functions in the corporate world and the public sector to what can be called the start-up side of the social transformation. In many cases, these services are knowledge intensive. The growing knowledge intensity – and political attempts to increase it even more – have also affected regional development. New 'development areas' have appeared. The presupposed indivisibility of knowledge development has attracted high-technology companies, consultancy firms and the development units and management functions of many large companies to knowledge-dense areas near universities and other educational and research institutes. In some cases, an attractive climate has also been a location factor. In the United States, there has been a move away from the 'rust belt' and into the 'sun belt'. Above all, the development of Silicon Valley has provided a model for many similar developments. Other famous development areas in the United States include Route 128 outside Boston, the Research Triangle in North Carolina and Orange County in southern Los Angeles. In Japan, there is Toshiba City north of Tokyo, in England the Cambridge area and the M4 corridor, in Germany the Stuttgart area, and of France's many 'technopolis' areas Sophia Antipolis outside Nice is probably the best known. In Sweden, the E4 Corridor north of Stockholm and to a lesser extent also the more recent developments of the Telecom City in Karlskrona in southern Sweden are the most important development areas of a similar character.

All these areas represent the centre of the new age, while the old industrial areas have become peripheral. Jobs in this periphery are disappearing as goods production is rationalised or possibly even moved to less developed countries. The new jobs are to be found in other industries – generally knowledge-intensive industries or services – which are plentiful in some industrial districts. This is reason for efforts to promote 'local mobilisation' conducted jointly by companies and local politicians trying to create local conditions for new knowledge-intensive operations. As will be seen in Chapter 4, we have studied three societal renewal projects within known development areas: Sophia Antipolis, Arlanda stad and Uminova stad.

The changes in their environments that companies now have to take into account are extremely complex. Short-term cyclical fluctuations are nothing new, and most actors are to some extent prepared for variations of this kind. But the long-term changes are something of which few people have any experience. Structural changes in industry such as those that occurred during the 1920s are probably familiar from hearsay, but attempts to compare them with the present situation are often regarded as exaggerated. However, some business leaders – in the steel industry for example – did point out as early as the 1960s that a violent structural change was under way.

The changeover to new forms for production is, if possible, even more difficult to visualise. The British must have found it difficult to recognise in the eighteenth century that they were involved in something as radical as the dawn of the industrial society. However, even if, against all expectations, people do recognise the change in progress, it is still very hard for them to imagine how it will affect their own lives. What is replacing the old order? There might not even be a relevant vocabulary to describe the situation?

The way in which modern society exploits knowledge appears to be particularly important. According to Joseph Finkelstein, who is both a historian and economist, we are in the midst of a third industrial revolution characterised by the widespread application of microelectronics and computer technology in production (Finkelstein 1986). In the first industrial revolution at the end of the eighteenth century, manual labour was replaced by machine power, particularly in the textile industry. Towards the end of the nineteenth century the second industrial revolution began with the introduction of electricity, soon to be followed by new chemical products and new means of transport, above all the automobile. Characteristic of this revolution was that industry now took science into its service. Characteristic of the third industrial revolution, which we are currently experiencing, however, is that science is taking industry into its service and industrial processes are being developed to serve scientific renewal. Rephrasing the Finkelstein formulation of the third industrial revolution, one might suggest that science and industry are merging to form a developmental unity emphasising renewal. One example of this is the biotechnology industry, in which production is currently relatively unimportant compared with research and product development.

Although arguments differ, there are several authors who claim that society is heading towards a new era, or that we are experiencing fundamental changes that will alter working conditions in companies and other organisations. Piore and Sabel (1984) discuss the so-called second industrial divide. According to their analysis, technology plays an important role and industrial divides occur when the path of technology development is at issue. The first industrial divide led to the development of mass production technology and subsequent development of institutions and regulations supporting mass production. Today, society is experiencing a regulation crisis in which mass production models no longer appear to be as efficient and appropriate as they once were. Companies respond to this in two different ways. Either they continue to develop a mass production model or they turn towards flexible specialisation. Of course, this choice is dependent on institutions and regulations and, consequently, areas in which mass production technology is less supported by institutions are more apt to respond to the development of new technological paths.

Storper and Salais (1997) present an action framework in which they distinguish between different categories of action and worlds of production. In addition to traditionally recognised industrial and market 'worlds', they also define interpersonal and intellectual worlds. They show that the different worlds coordinate action differently and that there are different conventions and different assumptions at work. Consequently, they criticise traditional theory on institutions and economics for being too narrow to grasp the full meaning of different 'worlds' but also for being unable to see new trends or emerging 'worlds' in today's society.

Christopher Freeman also speaks of the imminent radical restructuring of the economy, which will alter production processes in industry dramatically, as well as the production of services. Science is being used much more systematically (see, for example, Freeman *et al.* 1983). He warns of the difficult social consequences of this readjustment.

Unemployment, for example, may continue to be a problem for a long time. And, as it is not easy to predict today what kind of jobs will be needed as the new organisational forms take shape, various investments in education or other parts of the infrastructure may well turn out to have been wasted.

Thus, many researchers appear to agree that science and various aspects of knowledge formation and handling will occupy a new role in production. Finkelstein claims that science is taking industry into its service, while Freeman speaks of the more systematic exploitation of science in production. We need not choose between these interpretations here, since in one respect the result is more or less the same: there will be a broader interface between production (or industry) and science. This, in turn, will have important implications for all kinds of knowledge formation, whose extent, direction and organisation will all be affected. In particular, the balance between internal corporate knowledge formation and public knowledge formation will be altered. And the issue becomes still more complicated if one also takes into account the fact that relations between the permanent and temporary organisations of economic activity are changing. The total organisation of the traditional industrial enterprise is in question.

There are a great number of indications of a move towards higher levels of knowledge intensity in industry. Products that demand little knowledge input but a great deal of real capital are losing importance, while the volume of products requiring a large work input with a lot of knowledge is growing. Steel, pulp, paper and textiles are losing ground, while services, pharmaceuticals, computers and telecommunication systems are all engaging an increasing share of the production apparatus. Trends could be summarised as in .

According to all available indications, the main movement is towards activity with a high knowledge intensity (as shown in Figure 2.1). This is

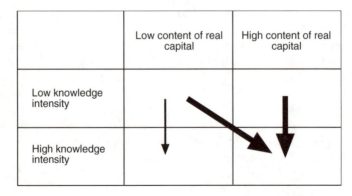

	Low content of real capital	High content of real capital
Low knowledge intensity		
High knowledge intensity		

Figure 2.1 The increasing knowledge intensity in industry.

usually combined with an advanced form of real capital, as more and more activities demand access to IT in the form of computers, the Internet and mobile phones, for example. This modern type of real capital is characterised by great flexibility, which provides scope for many different organisational solutions. Traditional capital-intensive and flow-process producing companies are combined with knowledge-intensive service activities offered by smaller organisations or smaller organisational units.

The increased knowledge intensity can be explained by a more sophisticated consumer demand and shorter product life cycles, but also by faster production cycles. In all three cases, most of the staff in the organisations will receive new impressions from the outside world at a faster pace. By involving co-workers in these developments and by diffusing knowledge to a major part of them, it will be easier to handle a fast stream of new situations. The tendencies we observe are, in other words, a question of 'knowledge widening'. However, whether or not knowledge in organisations is generally becoming deeper or more advanced or not is difficult to answer, although there does appear to be a trend (Sveiby 1997).

Service production today is quite different from the manual service transactions of an earlier age. The number of people employed in information and knowledge production has increased exponentially. A spate of new consultancy firms, particularly in the computer field, is providing services for the large companies and various institutions of society. Of the 19 million new jobs 'created' in the United States during the 1970s, only 11 per cent were in the goods-producing sector, of which 5 per cent were in the manufacturing industry while the remaining 89 per cent were in the information, knowledge and service sectors (Naisbitt 1982). In the 1980s, a considerable part of the growth in the service sector seems to have consisted of routinised and simple activities, whereas the general rapid growth in the US economy that is occurring in the 1990s has, to a considerably extent, consisted of knowledge-intensive activity.

In Sweden, corporate investment behaviour changed towards the end of the 1970s. Companies increasingly began to engage in non-material capital formation, i.e. investment in R&D, personnel and markets. Thus, the decline in material investment that occurred during the late 1970s was to a great extent compensated by a trend towards non-material investment. This was partly because the industries that were growing most rapidly, namely the manufacturing and chemical industries, were those with a high proportion of non-material investment compared with other industries. But it was also because companies in all industries are now investing more on the non-material side. And one reason for this is, of course, that they believe that the return on these investments will be bigger.

The knowledge factor has also gained in importance as internal corporate education (particularly advanced training schemes) has expanded, especially in the United States. Some large companies such as

IBM have internal education programmes similar in size to those of the major universities. N. P. Eurich has calculated that the scale of training in American companies easily matches the operations of the public colleges (Eurich 1985), even though, of course, the forms of training are different.

A comparison of the contents of advanced internal corporate training programmes on the one hand and academic programmes on the other reveals a number of differences. Corporate programmes are more operational, more goal oriented. Companies are concerned about technical solutions, new designs, new materials and new products. Commercially fruitful ideas are awarded the highest honours. In academic programmes, however, methodological knowledge stands the highest. These differences naturally stem from the entirely different conditions under which the courses are run. In the academic context, the presentation and underpinning of knowledge has an intrinsic value, whereas the corporate world, by necessity, is much more interested in knowledge that leads to decisions and action considered important for profit making.

If the yield on investment in corporate knowledge formation is as high in societal and corporate terms as is often claimed, we might well wonder why companies do not invest even more in this area. Economists explain why by invoking what they call external effects. Thus, Kenneth Arrow writes: 'A free enterprise economy will underinvest in invention and research (as compared with an ideal one) because it is risky, because the produce can be appropriated only to a limited extent' (cited by Boyle *et al*. 1984). Companies underinvest in research and training because their employees can always exploit this training elsewhere. It is not possible to put a patent on the knowledge stored in the company's all-too-slippery human capital. At the same time, it is presumably possible to reduce the cost for the company by handing over responsibilities for education and training to public institutions. An alternative option that also safeguards against the departure of key personnel might be to develop company-specific procedures or routines (knowledge of which is practically useless in another organisational context) and to invest in the training in such procedures. Such patterns are emerging in the computer and IT businesses. This dual tendency for knowledge formation may in any case be further strengthened if companies are dominated by temporary activities and if a corresponding employment situation develops.

To sum up this discussion on various aspects of knowledge intensity, one can claim that R&D activities have clearly been expanding, probably most notably in the largest companies. It is less clear how other forms of knowledge formation have been developing, partly because they are difficult to measure. However, it seems relevant to point out that new recruits increasingly tend to have some formal academic training in their background. And, as mentioned, there are also many signs suggesting that internal corporate training (mainly in large companies) is expanding. There are, furthermore, indicators that investment in market-oriented knowledge is extensive and on the increase.

Knowledge-intensive firms

Another development that confirms the growing importance of knowledge-intensiveness and temporary organisations is the evolution of what has come to be labelled *knowledge-intensive companies* or *knowledge companies*. Any discussion on this matter is complicated, however, by the loose and imprecise way in which the concept of the knowledge company has been used, especially in some of its details. The general consensus, however, seems to be that there is a kernel of usefulness (or truth if you so wish) in the concept of a knowledge company and in the descriptions in which that concept is used. One can say, however, that individually embedded knowledge of the staff is at the core of the knowledge company, much as in certain traditional institutions such as theatres or universities. According to Sveiby and Risling (1986), the 'real' value of the knowledge company cannot be inferred from a traditional balance sheet: its employees represent its value. The knowledge workers hold the real power in such a company and are frequently offered partial ownership in recognition of that fact.

The knowledge companies supply services to industrial companies and to public agencies and often start as the offshoot of an industrial company. People with special knowledge, perhaps in the computer field, establish a consultancy firm of their own. It thus becomes possible for them to utilise their knowledge in several companies at the same time. Consequently, the staff of a knowledge company is always knowledgeable in the sense that most of the time they are in fact on the very edge of knowledge in their specialised field. That does not need to be the case in a service company. The knowledge of a service company is mostly highly codified – idiosyncratic – but the main difference is that it fits only into a well-defined system. It is clear that logistics pave the way for a greater use of machines and automation. Note, for example, how hamburger chains have developed. The knowledge company sells a more differentiated range of *solutions*, which must necessarily be made customer specific and adapted to the specific circumstances at hand. For this reason, project organisation plays a dominant role.

Many companies and organisations (such as banks, hospitals and insurance companies) are engaged in the production of both services and knowledge. At the same time, a combination of services, goods and knowledge production is also becoming more common in the large manufacturing and IT corporations. Obviously, this must make heavy demands on control and management, since the production of knowledge is hardly likely to be very successful in a formal industrial organisation of a traditional type. A division of labour is sometimes introduced, whereby certain people are engaged in increasingly routinised short-term tasks while others concentrate on unique, long-term problems. It is this division that often provides the basis for an organisational split and a breakaway, whereby a separate organisational unit, and ultimately a separate company, is established for handling the long-term development problems, many of them specialised in handling time-limited projects.

Macro-level indicators

The tendencies referred to can also be confirmed on the macro level. The percentage of the workforce employed in industry (manufacturing/ transformative sector) has in the most industrialised countries decreased in recent decades. This is the case, for example, in the USA, UK, Canada, France, Italy, Germany and Sweden, as indicated below. Japan is different, however. At the same time there has been a sharp increase in what is called production services in all eight countries. These are services directly supporting industry (see Table 2.1).

Over the years and taking a long view, the changes have been drastic indeed. However, the table also indicates that changes are in fact very long term. The development of an industrial sector that is more dependent on services (and possibly also on knowledge in a loose sense) is slow, but, as indicated very clearly in the table, it undoubtedly exists. And even though there are clear differences between patterns in the eight countries, the general processes appear similar. A considerable part of the workforce is currently employed in service production in large industrial enterprises, small service companies and in knowledge-intensive infrastructure supporting industry. It has become apparent that the reduction (at least relative) in the number of industrial employees is actually compensated by a rapid increase in people occupied in industry-close service companies, i.e. independent companies working on project assignments for industry (Eliasson 1992; Illeris 1996). Taken together, this means that some institutions of the traditional industrial society are encountering difficulties

Table 2.1 The percentage of the workforce employed in the manufacturing and the production service sectors in eight industrialised countries

	1920	1940	1960	1970	1980	1990
USA	33 + 3	30 + 5	36 + 7	33 + 8	30 + 11	26 + 14
Japan	20 + 1	25 + 1	29 + 3	34 + 5	34 + 8	34 + 10
UK	42 + 3	*	46 + 5	47 + 5	36 + 8	27 + 12
Canada	26 + 4	28 + 3	31 + 5	27 + 7	27 + 10	22 + 11
France	30 + 2	30 + 2	38 + 3	38 + 6	35 + 8	30 + 10
Italy	24 + 1	*	40 + 2	44 *	41 + 5	30 *
Germany	39 + 2	*	51 + 4	47 + 5	*	40 + 7[†]
Sweden	25 + 1	34 + 2	42 + 3	40 + 5	33 + 7	28 + 9

Sources: Adapted from Singelman (1978) and Myhrholm and Ullström (1997).
*Information not available.
[†]In fact refers to information from 1987.
As sources have been combined, the information for the various countries is not entirely comparable owing to definition and measurement differences.

because much of what is important to them is in fact happening outside their boundaries. Thus, there are reasons to believe that the service sector percentages in Table 2.1 in fact reflect the transformation dilemma previously alluded to.

A transition to a neo-industrial economy does not mean, at least not necessarily, that the general production capacity of traditional industry will disappear – quite the opposite, as indicated previously. It is obvious, however, that the number of people directly employed in the production of goods will fall. In the very capital-intensive paper and pulp industry, for example, the proportion of employees in marketing, development, organisation and personnel has increased dramatically (Ekstedt 1988). In such a situation, changes in production technology will only have a very indirect influence on the work actually carried out. More and more people work in projects, and they will make use of flexible IT. This type of arrangement has great possibilities for all-round use by most people in any organisation – irrespective of level. Much of the renewal potential is transferred from the permanent organisations with flow production to the interplay between modernised, permanent organisations with modified functions and temporary organisations.

Increased project prevalence

Long-term development at both the demand and the supply sides thus leads to new opportunities. The demand for specially designed products, flexibility and closeness to the customer is increasing at the same time as technical developments are improving the ability of businesses to act quickly and differentially. But the question remains as to whether there exists the organising ability to cope with the new circumstances. The expansion of temporary organisational solutions of various kinds seems to be have been the answer to this. Seemingly characteristic of the neo-industrial economy, therefore, is the diffusion of temporary organisations and projects.

Utilising modern techniques and new organisational forms, even large corporations can meet diversified and close-to-customer demands. However, this scenario challenges the tayloristic work division in large enterprises. Although concern about production efficiency is still important, it is no longer the only or even the major controlling factor, as it was in the past. Two partly contrasting trends can be identified. Both an increasing use of loose or temporary organisational forms such as networks and projects and the growth of a minute, global work division structure specialising in the development and manufacturing of diverse components in different companies can be identified. Organisational functions are becoming more externalised. Components or complete systems for the final product are increasingly being purchased from companies all over the world. Mature companies in the industrialised world are concentrating on knowledge-intensive systems development and assembly (Hägg and Johanson 1982; Gareis 1990; Broström 1991; Henning and Norgren 1992).

Project organisation that in many respects is similar to that which traditionally has dominated in the construction industry is becoming increasingly prevalent in other lines of business. The multitude of consulting firms that provide large industrial enterprises with a variety of services work almost exclusively on a project basis. However, there are also many examples of companies moving to project solutions from routine flow-process operations. These changes can be attributed to the trend discussed above, i.e. customer orientation, with more and more complex and unique products, but the solution can also be the result of internal efficiency endeavours.

Within the ABB companies, both driving forces (or contrasting trends) are to be found. The heavy electrical equipment manufactured and delivered by the group is designed in close cooperation with customers with very particular demands. Every undertaking is viewed as a unique task with a fixed schedule. But, even in parts of the company that mass produce products, the element of project organisation has increased. The introduction of goal-directed groups has resulted in an increase in the number of people working on tasks that are time-bound and unique. Planning, coordination and execution of work is carried out by consensus within the groups themselves. The group members participate in the whole production chain, from order to delivery. Each order is handled separately, as a unit with a clearly stated schedule. In certain cases, the new organisation has led to communication problems, which have festered into rivalry between different professional cultures and resulted in the development of hierarchies with built-in class cultures. For example, it is not unusual for middle managers to encounter difficulties when working with former subordinates (Ekstedt and Wirdenius 1995).

Some traditional industrial enterprises – in striving for increased knowledge content and consequently increased product value – have also moved towards a project organisation in their operations. Several Ericsson units have, for example, moved from routinised manufacture and assembly of telephone exchanges to maintenance and development of computer systems. This change, in addition to necessitating massive retraining of the staff with regard to technical knowledge, required employees to become involved in all phases of the project and to come into close contact with customers. Before this dramatic transformation very few of the employees had ever conducted a serious dialogue with buyers about the product (Ekstedt 1991).

The growth of project organisation is also reflected by the dramatic increase in the membership of the US organisation that looks after the interests of project leaders, the Project Management Institute (PMI). In 1986, the institute had approximately 5,000 members; by 1995 that number had grown to roughly 17,000, and in 1998 membership stood at 32,000. It is likely that the International Project Management Association (IPMA) has experienced a similar trend in terms of membership. Project management has also received more and more attention as a general phenomenon. *Fortune* magazine designated project management as the '#1 Career Choice' in an article titled 'Planning a Career in a World Without Managers' in July 1996. And it is well known that educational institutions, public as well as private, are increasingly offering programmes or courses explicitly related to projects and temporary organisations.

So far we have presented more or less indirect evidence from various external sources as well as from our own case studies as to the increase in project-related activities on a massive scale. However, there have been a number of fairly serious definitional and measurement efforts to substantiate the claim that project organising is on the increase. Although all such efforts give different accounts of the problems of defining and measuring the phenomenon and the difficulty of finding relevant statistics, they have come to the same conclusion: project organising is on the rise and has been for some time (Boznak 1996; Dinsmore 1996; Eriksson 1997).

An implication of the transition to a project organisation is that the interfaces between different work cultures are widened while deep and long-standing relations may become weaker. However, it is certainly not unusual for network relations to 'hibernate' for a long time while the actors are busy with other things, and to be aroused to activity as soon as business opportunities present themselves. Individuals from different environments and professions are increasingly coming into contact with each other at the same time as their traditional roles in the hierarchical factory system is declining. The uncertainty created by this often results in greater emphasis being placed on tasks and business ideas. Top managers try to focus on or create certain common conceptions. In some cases, such efforts can lead to considerable friction between employees of different professional affiliation (Ekstedt *et al.* 1992; Lundin and Söderholm 1997).

Cultural aspects

There are many kinds of culture: professional, company or national. However, in all cases special norms are present. Concentrating for the moment on the original meaning of culture, i.e. national culture, it is clear that the changes in internationalisation that have occurred in recent years are associated with the greater closeness that has developed between producer and customer. It is now possible to travel great distances in a short time, making it far easier to visit other countries. And increasing customer demands for services and knowledge-intensive products also require companies to have an international presence. Thus, it is not only the quantitative expansion of internationalisation that is important:

changes in organisational forms are first and foremost of the qualitative type. More and more companies are participating in an international network of suppliers and customers. Moreover, recently the number of companies in direct control of different types of operations in several countries has increased markedly (United Nations Centre for Transnational Corporations, statistical information). It becomes possible to utilise the comparative advantages of different countries within the framework of a common enterprise system.

In Sweden – which traditionally has one of the most internationally oriented economies of the world – the period immediately after the Second World War was characterised by Swedish companies establishing subsidiaries abroad or acquiring foreign companies. These companies became the extended arm of the parent companies in the local markets. In many cases, the Swedish way of thinking and working came to be adopted. Recently these original so-called direct investments have largely been replaced by reinvestments in existing operations of foreign countries. As a result of this, the connection between the subsidiaries and the parent companies has grown weaker. Quite often the subsidiaries have become completely independent units with their own international network. In this transition from internationalisation of the first to the second degree, the subsidiaries can become the centres for a specific activity of the parent company (Holm 1994). The widening of cultural contacts can be attributed to the increasing centrality of the service industries. By tradition, most Swedish export companies have operated in the engineering and forest industries. As the knowledge and service content associated with these products increases, combined with increasingly sophisticated performance requirements on the part of buyers, the need for close contact with customers increases. Direct connections between the different company units on the one hand and the buyers on the other become a necessity. The direct interfaces between actors with different ethnic and/or regional cultures are broadened. In addition, relationships between individuals in different work organisations or from different business cultures may be strengthened. Both these dimensions are illustrated by the joint management responsibility of ABB and Polish manufacturers for railway signal equipment. Not only the mode of organising work, of doing business, but also everyday traditions, eating habits for example, are very different in the two countries, and these differences can create tension on both sides (Ekstedt and Wirdenius 1993). The changing nature of internationalisation thus increases the opportunities for cultural friction in a manifest way. This kind of friction – company experiences tell us – is easier to handle in a temporary organisation with a limited number of common points of interests than in permanent organisations. It might very well be easier for actors of different nationalities or from a different type of company culture to work together in projects, since that organisational form inherently brings a particular set of requirements.

However, project organisation at the interface between cultures varies from traditional international trade contacts in that it increases the demand for direct contacts of a more intensive type. Normally, international contacts of a trade character can be characterised as transaction oriented, but when international economic contacts diverge from simple trade, new types of cultural frictions might well appear. The project form of organisation, in particular, calls for an increased awareness of and special attention to the cultural friction dimension. However, project considerations are rarely to be found among international institutions, with the result that some kind of internationalisation dilemma could be said to be present.

Social/business intercourse between individuals or organisations with different cultural backgrounds is part of daily life in many companies. These differences often become most evident in international contacts, for example differences become manifest at the interface between Western European companies – usually operating in a dense supporting infrastructure – and Eastern European companies, which frequently have to operate in an institutional vacuum. Cultural differences between companies or professions can be also more elusive when – in contrast to the above-mentioned cases – they are not related to a national culture. The resulting friction then becomes more diffuse and tacit. Nils Elvander has demonstrated how, despite this, business culture can in certain respects override national culture (Elvander and Elvander-Seim1995). In areas such as construction and IT consulting, affiliation to the profession seems to play a greater role than national affiliation in industrial relations. Both kinds of activities are dominated by project organisations (Hofstede 1980; 1993; Ekstedt and Wirdenius 1993; Swierczek and Hirsch 1994; Elvander and Elvander-Seim 1995; Fukuyama 1995; Ekstedt and Henning 1997).

Why are project organisations becoming more common?

In order to understand better why project organising has gained such a prominent role in this new work division in industry, let us examine major trends at both the supply (production) and the demand side of the economy, i.e. push and pull effects, which could be said to be operating simultaneously. As far as the former is concerned, the discussion will focus on the expansion of communication and information technology, which affects both work and leisure time. The latter is concerned with new consumer patterns that are emerging from the fact that society seems to be becoming increasingly more individualised. These changes are also affecting the international division of work.

IT is a tool able to manage both time and space. It facilitates an intensive interchange of contacts in work life. It is possible to be informed instantly of what is happening at a certain place anywhere on earth by means of a number of new technical devices. In addition, modern automatic control engineering facilitates adjustments to production and special designs. It has become possible to respond to specific demands by individual customers. Products and services can be combined in many ways. Modern techniques of transportation, information transfer and control can be applied to almost any aspect of economic life and are increasingly encountered in everyday life (Beniger 1986).

Rapid development of communication and information technology thus influences the design of organisations in several different ways. Orlikowski and Robey (1991) use a structuration perspective, inspired by Giddens (see, for example, Giddens 1984), and show that relations between IT and organisations can be understood as a process of structuration. New technology thus interacts with structural properties and human action in the shaping of new organisational realities. In this respect, IT is one new component of organisations that, together with other organisational changes or contextual conditions, will be of importance for 'tomorrow's' organisations (see also Orlikowski 1992). The development opens up previously unheard of opportunities for organisational arrangements. Some writers even suggest that IT developments should be conceived of as driving and even unavoidable forces towards new and loose organisational forms (Rosenberg 1994; Yle-Antilla 1997). In any case, more effective and reliable methods of transportation have enabled economic actors from different activities and places to come together at their convenience. However, the relation between the development of IT techniques and organisation is less unequivocal. On the one hand, IT has made it possible to create large, connected organisational units that contain a wide variety of behaviours and modes of thinking. The cultural interfaces are widened. Expansion becomes possible through the fact that the IT can be used as a central control system, facilitating the direction of certain aspects of employees' behaviour. On the other hand, IT reduces the need for frequent, close contact between individuals and organisations. Individuals or smaller groups can carry through specific tasks on their own, often with a time limit imposed on their efforts. These activities can, in turn, be supported by information from various types of permanent organisations.

Work at home or at different customer locations is becoming more common. The role of a shared place of work is for many individuals diminishing, which in turn can create a vacuum that has to be filled with other arenas for activity. Thus, the capacity of IT to facilitate information exchange should not be allowed to prevent the development of more delicate and confidence-building personal contacts. Organisations as well as the markets in which they are operating ultimately determine relations between actors. It is, of course, in these organised behavioural systems that the foundations for economic exchange are laid (Snehota 1990).

In capital-intensive industries, such as the forest and steel industries, opportunities for changing logistics and organisation are limited. For example, refiners for pulp mills, which are produced by Sunds Defibrator (one of our case studies), can be modified to only a minor extent. They are manufactured specifically to form an integral part of a particular, long-term, large-scale and fixed production process. In such cases, hierarchies are the most natural way of organising activities. In contrast, many IT products have very broad fields of application. In addition, they can often be specially adapted for individual users. Providing the user has a certain level of competence, these aids can be applied in a very versatile and individual way. IT thus has a great potential for flexibility. It can readily cope with short response times and a geographically diverse customer base. Hierarchies, with their locking-in effects are too clumsy, not to say awkward. Markets, on the other hand, with their lack of embedded knowledge, are not prepared to meet advanced demands from customers (Williamson 1983). Hybrid forms of organising economic activity in between markets and hierarchies, such as projects or networks, are the obvious answer to this dilemma. In summary, modern IT increases the possibility of managing time and space, which in turn can be reflected in the design of organisations.

If IT facilitates an increased flexibility in organisational design, it is *the changed consumer patterns that promote project solutions*. Consumption rather than production is to be regarded as the main 'machine' of the economy. This generalised statement almost goes without saying (Jameson 1985). What is new on the customer side is the emphasis on the individual as a generator of needs and demands (Ingelhart 1990; Ester *et al.* 1994). The current individualisation process in Western industrial countries can be attributed to an increasing need for close contact between those who are producing and their customers, as well as between the actors in the production process. Customers want to be able to influence the design and quality of the desired goods and services and the sales staff have to offer products that hold an increasing experience and knowledge content (Wikström *et al.* 1989). To achieve the latter usually requires a far-reaching cooperation between actors belonging to different professions. Companies are increasingly turning such tendencies into active action, such strategies being termed customer focusing and/or service centring to mention a couple of the most popular labels. Sustained and often direct dialogue or negotiation between the actors in the market becomes a necessity. The trend can be described as a transition from an economic exchange characterised by *exit* mechanisms (of a take it or leave it type) to one characterised by *voice* and *loyalty*, to use the Hirschman terminology (Hirschman 1970). The transition to closely knit networks implies that the social, and not least the cultural, nature of economic transactions is becoming more and more important.

Service centring occurs in many different forms. For example, more and more people are employed in the areas of personnel, training, R&D, design, marketing and sales. In the largest Swedish companies more than half the staff are employed in these tasks (Eliasson 1992). The proportion of the Swedish labour force working with knowledge-intensive tasks has increased from one-tenth to one-quarter during the last three decades (Andersson and Sahlin 1993). The need to handle relations between staff and customers is reflected in the dense mass of consulting firms that is growing up around large companies. We are witnessing the emergence of a new breed of brokers as part of the projectisation trend as well as a new type of specialists. Computerisation of offices and shops has brought to light a number of organisational problems. Independent companies specialising in organisation and personnel development problems are supporting the large companies in their renewal projects (Ekstedt and Wirdenius 1995).

Many companies are trying to meet the diversified demands of different subgroups with great spending power, such as PC aficionados or practitioners of adventure sports, through customer focusing strategies. This increases the service element of businesses and, as services are difficult to store, direct contact between sellers and buyers is essential. The most salient example of close-to-customer activity is perhaps to be found in the computer industry, in which adaptation of products, the 'soft' software, is frequently carried out at the customer's premises. In Digital Equipment Sweden, for instance, another one of our case studies, an essential part of the work is done in direct connection with the various operations of large Swedish enterprises (De Geer and Ekstedt 1991). There are even researchers who argue that the involvement of the customer might grow and wipe out the dividing line between seller and buyer (Wikström *et al.* 1989). In any case, the tendency towards increased proximity between producer and consumer is placing stronger demands on actors' capability to understand and tolerate the thinking and acting of people with other backgrounds, as well as of collaborating with them.

Individualisation and increased purchasing power, together with new customer demand patterns, call for more complex and advanced products. Material goods are linked up with various types of unique services. It is not only mobile telephones that are sold along with more or less automatic services. This is true to an even greater extent of other IT equipment. It is common for service, training and support to be included in sales contracts. And among traditional manufacturers of goods, the Fläkt Corporation, for example, which has produced a long series of fans with specific technical performance data, has moved on to selling the somewhat imprecise service of 'climate', which naturally involves fans as an important element (Bröchner *et al.* 1991). This leads one to question whether there is any longer any point in distinguishing between goods and services. It is obviously the combination of both in a project that counts.

A number of indicators thus suggest that we have entered into a new all-embracing order concerning not only the national economy but also the world economy. The neo-industrial economy is spreading. A profound change of this kind naturally affects (or touches upon) many different social conditions, several of which will be alluded to in this book. However, we will focus mainly on the aspects of economic renewal, with respect to the actual transition to the new order as well as to the problems associated with the new mode of production, that is with the transformation dilemma and the renewal paradox. An important condition for the transition is the conceptions of economic organisations and economic renewal to be found among the representatives of economic activities. What, in more detail, are the theories of the practitioners and researchers? In the next chapter we will examine some elements of general organisational theory and project theory that we consider appropriate.

First, let us propose one more reason for the spread of the projectised order. It seems to us from our daily contacts with young people that project thinking is in line with the aspirations of the younger generation and with their way of thinking. Rather than planning for a life career, young people – at least those in the Western world that we have met – seem to encompass an ontology and a view of their life that consists in a series of experiences in time and space. Involvement in a set of projects further represents a string of challenges, through which one has to prove oneself. The challenge is to cope with the uncertainties, stresses and demands on stamina that appear to be a part of project involvement. Such challenges offer multiple opportunities to transfer a positive image of oneself, which is considered to be important for modern man (Lasch 1978). Project work might be considered as part of the post-modern movement towards fragmentation, in this case fragmentation in time and space, which is exactly what projects of a traditional kind lead to.

In the next chapter we will leave this macro view of developments and concentrate on the organisational level and on how theories take account of (or rather do not take account of) the challenges put forward in the previously outlined developments.

3 Shortcomings of present theorising about permanent and temporary organisations

The line of reasoning to be developed here is that theories about permanent and temporary organisations are unsuitable or even inept when it comes to accounting for some of the most crucial aspects of neo-industrial development. There is a need to develop the theoretical foundations for that development, and we intend to do so by outlining the present state of theorising in the field. However, when discussing theories-in-use (or espoused theories) as well as scholarly organisation theory, one has to make choices. Like Bishop Brask, we feel the urge to excuse ourselves, in this case from omitting in the present chapter any favourite theories that the reader might have. Essentially we have written this chapter to support the main points we want to make concerning neo-industrial organising in the hope that any omissions that we might have made are not too important in that particular respect.

Bishop Brask once upon a time signed a document with his seal, knowing that, if the king found the signed document, he would be executed. So, he was wise enough to put a small piece of paper under the seal with the text: 'I have been forced to do this.' Lo and behold, the document was indeed found by the king and that small piece of paper saved the bishop from sharing the unfortunate fate suffered by his less cautious co-signers.

It should be realised that theorising in this area (on organisations) occurs on at least two levels, or lives dual lives if you so wish. One such life is in the form of theory-in-use. On a practical level, theory-in-use is very important since, by definition, it guides people in their daily behaviours. And if several persons adhere to the same set of 'theories', then that set is undoubtedly important for the field and indirectly also for scholarly theory. In general, espoused theory (and to some extent theory-in-use) might be thought of as a mixture of influential theorising in the past and conventional wisdom at large and as constituting a powerful ontology in the management world, encompassing subordinates as well.

The second life of theorising on organisations and on organising consists in the theoretical 'debates' carried forward by researchers concentrating on theoretical advancement (and in pursuit of an academic career) rather than on practical issues. However, for a variety of reasons, it is certainly not easy to distinguish the two forms. All efforts to specify any boundary between them are almost bound to fail. Thus, it is probably fair to say that what is taught at business schools all over the world should be perceived as a mixture of the two. The mere notion of the 'powerful ontology' mentioned above has made us paint a picture of clear colours and with a wide brush initially in order to make some of the most obvious and crucial points and leave some of the sophistication for later.

For reasons that should be obvious from the first two chapters (and the preface) we concentrate on contrasting the permanent and the temporary when it comes to the usefulness in describing and accounting for the emerging meso-level system, i.e. the neo-industrial economy. We describe the developments from a micro-level point of view, i.e. the organisational level. Initially we allude to organisation theories and some of the traits that make them useful or less useful for our present purposes. Next we describe the most important ideas concerning projects and temporary organisations. The latter play a crucial role since projectisation is at the core of the interesting developments. Notions of learning, action and renewal are put forward as the essential aspects. Finally we outline some important traits of a theory of renewal through action and learning in a neo-industrial context.

Permanent organisation theories as rooted in industrialism

It is sometimes argued that we live in a thoroughly organised society dominated by organisations and organised interests, and it is in fact true that there are a great number of organisations in society today. Companies, as well as central and local authorities, are employers, and also producers of goods and services as well as exercisers of authority. Professional and industrial organisations take charge of the interests of their members, and put these forward in negotiations or talks with other organisations. It is also symptomatic that, when new issues arise (environmental issues for example), the standard response is the formation of new organisations (at ministerial level; new professional and industrial organisations) or organisational units (new units within the primary municipalities or within the large enterprises), whose aim is to reflect and deal with the new issues.

In other words, organisations are important. However, they do not necessarily reflect accurately what is crucial in society or in the individual organisation. The usual way of presenting the activity of an organisation, an organisation plan (or chart) with boxes and arrows seldom, if ever, tells us anything about what is actually done in the activities in which the organisation is involved. To an even lesser extent does it provide any information about major problems or opportunities within the activity described.

Nevertheless, it would be difficult to produce houses, cars or medical services if the necessary organisations did not exist. The coordination and collaboration between the different individuals and units that make up organisations could hardly arise spontaneously. Organisations are entities that we could not do without. Thus, organisations are needed. And we regard them as important not only for the production of goods and services, but also for our lives.

The problem with organisations, regardless of whether they are companies, public authorities or other kinds of organisations, is that the ideas that exist on how organisations work, how they are useful, how they are built up and managed, etc. are based on a number of implicit assumptions or axioms that describe the current situation very poorly. It appears that the axioms and assumptions stick in our minds and determine our ontological inclinations. Generally, there is a reinforcement of stability and normality rather than flexibility, adaptiveness and pattern change. As a result, renewal and development issues are handled in a less than ideal manner and are therefore problematic. The aim of this chapter is to demonstrate some of the deficiencies, and on this basis propose other directions for thinking on how organisations could be designed. It should be stressed once more that the shortcomings to be discussed are not just any old shortcomings but relate to renewal in the neo-industrial field.

Scholarly organisation theory could be said to be haunted by its traditions and by the general notion that knowledge in the area is additive (rather than subtractive), with no requirement that additions be a logical fit or consistent with other elements. Of course, most additions are in one way or the other useful for those of us who insist on trying to understand organisations, which means that scavenging is both difficult and questionable. However, the task of describing the present state of organisational theory from the neo-industrial point of view becomes a formidable job of imposing structure on what is quite nebulous. In what follows such an effort has been made however. Initially, we outline elements stressing hierarchy and behaviours as a background for a discussion of the conception of time as eternal in most of the theories. We further touch upon some more recent contributions, including the strengths that permanent organisations have in the neo-industrial development, i.e. in handling knowledge. A final argument before the sphere of project thinking is introduced is that permanent organisations are not action prone in the sense that renewal is facilitated in the neo-industrial situation.

Bureaucracy and renewal

A basic idea that has guided and is guiding the design of companies and public administrations is the idea of the (industrial) bureaucracy as a prototype. By this we refer to the observation that, in general, classical bureaucratic concepts are used when organisations are designed. Efforts are made to create an organisation with fixed spheres of authority that are hierarchically arranged, with general and specific rules for work tasks, and a more or less clear distinction between individual/employee and task (see Clegg 1990: 25–41). The employees are given uniform and clear responsibilities that are concentrated at different levels until the top and the executive of the organisation is reached. The chief executive officer (CEO) (or the top management group) is thus placed on top of a pyramid with integrated and entire responsibility for what is taking place at lower echelons. Those companies and administrations (i.e. our cases), which will be presented in the next chapter, do not deviate markedly from the description given above. The bureaucratic system is perhaps most obvious in public organisations, but Alcatel, IBM, General Electric, ABB, Volvo and Skanska also exhibit a clear bureaucratic structure with division of work and specialisation as essential elements. The tradition of the industrial bureaucracy dates back to the breakthrough of industrialism, and was given a more clear and definite form by Weber, Taylor, Fayol, Gulick and Urwick, among others, who made explicit the conventional wisdom of their times.

There are several functional, logical reasons why companies have come to be designed and conceived of in this way. For an activity that is strictly production oriented – in which what is called the value chain is sequentially built up from the acquisition of raw material, via storage and production to sale – it is often particularly efficient to design the organisation as a bureaucracy. To create security in the process itself and to ensure good production results it is important to make the responsibilities for different parts of this process clear. Stabilising expectations becomes an important part of organising under production orientation circumstances.

It has been suggested here, for example, that the method of organising is dependent on the environment within which the company is operating. In a stable environment the organisation should be designed like a mechanical machine, i.e. with a large proportion of standardised routines and processes, while a dynamic environment requires a more flexible organisation that is more organic in its functioning. On the whole, it has been an important theme in the organisational literature to analyse in what way the structure of the organisation is well tuned to the tasks to be performed, on the one hand, and to the characteristics of the environment, on the other. Concepts such as technology, culture, structure and individual can be used to describe central components in the world of organisations where organisational form is considered as contingent upon the environment.

Thus, organisation theory as well as practical leadership have been characterised by issues concerning how to build systems that can ensure the continued existence of the activity, in other words systems that are well structured, where technology and people function together, and where that which is produced also has a market outside the organisation. Strategy and strategic management are thus something that is designed and exercised with the aim of ensuring the continued existence of the organisation, its long-term survival. The drill in organisation structures, which often is to be found in textbooks about companies, organisation and management, is another manifestation of this. Several research directions have, in the course of the decades, supported the great interest in companies as structural systems, developing in some form of symbiosis with a variety of environmental demands (see, for example, Burns and Stalker 1961; Lawrence and Lorsch 1967; Pugh and Hinings 1976). The stable and constant state is the aim. Not only does change become a marginalised problem, which arises when the organisation for some reason is not in phase with its present conditions, but the notion of change as something special seems to reinforce the concentration on stability by offering the world view that stability is normal, whereas change is not.

Focus on decisions

The concentration of interest in formal organisations, structures and simple exchanges with the environment also maintains the view of management chiefly as a decision problem. To manage organisations is about making correct decisions, and these should be rational according to the norms implied in many theoretical discussions. The basis for focusing on decisions is to be found in the microeconomic 'economic man' assumption, which is still considered important in the most popular managerial economics textbooks. The notion of the economic man has been reformed to an 'administrative man' idea in the post-war period. The latter concept (Simon 1947) was pushed forward as a consequence of the fact that the unreasonable assumptions underlying the economic man concept were impossible to combine with any practical experience whatsoever, or any empirical research on how decision making was really occurring. Cyert and March (1963) later showed how it is possible to develop a more behaviour-oriented theory of organisations by relying on different types of theories on decision making. Their theory is thus still basically decision focused.

In a practical sense, the strong influences of different forms of decision theory become apparent with the great number of decision aids that are available. Systems for evaluating investments and product calculation *ex post* as well as *ex ante* are such examples of applications, illustrating the belief in the decision as the central, rational managerial activity. There is very little empirical evidence that supports the practical use of such decision aids (see the discussion in Jansson 1992), but it is the rational decision making that is strengthened as a norm. Furthermore, in decision models it is usually assumed that action automatically follows upon decisions made. It is thus a consequential logic that is expressed. If the models are founded on such assumptions the renewal problems will also be disregarded. Any one who has worked with renewal questions knows that decision and ensuing action are not directly causally related, a circumstance that the research in the field has confirmed (see March, 1988, for example).

Time as eternal

Common to both the decision orientation and the system building is that time tends to be conceived of as an endless resource to such an extent that eternity is the horizon for organised activities. The systems are planned to exist, if not forever, then for the foreseeable future. To maintain that the organisational renewal carried out recently is only temporary or that the decision just made is valid for only a short period of time does not accord with the world of ideas that has produced the new organisation structure or the specific decision. Even if people in practice (particularly in retrospect) can understand that no specific organisational solution can be valid forever, it is still difficult for them to admit that in the presence of others. This is especially obvious when they are working on organisational change. Admitting that the solution they are currently considering is not a permanent one would be tantamount to saying that they are not very serious in what they are doing. Matrix organisations or divisionalised organisation structures are simply not introduced on a temporary basis, because such a line of action or reasoning could, for example, be regarded as detrimental to motivation.

Information and economic systems function in the same way. They tend to have eternity built in as an assumption. Economic systems effectively break up history as well as the present and the future into delimited months and years, which can be treated as a long series of similar months and years. Also, annual budgets, balancing of the accounts and audits are built on the same conception. The link to market, customers, consumers, clients (or whichever word is used in a particular activity) is usually also based on similar stereotyped time perceptions. Customer accounts are added up per year (or some other time period) and salesmen have sales targets per year or per six months. The market development is generally described as a trend over time in various decision support systems and the important information is to be found in the long-term incremental development within different relevant markets.

In other words, in the many different systems that build up in the company or the administration, time is more or less uninteresting as a variable (except when it comes to formalised models for investments and the like in managerial economics, as alluded to above). Production goes on, years are added to years, minor changes are made, time continues, and by means of a great number of decisions the activity is kept together, develops and lives on.

Some theoretical attempts at handling organisational renewal issues

Organisations, despite being rooted in the ideals of industrialism, are less stable than they might seem. It is almost a prerequisite that things will happen to cause the eternal perfect system or the perfect organisation structure to break down or at least to be viewed as no longer very successful. In other words, and as has been claimed with increasing emphasis in recent years, what are regarded as relevant and modern ideas of how organisations should be designed are also changing with the result that individual organisations are trying to find new forms for their activity (Powell and DiMaggio 1991).

The above discussion should not be interpreted to mean that industry and local authorities are completely unaware of the need for renewal. The point is that the systems they use originate to a great extent from views and lines of thought that have a stable eternity as an implicit assumption. Renewal is, therefore, an anomaly, something that is not normal and something that cannot easily be incorporated within stable structures. However, renewal has come to be an important theme and a matter of preoccupation for both theorists and practitioners.

Renewal theories and renewal models, which try to derive normative statements from descriptive experiences, aim either to change one structure into something else or to make a particular structure more flexible and renewal-prone. The former could perhaps be considered the classical renewal approach, for example to change a functional organisation into a matrix organisation, whereas the latter, which attempts to make the organisation into a 'learning organisation', has aroused more interest during the past decade (Senge 1990a).

When the intention is to change one structure into another, it is usually because a problem in profitability or direction has been identified and it is hoped that it will be solved by a new organisation structure. The literature in the field is voluminous but often describes some form of unlearning–relearning sequence, in which a period of renewal is undertaken with a view to stabilising the new situation thereafter. The popular sequence 'unfreeze, change and refreeze' further reinforces the notions of stability by the implicit exhortation to 'keep it frozen'. The management issues that are brought into focus have a considerable effect on new structure, requiring decisions about the design of the new organisation and the method of organising different bureaucratic functions (responsibility, hierarchy, division of work, etc.). Such renewal efforts could easily be viewed as being decision driven in that, once a decision on the new structure is made the important work is done and the realisation is then a relatively simple procedural matter.

The second renewal approach, which aims to make an established structure more renewal-prone, faces similar problems. In this case, though, overall structural renewal is replaced by the introduction of new routines and adaptive systems in the organisation. Autonomous groups, learning organisations (with Japanese models, for instance), systems for continuous improvements and even disposable organisations (March 1995) are some examples. The aim is to increase the sphere of responsibility of individuals or groups within the organisation to include also current changes and to increase competence and comprehensive vision among organisation members. The underlying arguments are that the pace of renewal in the world around is high, that production must be more customer oriented, that quality is central and that throughput times have to be reduced. Such a situation is associated with a considerable amount of uncertainty and is difficult to plan. It is not possible via a central management function to foresee or plan for all possible problems or opportunities that may arise. In other words, it becomes necessary to increase competence among those who have a direct contact with production, customers, suppliers and others.

It is also possible that an increase in flexibility may result, but still this approach is about building systems or structures, albeit systems containing components that allow for incremental change over time. Incrementalism is one way of learning, but it will not lead to a major change in organisational structure or to a radical shift in organising patterns. It is more likely that an incrementally developed learning organisation will do 'more of the same' although with time it might do so more effectively. In other words, the solutions sought are in the same direction as in the traditional models of thought originating from industrialism. The goal remains stable and permanent systems, even if the requirements are different.

Empirical observations that companies cooperate in various ways (while simultaneously competing in other areas) have prompted several attempts to use networking as a metaphor for describing and analysing not only intraorganisational but also interorganisational relationships and behaviours (Johansson and Mattson 1987; Powell 1990; Jarillo 1993). Intuitively, the use of the network metaphor would seem to imply flexibility and renewal and, indeed, some theoretical contributions of that kind can be found. However, flexibility seems to be confined to interorganisational relationships in the form of adding (or possibly subtracting) partners in the network. In addition, the effects of the overall network structure are the main concern. Stability is in general regarded as the norm for the network and the set-up of any individual organisation is not considered to change very much. At the same time, renewal is of relatively little concern in that line of research. Nevertheless, the processes involved in 'networking' as an activity are of some interest for the phenomena that are the focus of this book. Projects could be considered as examples of concentrated networking and project theory in some respects could be regarded as a form of action-oriented network theory.

The relationships between individual organisations and their environment have long been of interest to resource dependency theorists (see Pfeffer and Salancik 1978 for a description). In this area, work has focused on the implications of the environmental resource dependence for the internal affairs of individual organisations. Thus, the perspective is primarily an outside-in one, in contrast to the inside-out perspective commonly adopted in neo-industrial developments. This means that resource dependency theory adds to our understanding of organisations *per se* but does not appear to be particularly useful in the present context.

However, there have also been some attempts to change the established view of organisations as firm, delimited and system-dependent units, and to do it in a fundamental way. The concept of virtual organisations is such an attempt (Davidow and Malone, 1992) to describe formal organisations in a new, more meaningful way, as loosely linked units in which the interesting work is taking place across traditional organisation boundaries (also compare with imaginary organisations, Hedberg *et al.* 1997). Virtual organisations will come into existence if a company farms out its product development to another company, for example, and the development process then is carried out in close collaboration between them; or when the custom-order systems of different companies are linked together in such a way that production orders are transmitted to subcontractors and other actors in the production chain. Several variations on the same theme are conceivable, but the common feature is that the virtual organisations reflect existing market needs. Virtual organisations are primarily a normative fiction in the present situation, however. Even if empirical examples in the literature are not missing, the examples are of a curiosity type rather than indicative of any widespread occurrence.

Nevertheless, concept formation in the direction of virtual organisations does not break the deadlock that thinking in terms of formal organisations usually implies. For this reason, the virtual organisation is more interesting as a metaphor than the network (which of course is an alternative concept that could be used to describe the same kind of phenomena). The components of the networks are individual organisations, and between them there are different types of connections. Network theory recognises a qualitative difference between what is taking place between organisations and what is taking place within organisations. Virtual organisations are defined by the arena of the linked activities – i.e. those of interest to the customer – irrespective of whether they are organised within or between formal organisations. The focusing on individual formal organisations that exists in network theory is thus largely historical in terms of the concept of virtual organisations. Although thinking on virtual organisations has freed itself from some limitations, the concept of an established, constant organisation remains dominant. Once an organisation has been established and given a working framework, it forms the basis of the firm systems of virtual organisations, which must function and develop incrementally. Thus, the notion of the virtual organisation can be viewed as a very special case of resource dependency alluded to above, the difference being that, whereas resource dependency seems to stress outside-in aspects, the virtual organisation concept stresses inside-out aspects by virtue of its managerial involvement. All in all, virtual organisations, although they do not achieve the reality of a neo-industrial organisation, are a step along the road, introducing elements of fluidity or adaptiveness not found in traditional bureaucracies.

Organisation and culture

Culture and ideology in various forms have also affected much of the thinking and research on organisations and renewal in recent decades. The theory has achieved a very high degree of practical penetration through Peters and Waterman (1982) and has dominated much of organisation rhetoric and research. Since then, more well-thought-out and empirically founded research has been carried out (see Smircich 1983 for example). In short, cultural thinking implies that – beyond that which is openly expressed and observable – there are different norms, attitudes, symbols and values that guide and affect the way of organising, working and being together within organisations. Organisational symbolism, for instance (Pondy *et al.* 1983), has become a field in its own right within cultural research.

That cultural aspects influence the work within an organisation, in great as well as in little things, is self-evident. However, to what extent it is national, regional or company-related culture that is most influential is seldom as obvious. All theories, from Weber's Protestant ethics to Peters' seven-s-framework, are, as explanations, equally believable or unbelievable. The contribution of cultural research to questions about organisational forms or systems is therefore small. Analysis of organisation culture tends to be caught in the same trap as traditional systems theory, i.e. it is based on the study of supposedly uniform organisations. Although the global picture of cultural research is different from that of systems theory, for example, this does not enable other conclusions to be drawn about the organisation as a relevant unit of analysis. In addition, there are obvious difficulties in explaining convincingly, from a cultural perspective, the renewal that takes place regardless. It is worth noting that one of the seminal works that paved the way for cultural research (Turner 1971) dealt with what is more commonly called industrial subgroups rather than organisations as such.

However, there is no lack of critique of the organisation as a relevant unit within the research tradition that is represented by cultural research. Critique can also be found within other research areas with kindred ontological points of departure. Companies have been described, for example, as being composed of many different cultural contexts, sometimes of a conflicting or competing nature, and so the idea of the company as a uniform unit usually falls down. Unfortunately, explanations about what constitutes other cultural contexts, are largely lacking apart from references to general class theories or otherwise socially institutionalised conflicts recurring in individual companies (see Schein 1996 for example). In terms of practical applications, cultural theory has most often been used either to create a uniform organisation culture or to resolve conflicts between different cultures. Thus, cultural theory, either theoretically or practically, cannot truly be said to have abandoned the idea of the organisation as the primary unit for analysis.

Institutions, established conceptions and the possibilities of management

Whereas cultural theory seeks explanations internally within the organisation and in various groupings within the organisation, institutionalism could be said to move in the opposite direction. In brief, those who are called the new institutionalists (Scott and Meyer 1994, Powell and DiMaggio 1991, among others) maintain that stability is after all the natural state and the one that prevails in organisations or that organisations tend to aim at. Renewal is not particularly common and, when it does occur, does not happen quickly. The explanation for this is to be found in the fact that organisations are part of a wider environment of organisations, within which ideas about activity are shared and maintained in the form of routines, rules, norms and structural orders. Such rules evolve only slowly, and changes are seldom prompted by needs or demands formulated in individual organisations. More likely, new legislation, new professional rules, change in business codes or suddenly emerging opinions will be the cause of such a renewal. When renewal does occur, it is usually to be found occurring within several organisations simultaneously, and may affect only external, structural aspects, leaving the actual activity unaffected. Frequently, the decision theory underlying the course of events is the logic of appropriateness rather than the logic of consequentiality (March and Olsen 1989). In other words, what is experienced as urgent and appropriate is more important than what could be said to be needed according to technical or market-oriented arguments.

Institutional organisation theory has a considerably greater value than culture theory or systems theory, for example, when it comes to explaining what actually takes place in organisations. Moreover, organisation theory takes into account the conceptual environment of organisations, and its values and norms, which are transferred between organisations, aspects that are (almost) absent from culture theory. However, formal organisation structure constitutes an important part of the theoretical analyses, i.e. through studies and analyses of formal organisation structures it is possible to determine how different organisation models are disseminated. Research in the field in recent years has widened the theoretical and empirical focus of the analyses to include also behavioural aspects within organisations (see Czarniawska and Sevón 1996 for instance). In some recent developments the notion of institutions as being stable and in existence for a very long period of time and over a wide range of fields has been challenged (Røvik 1996; Sjöstrand 1993). However, the roots of change or deinstitutionalisation lie not in action *per se* but in movements in the field.

The newer form of institutionalism differs from the earlier version (Selznick 1957) by, among other things, the little weight attached to consciously formed and maintained institutionalised patterns. Institutions have become more impersonal and are not, according to the newer theory, within reach of an individual management team, even less so of the employees. This, in turn, can be said to reflect the increasing complexity in society. More and larger organisations, more organised interest groups and increasingly diversified demands from unions, owners and state and commercial interested parties result in the emergence of institutionalised conditions in a network of conceptual relations between actors of a different nature.

On the other hand, in a complex network of ideas, commercial exchanges, professional groups and conflicting demands, it can be asserted that the need for competence at the managerial level in handling this network can only increase. It is certainly not the case that individual management teams can choose what they want to do (they are, as mentioned, dependent on dominating ideas within the field), but they can use various means to deal with the incompatibility of different ideas: they can, by the clever use of rhetoric, word internal messages in such a way that certain views relative to the institutional environment are more strongly stressed than others and they can, more or less consciously, choose to present one view to the outside world while internally working to a different agenda. Moreover, some ideas or ambitions can be expressed by structural design, while other ideas can be manifested by the design of routines and procedures within the organisation. In such a situation renewal issues will necessarily become natural to managers and, instead of a simple diffusion between different organisations, renewal becomes a question of translation between the 'global' and the 'local' (see Czarniawska and Joerges 1996: 23–24). The translation – and with it the renewal desired – is neither planned nor given by the environment. Instead, it is a mixture of intentions, demands, institutionalised ideas and pure chance that results in empirically observable renewal.

Renewal beyond the fashionable words

The management questions change when the reasoning above is taken as a starting point for trying to understand how organisations function. On the one hand, there are many societal indicators of the need for new organisation models and renewal patterns that break away from ingrained principles; on the other hand, there are relatively established models of how organisations should look, and these models are widespread and difficult to change. In other words, if one still wants to renew an activity it is necessary to take account of the complexity of the external as well as the internal environment.

Eccles *et al.* (1992) argue that it is necessary to look beyond the superficial meaning of the management buzzwords that prevail among consultants and updated managers. For example, consider the current fashion for 're-engineering'. it is not re-engineering *per se* that is important in order to achieve renewal; however, the term re-engineering describes what one is trying to achieve and is one example (in a long line) of the importance of rhetoric. Rhetoric is just words, though, and words, although important, are not sufficient for understanding how renewal takes place. Action is also necessary and, for this action to have any effect, an identity within the activity is also needed. Eccles *et al.* (1992) recommend an action perspective to understand management. They claim that one should conceive of management as composed of action and processes rather than of state or structures (Eccles *et al.* 1992: 13). Their theory thus includes several elements that are consistent with our argument of the irrelevance of static organisation theory and the limitations of renewal theories. Eccles *et al.* are not, however, particularly inclined to conceive of renewal as a theme of its own, even if they stress dynamics and processes. In addition, they say little about what should be the object of renewal, and they do not, therefore, come to any particular conclusions about the specific renewal problems of organisations, or which fields are especially difficult to renew.

The necessity of action in renewal theories

In other words, it is not sufficient to apply an action perspective; this perspective has also to be given a direction – a value if you like – as to what is to be the object of action. If managers concentrate their action on continuing to exchange their machinery every fifth year not much is gained from a renewal perspective. To act as a point of departure therefore requires the addition of a time dimension, keeping in mind that the target is renewal. Of the theoretical directions touched upon above, none satisfies this in full.

The discussion above has criticised a wide variety of established theories with reference to the issues presented in Chapter 1, i.e. how different organisational theory approaches manage to question the idea of the permanent organisation, and which aspects of traditional theory can be used to build a more discerning understanding of the distinctive character of the temporary organisation. The exposition is naturally not complete but has demonstrated: (i) that a basic conception of organisations is that they should be built up around stable systems and structures, (ii) that organisations are driven by decisions and (iii) that they are conceived of as acting with eternity as the time horizon. There are few direct lessons that can be drawn from this type of theory to explain or develop the understanding of the different cases to be presented in the next chapter. There are, however, many indications that people active in today's companies and administrations conceive of their organisations in the uniform and structure-bound way that has been described in this chapter, and thus are directly responsible for making the renewal endeavours more difficult. It is already obvious that action should be a given element in the understanding of renewal efforts. Within what can be termed project theory, or perhaps project science, action is emphasised as something central. Projects can therefore serve as a starting point when dealing with the need to understand action. Furthermore, projects imply – at least on the surface – that time is regarded as limited, thus responding to the criticism raised above that the organisation theories tend to conceive of time as eternal.

The sphere of project theories and project thinking

The origins in practice

In general, it could be said that project theories do not emanate from traditional organisation theories or from recent developments in scholarly theories of organisations. Rather, project theories appear to have developed more or less entirely out of practical considerations and practical experiences and among project managers rather than from deliberate work among organisation researchers. This conjecture is supported by at least two facts: (i) practitioners in the project field have united in professional organisations and are organising worldwide conferences on project practices, on project management and on project 'theory' (in a practitioner sense) and (ii) notions of temporariness or of the need for a time limit for human organised efforts have been quite absent for researchers in the organisational and behavioural sciences. Among people working with projects on a regular basis, time limits have often become regarded as almost equally important as the task to fulfil.

Of course, some elements of the thinking concerning permanent organisations can also be applied (and are applied) in a temporary setting, which makes questions about temporariness and about the origins and consequences of time limits even more difficult, even fuzzy, from a theoretical point of view. In practice, the borderline between theories on permanent organisations and theories on temporary organisations (or projects) is ambiguous and quite debatable in the present context. The main point we want to make here is that organisation theory and project theory appears to have developed out of quite different traditions of research and/or of human experience.

Development (and application) of a general organisational theory and a project theory appears to have occurred in parallel and with very little overlap during the course of history. Furthermore, practitioners (i.e. actors such as project managers and project owners) appear to have played a more prominent role (or possibly the only prominent role) in the development of project theories compared with traditional organisation theory. To make the same point in other words, one might say that espoused theory and theory-in-use among practitioners dominate the development of project theory in a relative sense. Scholarly theory in the projects sphere is quite scant under the present circumstances and has played a very insignificant role in the development of the project field over the years.

This means that the theory that does exist in the project area has been very much influenced by practical work and by the work situations that have emerged during the course of that practical work. The label 'project' and the work situations leashed together with that label have been the basis for the development. However, very early – or even in the original formulations of the area – the notion of project management and the normative aspects of project theory were put forward and dominated the field. Before we delve any further into this area, we will allude to the multitude of phenomena that have the potential of being inspirational for the development of the field. Projects are important for human life.

Projects as important phenomena

Regardless of the facts related above, projects and temporary organisations have no doubt played important roles in the history of mankind. In fact, all major efforts in our history can be regarded as projects and we also tend to think of them as projects. Each 'business' expedition that the Vikings undertook was most probably regarded as an isolated project. Of course, the time limits involved were probably quite vague when the trip was organised and the purpose apparently owed more to fantasy and wishful thinking than precise goals. The only project ingredients appearing to be very well defined were the resources in terms of ships, weapons and the team (human resources) at the time of departure. In any case, these expeditions played an important role in Viking society and appear to have been essential themes of tales told in Viking circles and during Viking times. Even if the plundering of the Viking age is not something in our history that we are very proud of, the example serves to demonstrate a particular type of an original project kind.

'Viking trips' of more modern times consisted in expeditions to the North Pole and to the South Pole and similar major efforts whereby groups of human beings challenged the extremes of temperature, winds and other forces of nature. Similarly, the Apollo projects and the trips to the moon were undertakings of a spectacular kind. Unlike the Viking expeditions, the purpose of the efforts were explicitly and unequivocally stated, and thus it was very easy to evaluate whether the efforts were successes or failures. (Viking trips that did not bring home riches were probably labelled as failures regardless of the fact that the purposes of the trip stated initially were somewhat vague.) Unlike the Viking trips, these modern ventures are matters of concern for nations (and not only for the Viking team). Similar ventures (but somewhat less publicly attended to) are submarine activities to uncover what is in the depths of the oceans.

These expeditions have heroes, as does almost every project of this spectacular type. Göran Kropp – a remarkable Swede – is a modern hero. He undertook a most extraordinary project of a personal type by cycling all the way from Sweden to Nepal, climbing (and without the aid of oxygen) to the top of Mount Everest (succeeding where multimillion dollar expeditions have failed and resulted in a multitude of deaths among expedition members) and then, after not much more than one day of rest, spending more than half a year riding his bike back again to Sweden. Upon his return to Sweden, the project manager of this one-man team demonstrated his drive to challenge nature by making public his plans to sail alone in his little boat all the way from Sweden to the Antarctic region, to ski cross-country to the South Pole and then return in his boat. Like most project managers (heroes) he demonstrates not only stamina in what he is doing but also a willingness to take on impossible tasks.

We all know of some less conspicuous projects that have had fundamental effects on the fate of mankind. Remarkable discoveries, such as X-rays or penicillin, might not be described as proper projects today since the purpose of the work was not too well stated initially. However, the similarities with the Viking expeditions are striking. The efforts were guided not by a clear understanding of the goal but rather by wishful thinking and faith in creativity. The aftermath and tales of these inventions usually reveal a hero as well. In this case, the hero is not like Göran Kropp, i.e. someone who is fighting nature, but rather someone who has to fight the scientific or commercial community if not society at large.

Innovation work aiming at developing a new version of a car is similar to modern expeditions or trips to outer space in that the goal of the endeavour is defined relatively clearly. However, the stakeholders of such an effort are to be found within a company rather than in the society at large. As such, product development is certainly something that fits almost all modern definitions of project work (to be alluded to later in this chapter).

To finalise our account of projects as important phenomena, we should point out that our modern environment contains many examples of routine projects, such as constructing a new building, putting on a theatre production or developing (on the margin) a consumer product. Thus, our world is filled with unique projects, such as cleaning up after the Chernobyl accident (making nuclear power plants in Russia safe), or, even more difficult, putting together Agenda 21 (the Rio document), which sets out a programme for sustainable development in which environmental concerns play a significant role.

Despite the different guises that projects can take, it seems that projects were even more dominant at the beginning of time than at present, at least in terms of economic activities. In fact, the enterprise vocabulary was used for time-limited efforts rather than for businesses. To take one example, in Sweden the East India Company did not start out as a company. To begin with each trip was regarded as an isolated enterprise to be evaluated on its own merits. Numerous trips to India took place, and each trip had its own organisation. The East India Company was eventually formed to stabilise operations, to store resources (in terms of company equity) and to adhere to the general change in the conceptions in society about organising economic activities.

Notions about permanent business organisations were in our opinion formed during the era of industrialisation, with its demand for heavy investments and with its concern for stable production operations. A mixture of permanent and temporary organisations was created, but in due course research interests came to concentrate on the permanent. In other words, the fight for attention between permanent and temporary organisations was won by the permanent. The reasons for this are probably manifold. Long-term employment is much more interesting to most than short-term employment. And it is easier for actors in the context of an organisation to focus on what is regarded as permanent rather than what is regarded as temporary. The notion of trust, for instance, seems to develop more easily among persons or companies than among temporary units (Huemer 1998). And permanent organisations are most certainly easier to study than temporary ones (as the latter evaporate when their task has been fulfilled). To us it appears, though, that interest in temporary organisations is now growing. We will now consider the theoretical development and the foci of project thoughts.

Theoretical origins and projects

One alternative to organisation theories for describing, explaining, predicting and prescribing activities in the industrial economy might be theories about organising (in contrast to theories about organisations). The use of the word organising implies that a process is focused (see Weick 1969). In particular, it focuses attention on the notion of time. In the temporary organisation (or, to use the alternative and more common term, the project), time takes on a very specific role. In a project, effort is directed towards achieving a specific task, and according to the prevailing, mostly normative, theories about projects there is a fixed time period in which the task must be achieved.

Time limitation creates a sense of urgency among the members of the project team and provides a distinct focus for all their activities. In fact, actions other than those directly aimed at completing the task during the allotted time are regarded as illegitimate. The combination of the time limit and the task involved makes the project a much more coherent phenomenon than an ordinary organisation. The multitude of goals ascribed to any ordinary organisation can sometimes confuse members of the organisation, and the lack of definite time constraints further diffuses efforts and fosters the attitude that everything can be handled later. Postponement of action is a serious threat to any project, but in a permanent organisation postponement is not necessarily even regarded as a problem. Postponement might even be seen as a virtue. Thus, the temporary organisation has some desirable attributes by comparison in that it is more clearly defined in time and in space. In fact, the tendency to isolate a project from its environment appears to be one important explanation for the 'getting-things-done' quality of projects (Lundin and Söderholm 1995). Moreover, in an achievement-motivated society, the norms that guide the temporary organisations appear to be very much appreciated.

A common denominator of project theories is a focus on defining projects, and on defining them in such a way that the definition is useful for the problem to be solved or for the task to be fulfilled. Most of the time, the definer is preoccupied with defining projects not in relation to permanent organisations but in such a way as to discriminate them from other phenomena that should not be mistaken for projects. The question to be answered seems to be 'How do we know that the phenomenon at hand is a project?'. The implication seems to be that the definer needs to know whether or not the phenomenon can be handled as a project. Or, rather, if a particular phenomenon cannot be viewed as a project the implication is that it might be wise to transform it in line with the common definition. One common definition of a project states that 'a project is a major and significant undertaking or task to be fulfilled within a limited time and with a given set of resources' (Engwall 1995: 43).

In other words, project thinking is also based on a certain set of values (not necessarily explicitly stated), for example the concept that action is desirable. According to project ontology, project work should be handled in accordance with the definition of a project given above. Achievements are measured by, or are perceived as equivalent to, action. In other words, project theories and theories about temporary organisations have some ingredients that are very desirable in an industrial setting, e.g. 'getting things done' rather than discussions or even just talk is a major preoccupation for most prominent actors in the field.

Some traits of project theories

To return to definition issues, most definition efforts have some features in common. As mentioned above, a project is usually defined by the task that it is designed to fulfil and by the time constraint attached to that task fulfilment. The idea of forming a team to 'take care' of the task within given constraints appears natural. In that sense, regardless of the definition, the project is regarded as a whole and as coherent in comparison with permanent organisations. It is then relatively simple for all members of the project team to understand the project in its entirety, in other words the project typically is transparent and unambiguous. The most common complaint expressed by members of any ordinary organisation is that they do not understand some aspects of their own organisation; this lament generally is not to be heard among project team members, at least in relation to the project on which they are currently working.

However, other than the need to specify task, time and team, theories pertaining to temporary organisations and project theories are dissimilar. In addition, project theory and practice vary greatly between industries. However, conference organisers at least seem to have 'solved' the problems of differences in project thinking by identifying the industries in which projects are believed to be important and catering for them. For example, PMI annual conferences are subdivided into different conference tracks along industry lines. In 1994, the theme of the main PMI conference in Vancouver was 'leadership in a world of change' with different, parallel tracks for utilities and energy, transportation, urban development, construction, oil and gas, information systems, telecommunications, pharmaceutical, manufacturing, financial services, aerospace and defence, etc. In other words, thinking about projects tends to be either very industry specific or extremely specialised in terms of tools and methods in professional circles.

The implication is that contemporary theories on temporary organisations are considerably less coherent or in alignment with each other than are corresponding theories focusing on permanent organisations, as alluded to above. Fragmentary project theories are seldom viewed as viable alternatives. One explanation for this might be that very few theorists have been involved in studying projects and that practitioners do not regard fragmentation as a problem. The result is that different versions of research in project work and project management live parallel lives in peaceful coexistence. The tendency appears to be to regard them as complementary rather than as alternatives or competing.

Project theories of the PMI type

The most conspicuous and widespread theory type when it comes to temporary organisations is normative. Project management is a label widely used in professional circles to describe the main concerns of project professionals. 'Certified knowledge' in the project management field has been documented in the pmbok guide (1996), which is the official document provided by the standards committee of the Project Management Institute – the organisation for professionals in the field (most members are in the US). The pmbok publication has existed in different versions over the years. The publication of each new version resembles a project, with a strong emphasis on the procedure to be followed. Thus, the 1996 guide was preceded by an 'exposure draft' in August 1994 that was the subject of an organisation-wide discussion.

Normative project theories have, as indicated, a great deal in common, i.e. an emphasis on time, task, team and resources. However, they also share several other traits. The most important of these is the inward-facing perspective that is typically adopted. Problems to be resolved are thought to be almost always related to the functioning of the project group or how to manage the project work in such a way that the project task is fulfilled on time. The reason for this might well be that, from the outset, the aim of project theory has been to analyse how to simplify project work and how to manage projects. The inward-looking perspective is of great interest for those actually involved in project work as it focuses on the problems that they encounter in their daily work.

Outside perspectives on projects are rarely considered in project theory of the normative type. An outside perspective might be guided by interest in the effects of projects at a societal level or the implications of an increase in project work on the workforce, employment or the measurement of national economic indicators, and so on. The only time that normative project theory adopts an outside perspective (relative to a single project) is when project dependencies are at stake, i.e. when management of a set of projects is the normative problem to be solved and when scarce resources are to be distributed to a set of projects for which the manager is responsible.

Leadership issues are also important in the normative orientation of the dominant literature. One reason for this is probably the culturally bound American fixation on leadership issues (as opposed to participative issues). Moreover, the established 'theory' of project management was developed out of the military–industrial complex (see Engwall 1995: Chapter 4) with its close association with military operations. With project management literature presented in this way, it seems quite natural for project management theory to concentrate on internal aspects, with relationships with the environment usually viewed in terms of management problems for the project manager. Other environmental aspects are almost entirely lacking in the normatively oriented literature. As a result, headings such as management of time, cost, scope, quality, integration, human resources, communications, risk and procurement appear logical (see the pmbok guide 1996).

The problem situations for which normative project theories seem to be designed can be classified as fairly closed on a scale from open to closed. The emphasis is on how to handle well-defined problem situations; as soon as questions stray somewhat from well-defined situations, normative theories either become vague (and merely indicate a problem area) or ignore the situation altogether.

The origins of PMI project theory

The techniques available for handling project work give the clear impression that normative project theories have a basis in engineering. Research on the origins of project management thought (Engwall 1995: 40–75) indicates that engineering plays an important part and that the organisation of major efforts in the military–industrial complex plays an important role in the development of project management theories of a normative type. This further indicates that project organisations are often created in environments in which a sense of urgency prevails or in which a sense of urgency can be instigated.

In prescriptive project theory, planning plays a dominant role. The underlying assumption is that planning of the entire project is possible as well as desirable. There are essentially three prerequisites for that assumption. One is that humans can control fate at least to some extent. Measures and activities undertaken in the present are believed to have effects some time in the future, which implies that measures and activities should follow a plan if the resulting effects are to be beneficial. Furthermore, means–ends relationships are, if not known at the time, at least possible to determine. Each means–end problem is believed to have a solution. Finally, the aim of the project is well understood and one-dimensional. It is obvious to everyone when the task has been fulfilled.

In project management theory it is assumed that the task and the effort required to achieve the task can be separated from everything else. Normative project theory works in situations in which there are many givens or in situations in which all other concerns are considered to be secondary to the project task (as during the Second World War or on occasions during the Cold War). Also, the norm seems to be that each project team member concentrates on his or her contribution to the project. The task to be fulfilled is dictated by someone else (i.e. other than the project manager or the team) and, when the task is accomplished, the project and the team are disbanded. Undoubtedly, the view that the project can be separated from the rest of the world is simplistic to say the least. In that sense, project thinking is an extreme form of social engineering. Recent research work of an empirical as well as a theoretical nature has focused on decoupling, i.e. where projects come from and the mechanisms by which a project is formulated and separated from its environment, and recoupling, the process that occurs when the project mission and the project group are dissolved.

In short, it could be said that project management literature since the 1950s has been dominated by notions about the need for control of projects, norms for that control and techniques and tools to fulfil the task within the given restrictions. Project management theory as an espoused theory was born. However, project thinking now appears to be drifting away from its original assumptions.

Deviations from pmbok thinking

Some of the problems of project management theory have recently been addressed in work related to the project field. One change has been to view projects less as based on techniques of an engineering type and more as based on issues such as group processes, motivation and exploration. Such issues are most important for unique projects. One recent development is the finding that people who regard their current project as unique tend to behave differently from those who view their projects as recurrent or even repetitious. That finding is well in line with what Gioia and Poole (1984) found: they envisaged a continuum between a novel situation and a stereotypical situation, in which the former is characterised by unscripted behaviours and the latter goes by a strong protoscript and mindless behaviour.

The idea that activities can be separated from everything else has been the subject of several empirical research efforts. Thus, the notion of the project environment as comprising both preproject and post-project links to the work itself (a process that has been called 'bridging') is a recent addition to project thinking.

Moreover, scrutiny of developments in the area, as reflected in discussions at professional meetings, reveals new themes (that is new to the project area). One 'in' concept in recent years has been the notion of 'empowerment'. Through some form of delegation, project team members should be empowered to take their own decisions and to act more freely in the course of the project work. This might appear to be a departure from the prevailing belief in the importance of leadership. However, one should recognise that empowerment also implies the existence of someone with the power to empower, which suggests that traditional notions of leadership have merely taken on a different form. However, those who have analysed the European concept of *Mitbestimmung* might feel that the notion of empowerment is not particularly new, either in the project field or in permanent organisations.

All in all, current project thinking seems to be deviating from traditional beliefs, with the result that more philosophical questions are posed. In fact, practitioners themselves seem to be partly responsible for this by openly admitting that they do not always practise what they preach. Theory in use is developing in different directions from that proposed by the traditional project management literature. In essence, there seems to be a deviant tendency in project management thinking among practitioners, and this trend is supported by scholarly research on project work.

Project theory weaknesses in a nutshell

Project theory is not scientific or scholarly, and the use of the word theory in this context might even be controversial. The term is instead used to describe a collection of models followed by practitioners or, in other words, a series of rules of thumb that are actually used in real-life situations. Moreover, project theory is not in any sense unitary or unified but is rather a hotchpotch of bits and pieces of theory that have survived the scrutiny of practitioners over the years. And, as indicated previously, different practitioners subscribe to different bits of theory. The difficulties from a scientific point of view that we want to highlight emanate from a variety of perspectives and essentially represent the weaknesses (aside from fragmentation) of project theory:

1   It is normative rather than descriptive (or explanatory). A practical consequence of this is that project theory is not questionable. It resists any attempt at empirical testing and represents the truth for practitioners. Even negative evidence (when normative advice does not work) is regarded as something that strengthens beliefs in the theory.
2   Inherent in project theory is the idea that partitioning (of the real world) is not only a matter of convenience but also something that can be carried out in an indisputable manner.
3   Project theory represents a powerful ontology. It suggests not only that the world can be viewed as a set of projects but also that such a view of the world has an intrinsic value.
4   Classical project theory does not take into account relationships with the project context. For instance, it cannot answer questions of the type: Where do projects come from?
5   Project theory rests on a very strong belief that means–ends relationships can be found in the practical world. Genuine uncertainties can be 'planned away'.
6   Project theory seems to be overconcerned with leadership (which is certainly one way to achieve partitioning). The overconcern is based on the dual notion that leadership is both possible and desirable.
7   Project theory is one-sided in the sense that it takes only an internal perspective on projects. A corollary to the main rule that project leadership is the most important problem area is that project theory can only deal with projects from the inside.

Learning as absent

However, the most severe criticism that can be raised against project work and project theory is the absence of learning. Two kinds of learning could be said to be involved (or not). In both cases, the lack of learning can be attributed to the time limits that are imposed on temporary organisations and the dissolution of the project team once the task has been fulfilled. The first kind is learning about the project approach and work procedures, i.e. learning that is relevant for project thinking and for the project way of organising work. The second kind is learning about the area that is the subject of the project, i.e. the practical problem at hand or what the project is all about. When individuals working on a project solve problems, the solutions are, it is to be hoped, put to use in the current project, but the only learning involved aside from the practical application of the problem solution is individual. Retrieving knowledge is thus only a question of individual activities.

In summary, neither projects nor project theory have room for how to handle learning. As projects are of limited duration, they do not include any means of storing knowledge. Learning is reduced to an individual matter.

Towards a theory of action and learning

This chapter has dealt with the shortcomings of contemporary theories on permanent and temporary organisations. It appears that these two (dichotomised) forms of organisations demonstrate deficiencies in exactly those areas where theory has either no answers or at least not very good ones. For example, permanent organisations usually demonstrate an inability to act and, in the same way, organisation theory does not encompass action as a central ingredient. Similarly, temporary organisations appear to be disabled when it comes to learning and project theory does not have learning or mechanisms for learning as a main ingredient or concern.

From a neo-industrial perspective, there appears to be a need to combine the strengths of permanent and temporary approaches in order to eliminate weaknesses or at least to ameliorate the situation. Projects or temporary organisations (as well as theory in that field) are very strong in at least three respects:

1 Projects are action oriented. They place value on getting things done as well as on work procedures designed to make things happen.
2 Projects are task oriented. The only results that count are those that were aspired to. The task is to be fulfilled within restrictions of time and other resources. Projects thus create focus.
3 Projects are flexible at the outset and can be adapted. The form of a temporary organisation can be designed with an exact purpose and only that purpose in mind. And it can be redesigned even though the popular belief of a traditional project manager says that projects should never be redesigned.

Similarly, permanent organisations have strengths (and theories to account for them) in the following areas:

1   Permanent organisations have mechanisms for learning and, even more important, for transforming learning to knowledge in a retrievable system. In this way, they have a definite instrument for progress.
2   The decision orientation of permanent organisations says that they have an explicit apparatus for deliberating decisions and generating and evaluating alternatives. Action can be based on solid grounds.
3   Permanent organisations typically stress rhetorical aspects of their activities. Organisational culture is an important input to the rhetoric processes as well as an important output of the rhetoric.

One limitation common to both project and organisation theory is their tendency to regard projects and organisations as distinct entities and, consequently, to favour linking explanations, theories and models to these entities. One general conclusion of the first two chapters of this book was that formal organisations and single projects as separate units are of less importance in a neo-industrial society. Instead, boundary-crossing (or boundary-spanning) activities and the explicit linking of a multitude of organisational forms seem to be a central characteristic of neo-industrialism. A limitation of contemporary theory is thus its a priori assumption that organisational phenomena are either formal organisations or projects. We believe that a more appropriate theoretical understanding has to be developed along other lines. Instead of focusing on organisational forms as the most important issue, we propose, as argued earlier, that action and learning are two of the most important aspects to be addressed in the neo-industrial context. These aspects will be foci of special attention in Chapters 5 and 6. In Chapter 4, the empirical food for thought that we have been utilising will be described. That chapter will provide an overview of our empirical base for the statements concerning the developments of the neo-industrial economy.

4 The project landscape – our empirical base

A wide variety of phenomena could be labelled projects. However, not all of them are interesting from the perspective of neo-industrial organising as we have alluded to it previously. However, the 25 cases that will be briefly described illustrate various aspects of a neo-industrial way of organising. They all exhibit some kind of renewal effort in which action and learning or knowledge formation are important components, and they illustrate some of the difficulties involved in dealing with the renewal paradox or transformation dilemmas. They are also evidence of management ambitions to reform businesses activities or the like.

It should be stressed that it was the empirical impetus that initially led us to the notion of the neo-industrial economy, in other words case selection was crucial. We do not intend to describe the research process in detail, but since the selection phase turned out to be crucial we will describe this phase fully. Originally we set out to find a selection of projects (or temporary organisations) that would improve our understanding of how projects work internally. Thus, at that point we selected pairs of projects that we expected to have some common traits but also evident differences. The aim of the initial selection process was to provide broad input into our efforts to understand the working of projects *per se* utilising the conceptions of similarities and differences that guided the selection. What traits, if any, do projects have in common? Are the processes similar, etc? Simultaneously we conducted a literature search.

During our discussions of the cases (when we found the variety to be very useful) as well as during our discussions of the literature in the field, we realised that we were drifting away from our original aim, i.e. to understand projects internally by relating the theoretical literature to what we were experiencing empirically. As a result, we increased the number of cases from which we collected data. In fact, as many as 16 out of the 25 cases presented came from the additional set. Eventually, combining and comparing all the cases made us prone to synthesise (rather than analyse) at a level far and above the individual case level, concentrating on the role projects seem to play in the industrial context on a grander scale. And the name we coined for that synthetical level that we felt we observed is neo-industrial organising. In retrospect, one might say that the selection of cases was an example of theoretical sampling in a Glaser and Strauss (1967) sense. This is true at least of the second half of the study, when the selection of cases was guided by emerging concepts.

Now that projects appear to be very important from the neo-industrial perspective (what is actually new is project thinking), this means that we could easily continue to use the project level to illustrate our reasoning. To argue more strongly, one might say that our aim was to abstain from the general tendency to describe primarily permanent organisation(s). That is why the principal focus of this chapter is a general description of projects rather than of host organisations. Rather than envisaging projects as subordinate to the permanent organisation, we prefer to view the permanent organisation through the projects. The choice of projects as the prime representations of the cases is in alignment with the essence of our findings. The neo-industrial way of thinking comes increasingly into focus when using the project as the starting point. In addition, most of the projects we analysed initially turned out to be useful also for the kind of meso-level synthesis that we have indulged in. And the variety of contexts in which our projects were to be found seems to demonstrate the general truth of our conjectures and findings (even though considerable variation can be found). The neo-industrial pattern seemed very consistent.

For a while we tended to be highly critical of these general ideas of neo-industrial organising, especially as they tended to get carried away by the mental constructs that we ourselves put forward. In fact, we made very conscious efforts to find viable counterarguments or counter-examples. However, the notions seemed to survive all simple and straightforward attempts to nullify them – empirically as well as theoretically. We further extended our literature search to encompass the meso-level where our discussions had taken us. However, not even at this level did we find substantial counterarguments or contrary evidence. Instead, the development as we came to describe it seemed to be in line also with what meso-level theorists and futurists in the field were saying.

The cases we present fit the current purpose to illustrate forms and aspects of projects that seem to play a role in neo-industrial organising. The text should also function as an illustration of the variety of forms that projects can take, especially for those readers who are not all that familiar with projects. Thus, the reader should be able to grasp some of the main notions of each project. The descriptions also provide some indications of the bases for our claims. The cases have most certainly served as good sources of inspiration for us. Notwithstanding the efforts mentioned above to be critical in a very serious sense, the cases presented here should not be taken as proof of the phenomenon we discuss. There are several reasons for this, two of the most important being: (i) neo-industrial organising emerged as an output or as a perspective from the cases we have been working with and (ii) the cases will not be described in so much detail that the descriptions can be used directly to corroborate our claims.

Next we discuss the practical aspects of how the cases (projects) described in this chapter were chosen and how they are presented. The projects are then described in a summary form with the emphasis not so much on the internal functioning of the projects but on the contexts in which they were undertaken. The contextual dimension is used to group the cases into five different subgroups. For obvious reason each case is described only briefly. However, we have not attempted to form all descriptions in the same mould: some are longer than others. In most cases write-ups are available, some published as working papers, though. The reader who is in a hurry should use this chapter for reference only and head directly to Chapters 5 and 6, which discuss action and knowledge formation respectively. Those are the two aspects that we want to stress as important in the neo-industrial context of renewal.

General aspects and choice of cases

The reasoning in this book is largely based on longitudinal studies that we have recently carried out within a number of organisations in Sweden and elsewhere. Our aim is to paint a broad picture of renewal initiatives taken in a contemporary economic and industrial situation. We did not look specifically for success stories or for examples of best-run companies or anything of that kind; instead we concentrated on projects conducted in host organisations that are known to be in the front line concerning development ventures, projects that at the time were also attracting attention in professional or public circles. In a few instances we were explicitly invited by organisations to participate in research on their contemplated transformation projects. With few exceptions (see below) the projects were *de facto* initiated by top management with the immediate or ultimate purpose of renewing the organisation.

The chosen projects relate to many different situations and contexts. Some were carried out in a general societal environment (e.g. urban renewal and renewal within the Swedish defence programme). Many are examples of projects taking place within a clear-cut and typical industrial setting, whereas a few others represent the public sector. A couple of cases are drawn from the cultural/artistic field (theatre production), which should serve to illustrate the wide applicability of neo-industrial ideas. In two instances the project was launched in a foreign environment (a major French research park venture and an East European industrial endeavour). Other projects are taken from the Swedish domestic scene. However, many of the host organisations are corporations with worldwide operations (ABB, Ericsson, Skanska, Volvo, Saab Aircraft, Digital Equipment, Sunds Defibrator) so their experiences should mirror operations outside the Swedish context and have a bearing outside Sweden as well.

The projects are drawn from both non-project-based and project-based organisations. The host organisations thus represent two principal forms of organising operations: flow-process organisation and projectised organisation. In the flow-process situation, regular experiences of project organisation are somewhat rare, or at least not in focus, as opposed to the projectised situation. Generally, one permanent host organisation sponsored the project, but our cases also include a few examples of joint sponsorship or partnering in a societal–interorganisational project. In addition, some of the cases chosen are recurrent product development or production projects that were transformed into some kind of unique renewal project with the ultimate view of influencing the total organisation and its future functioning.

The level of renewal, that is the degree, pace and scope of efforts, varies from one project to another depending on the ambitions in the particular case. Aspirations range from moderate to radical transformation of the project target, and efforts could be geared to incremental change or to change in one go, i.e. piecemeal adjustments made over a long period of time or a concentrated major effort. Renewal can also be more or less organisationally all-embracing: the project could concern an organisational sphere of society, a business or public organisation (or group of organisations) or an organisational unit.

The target or focus of renewal endeavours ('what to renew') is also a source of variety. A common aim of renewal projects in organisations is to improve relations with customers and other recipients of the 'product' or, more generally, as the PMI puts it, 'to meet or exceed stakeholder needs and expectations from a project' (pmbok guide 1996: 6). This can be achieved by targeting the work behaviour of organisation members and other actors involved and, in so doing, improving also the general functioning of the organisation. As the examples will demonstrate, this aim can also be achieved directly by focusing on the qualities of the product or service produced, e.g. by improving the design of the product and adding new technical and other features.

The projects studied are thus examples of rather exceptional ventures, in which great expectations of renewal are entertained. They are also projects designed and launched to further general organisational renewal as an ultimate objective. Their direction is visionary rather than well structured in the details, and consequently the level of uncertainty and risk at conception must have appeared high. They are in glaring contrast to the regular, recurring projects that we have studied previously, e.g. in the construction industry, in which the renewal paradox (as discussed in Chapter 1) is manifestly evident in almost all projects.

Characterisation of cases

The frame of reference to be used in presenting the renewal projects studied is summarised below. The projects will be characterised according to certain crucial dimensions, i.e. context, scope, pace and prime target of renewal, as shown in Table 4.1. These dimensions are crucial as they determine much of the character of the project.

A project, according to the PMI, is 'a temporary endeavour undertaken to create a unique product or service' (pmbok guide 1996: 4). If we subscribe to this general description of a project, we can elaborate the project concept by making a distinction between regular, *recurring* projects and special, *unique* projects as follows. In a recurring project the team members in general feel that they have substantial experience of similar projects and apply existing knowledge to create a unique product or service, whereas in a unique project they feel that the situation is novel and requires new knowledge. Refinement is natural (or possible) in the first case, renewal in the second (see Lundin and Söderholm 1995: 441).

The various forms that the two types of projects could take in different organisational contexts are illustrated in Table 4.2.

The renewal projects studied will be classified according to the form of organisational production system in which they were carried out – flow-process, projectised or societal–interorganisational projectised – and also according to the scope of the project. This results in five major groups of renewal projects (see Table 4.2):

1 total organisation (flow-process)
2 part organisation (flow-process)
3 total organisation (projectised)
4 part organisation (projectised)
5 societal–interorganisational (projectised).

Table 4.1 Classification of projects concerning organisational context, scope, pace and prime target of renewal

---

Organisational context
*   Flow-process organisation
*   Projectised organisation
*   Societal–interorganisational (projectised) organisation

Scope
*   Sphere of society
*   Group of organisations
*   Individual organisation
*   Part-organisation

Pace
*   Incremental
*   In one go

Prime target ('what to renew')
*   Work behaviour of actors involved
*   Qualities of the product or service produced

Table 4.2 Project types common in different production systems

Dominating mode of operations	Regular, recurring projects	Special, unique projects (scope of renewal)
Flow-process	Development projects (e.g. concerning product features, production processes, individual competence)	Total organisation Part organisation (transformed development projects)
Projectised	Production projects Development projects (e.g. concerning product features, production/project processes, individual competence)	Total organisation Part organisation (transformed production or development projects)
Societal– interorganisational projectised	Production projects Development projects (e.g. concerning societal functioning, features of societal object)	Societal organisation or object (trans- formed production or development projects)

The most typical cases in each group will be outlined in more detail. Table 4.3 provides an overview of the classification the 25 renewal projects described in this book.

Group 1: projects concerning total organisation renewal in a flow-process context

Projects in this group are initiated by top management and have the aim of total organisation renewal. This group includes the following cases with their permanent host organisation:

Project	*Host organisation*
'T50'	Swedish ABB Group
'We are Building Control'	ABB Control
'K-Concept'	Sunds Defibrator Manufacturing
'Poland Project'	ABB ZWUS Signal–Swedish ABB Group
'STIS 2000' (Study Support Information System)	Central Study Support Committee (CSN)
'EPQ' (efficiency–productivity–quality)	Västerbotten Medical Care Area (VL)

Table 4.3 Characteristics of the renewal projects presented

Organisational context (host)	Scope				Pace		Prime target	
	Society	Group	Org	Part org	Long run	In one go	Behav	Prod
Flow-process								
Group 1								
Swedish ABB		×				×	×	
ABB Control			×			×	×	
Sunds			×			×	×	
ABB ZWUS			×			×	×	
CSN			×			×	×	
VL	×					×	×	
Group 2								
Saab JAS 39				×		×		×
Volvo 850				×		×		×
Saab 2000				×		×		×
Projectised								
Group 3								
Skanska		×				×	×	
Diös		×				×	×	
Diös Östra			×			×	×	
Kullenberg		×		×			×	
Ericsson				×		×	×	
Digital		×		×			×	
Young Klara		×		×			×	
Group 4								
Royal Opera				×		×	×	(×)
Young Klara				×		×	×	(×)
Skanska Stockholm				×		×	×	(×)
Skanska Norrland				×		×	×	(×)
Kullenberg				×		×	×	(×)
Societal– interorganisational								
Group 5								
Arlandastad	×				×			×
Uminova stad	×				×			×
Sophia Antipolis	×				×			×
JAS 39	×				×			×

Org, organisation; Behav, behaviour; Prod, product.

'T50' – Swedish ABB Group

ABB's T50 project (Ekstedt and Wirdenius 1995; Wirdenius 1994) is a massive project initiated by management with the aim of renewing traditional industrial production within the corporation's subsidiary companies. It adopted a combined approach aimed at bringing about both fast, radical and long-term, incremental transformation of subsidiary company operations. Thus, the chief target of renewal was the work behaviour of all organisation members, but effort was also directed towards influencing business partners. The objective was to develop modes of action that would secure future continuous improvement in the quality, cost and delivery times of products and services, and in this way increase customer satisfaction. At a later stage the technical qualities of the products also received attention.

The principal renewal action undertaken by top management was the introduction of imperative rules (e.g. reduce order-to-delivery times by 50 per cent, which led to the acronym T50) and thus new work roles. Different kinds of professional expertise were utilised in the design and steering of the project, e.g. specialists from international management consulting firms. They supplied knowledge on change processes and assisted in the extensive training activity needed, and thus were instrumental in achieving the desired mental and behavioural changes. Renewal initiatives were expected from the subsidiaries, although the reception that the change message from top management received varied from company to company. However, generally corporate project goals were felt to have been achieved. One of the subsidiary companies, ABB Control, which was a main innovator and inspirer of this corporate project, is the subject of a special study reported below.

The T50 case in brief

The initiative to start a radical renewal effort in the Swedish ABB Group was taken by its CEO. He had become interested in the new management model called 'time-based management' and had seen the promising results of experiments with goal-directed groups in ABB Control. The foundation for the transformation of company operations, however, had been laid by the president of the ABB Corporation, Percy Barnevik, who carried out a decentralisation and debureaucratisation drive in Asea (one of the companies forming ABB) following his appointment.

Senior managers promoted their renewal message primarily by referring to the increasing competition in the world market: 'We are shooting at moving targets all the time. Markets change, customers change, competitors change. We have to take part. That is the only security for jobs.' (Boman 1992). Moreover, they pointed out that industrial work is often seen as boring, monotonous, strenuous and lacking freedom. Therefore, the vision presented by managers was of a company realising the goal of 'satisfied customers and motivated co-workers'. This called for a new method of organising production. T50 was expected to realise this vision.

The renewal message sent forth by senior managers emphasised the following aspects of ABB's operations:

- The customer is always the focus of work.
- The role of workers is changing.
- Continuous improvement of operations will be achieved by the application of a number of recommended 'tools'.
- Radical reduction in throughput times is the aim.

Consideration of customers' needs and demands formed the basis of action. Meeting delivery times, quality specifications and competitive cost requirements was a minimum demand. Instead, exceeding customer expectations was the determining competitive factor.

The renewal effort implied a 'cultural revolution', a mental change in all members of the old, solid and engineer-dominated organisation. It required the development of a new view of labour, a new leadership based on trust and confidence in each individual.

One challenge was to make the transformation permanent, to develop a lasting process of continuous improvement. Moreover, all improvements had to contribute to the final result and in the long term to increased profitability.

A number of means, 'tools', were recommended for application in the renewal effort: goal-directed groups, time focusing, benchmarking (looking for good examples), competence development, etc. A comprehensive information pack was also available, showing employees how the renewal work could be carried through in the subsidiary companies.

A primary objective of the effort was that order-to-delivery-times would be halved by the end of the third year (on average). This was a non-negotiable target as it was embodied in the title of the project. To put a quality stamp on the renewal initiatives of the subsidiaries, criteria for so-called T50 authorisation were developed (for example well-defined objectives in terms of customer value and delivery times, concrete plans for projects, involvement of a fairly large unit and a reasonable number of organisation members).

A central group with one vice-president as a project leader was set up to support subsidiaries in their renewal work. This group assisted with education and training, information, exchange of experiences and development of the renewal programme. At the subsidiary level, the renewal work was expected to be initiated by the managing director, who would act as a local project leader. Customers and suppliers were to be involved in the renewal process with a view to deepening the collaboration with them. (For a more comprehensive description of the T50 renewal project, see for example Steen 1991; Boman 1992; ABB 1994; Hart and Berger 1994; Wirdenius 1994. For an analysis of the relationship between corporate change in ABB and learning, see Lundin and Söderholm 1993; Shani and Stjernberg 1994.)

'We Are Building Control' – ABB Control

ABB Control was the first company in the ABB Group to introduce the concepts of flow-time focus and worker involvement, as well as goal-directed groups. This development project ('Time 88') was in fact initiated before the T50 programme was launched by group management.

The change programme continued and was named 'We are Building Control'. Organisational changes were combined with extensive competence development programmes. The T50 message actually confirmed and articulated a continuous process of progression. In fact, many of the ideas included in the T50 programme had already been accepted and achieved by employees working in production. There are indications that the motivation and commitment of employees, as well as their self-esteem, were increased. Certainly, T50 provided them with new tools for a continued renewal process (Hart and Berger 1994).

The most visible aspect of the We Are Building Control programme was the introduction of goal-directed groups. These could be viewed as companies within the company. The group members are responsible for directing and distributing work among themselves and for liaising with management, as well as with suppliers and customers. It goes without saying that the groups also take full responsibility for the quality of production. The company has received the ISO 9000 certificate, which both stimulates and rewards quality efforts.

This new method of dividing up work has increased the demand for communication skills in the workforce compared with the traditional line organisation. This calls for further training, which is arranged by managers in consultation with the groups.

The role of white-collar workers has changed dramatically as much of their traditional work has been transferred to the goal-directed groups. Lower-level white-collar workers are most affected by these changes. Salaried employees at all levels have been assigned an active role in supporting production staff. These new roles have not yet assumed their definite shape, but managers are exploring possible competence development initiatives for this group.

'K-Concept' – Sunds Defibrator Manufacturing

This project, initiated by Sunds Defibrator (Ekstedt and Wirdenius 1994a,b), was an enterprise renewal endeavour similar to that undertaken by the Swedish ABB Group but differing in several respects. Conceived as a relatively short-term, once-only effort, the initiative lost its clear and stable focus when the initiating CEO left the company. The prime target of renewal was general work behaviour in the company. The ambition was to 'develop competitive power to win customers' by raising the level of knowledge in the organisation. The K-Concept, stressing the importance of knowledge, was thus a basic tool of the improvement programme. The approach used by senior managers to accomplish change was an introductory physical restructuring of the workshop, followed by some institutional measures involving changes in work roles. The major initiative, however, was a massive training programme for every individual. The project increased commitment and action, at least until the initiating chief executive left the organisation.

The K-Concept case in brief

The company had for a long time existed under the protection of a major paper and pulp corporation (SCA). When it was sold to a Finnish engineering group, Sunds suddenly found itself facing tough international competition. The new managing director soon found that the workshop was very unprofitable and instituted a radical renewal programme. The renewal effort was viewed by the managing director as a relatively short-term development, 'improvement work' to be carried out by line managers as project leaders, with himself as project manager/sponsor/supporter/owner.

The company manufactures large machinery and systems for the paper and pulp industry. Shop operations had been designed as one-piece production within a traditional functional organisation but senior managers wanted to develop a process or flow arrangement within the framework of a project-organised production.

The target for the renewal effort set by top management was to halve the through time within the organisation, trebling the stock turnover rate and reducing the cost level. The basic objective was to guarantee delivery and quality assurance. The vision stated for the renewal work reads as follows: 'we are to work with continuous improvement in order to become the best in the industry' and 'we are to set up a record'. The following steps were taken to realise this vision:

- The workshop was physically rearranged and a production structure that could develop into flows was created.
- The new units within the workshop were manned by teams of operators in an attempt to develop a new organisational form with an emphasis on teamwork rather than individuals. The position of shop manager was abolished and supervisors were made project leaders of operator teams.
- Training programmes were arranged to teach operators how to run several machines and to introduce them to the new approach to speed up flow and shorten through times.
- A customer–supplier attitude was developed.

The so-called K-Concept was formed as basic tool for achieving the improvement programme. According to the K-Concept, the company can, by continuous improvement of quality, capital, cost, communication and knowledge, develop competitive power to win customers (in Swedish the underlined letters are k rather than c). The K-Concept thinking and way of work was conveyed via external seminars to all members of the organisation, with the managing director as a primary actor. The participants brainstormed improvement ideas in small groups, gave priority to selected ideas and drew up a list of ideas. In support for improvements in line with the K-Concept, senior managers determined norms for leadership, role of production leader, teamwork, role of coach and team tasks.

'Poland Project' – ABB ZWUS Signal

We have studied one enterprise renewal project carried out in a foreign environment. This renewal venture – termed the Poland Project – was undertaken by ABB ZWUS Signal, formed by the merger of ABB and a Polish engineering company (Ekstedt and Wirdenius 1993; Nish *et al.* 1996). This project is an example of a radical once-only transformation approach followed by piecemeal refinement efforts. The prime target of renewal was general work behaviour with the aim of increasing the general effectiveness of the organisation and thus also increasing product quality. However, the objective was not only to increase customer satisfaction through increased quality of products and service, but also to influence customers to demand higher quality. The approach included investments in new machinery, Swedish consultancy services and recruitment, education and training of managers and other personnel with a view to introducing new knowledge. This is a case of successful cultural and professional transformation with a high level of commitment.

The Poland Project case in brief

The problems of organisational renewal are particularly complex in another culture, as in the ABB ZWUS venture. How can modern organisational and technical knowledge, market thinking and customer orientation be transferred to a culture with cemented attitudes and work behaviours stemming from 45 years of Communist rule? The principal challenge in this case was to find ways of changing people's behaviour rather than to change machinery and equipment.

The approach taken by the ABB project manager in charge was to make the five division managers the prime motors of change. He exerted pressure on the division managers from both the top and bottom of the organisation. This was accomplished by setting specific goals and at the same time making employees on the shop floor aware of the need for change and the opportunities involved in change by giving them special training.

The divisions were organised as 'firms within the firm'. The aim was to create an internal market economy and to make all members of the organisation aware of costs. The transfer of ideas from the Swedish ABB to ZWUS was primarily achieved by the project manager and a large number of ABB consultants specialising in, for example, marketing, production, quality, organisation, training and information, purchasing, computer systems, economy modelling and control and technology transfer. All employees attended a training course on the role of the company in a market economy. During the training course, the division managers entered discussions directly with employees from the shop floor for the first time. Middle managers also received formal training, e.g. on the psychological aspects of management.

Through this organisational design the division managers became the key actors in the restructuring process. They came to understand the intentions underlying the ABB philosophy and also developed the ability to adapt them to the Polish situation.

A particular difficulty for the Swedish consultants was the differences between the national cultures of Sweden and Poland. Therefore, the consultants were allowed an ample introductory period to familiarise them with the local thinking before suggesting any changes in operations. The major goals set out by ABB were achieved. However, the relearning process at the shop floor level will probably continue.

'STIS 2000' – Central Study Support Committee

This case study concerns a public organisation operating in a flow-process organisation context (Ekstedt and Wirdenius 1994a,b). The CSN project STIS 2000 was sponsored by a fiery top official. It was a radical, once-only initiative ultimately targeting the quality of the service rendered to 'customers' (students) in the form of more comprehensive information. The work behaviour of the office staff was the prime focus as a means of ensuring that the quality of the service comes up to standard. In order to achieve this, a major initiative to improve the present IT system was undertaken, involving the introduction of an entirely new system with maximum use of modern technology. The approach was to use external and internal expert help to train the entire staff in the new technology. To a great extent, this involved both unlearning and relearning, as the new system was different from the old one in a very basic sense. The change process was hindered by delayed political decisions, but on the whole the new technique has been received with acceptance and moderate commitment.

The STIS 2000 case in brief

CSN is a national decentralised service organisation established to administer state study grants. To meet current and future demands for efficiency as well as customer and market orientation, CSN needs an effective and flexible information system. The computer system that was in use before the STIS 200 programme dated from the 1970s, and its structural and technical design was such that it was difficult to modernise work organisation and business operations. Working routines were computerised step by step over the years. Several different systems were added to the old ones. Eventually the multitude of systems and the lack of compatibility between them became so great that logistical problems and inefficiency were the result. Amending the existing system would have required a very expensive investment. It became evident that a totally new system had to be developed and implemented in the organisation. This, in turn, would provide senior managers with the opportunity to reorganise and extend the area of activity.

A major effect of the proposed new system was that fewer administrators were required. However, it also expanded the role of the administrators, who had to be willing and able to do everything. All-round competence was therefore an advantage. Furthermore, employees were expected to replace authority-based performance by customer-oriented behaviour, i.e. to adopt a service attitude. Moreover, the new techniques necessitated a different type of structural thinking, one that demanded unlearning as well as new learning. The new information system required a radical mental reorientation on the part of administrators/users.

Senior managers – represented by a dedicated person (the Deputy Director-General) – decided to make a radical move and rebuild the whole system using up-to-date technology. Project groups were formed to analyse the situation. They delivered a report containing a detailed description and specification of the new information system required. Top management commissioned the group to achieve the plan.

Pilot studies were undertaken to select possible information tools. These were then developed in collaboration with users (development of windows, dialog boxes and icons). The development work also required detailed job specifications to be drawn up and suitably qualified persons selected. Implementation of the system with final users/administrators will be carried out in several stages following final user tests and a comprehensive user training. The new system may also require organisational changes in the local offices.

The renewal process was to a great extent influenced by the technology of the system, with the project team determining the choice of technology and its implementation. Their approach was to try to adapt people concurrently with the building of systems. This was achieved through extensive training and development programmes for developers (selected qualified persons from the old environment). Thus, the design and implementation of change was characterised by broad user collaboration, controlled by the project management team.

The project manager regarded CSN as an organisation prepared for and competent to change. Staff there have passed through many transformations over the years. Renewal work is thought to have been facilitated by the fact that the staff is a relatively homogeneous professional group with similar values and competence.

However, the renewal project has been delayed and ambitions have had to be lowered. That is because politicians have not decided on the new rules of study support as expected. The new information system that is to replace the old patchwork system was designed to implement the new rules. The delay makes this impossible, and to wait for a decision is not feasible on grounds of economy. Fortunately, as a result of new technological developments, it is now possible for the old and new information systems to exist side by side, and the old system will be replaced gradually.

The renewal work in this case was facilitated by the fact that it was technology led. Technology was imperative. The new technology was quite different from the old system, however, and therefore some unlearning has to be undertaken before new learning could begin. At this time, the new information system is in operation, but is undergoing a running-in period.

'EPQ' – Västerbotten Medical Care Area (VL)

This case study also concerns a public organisation operating in a flow-process organisation context (Lundin and Söderholm 1997). The VL project EPQ, (efficiency, productivity, quality) was an attempt at radical reform in a major public service organisation. It illustrates the application of a process-oriented, long-term approach with a view to renewing traditional work behaviour in various divisions of an organisation. The underlying aim was to increase the quality and reduce the cost and time taken to supply the service. The process required a gradual change in old habits and ways of organising health care. The general approach used was based on reorganisation and rules regarding finance and modes of operation. As the renewal initiatives were undertaken locally, their reception varied considerably depending on the current situation in the organisational units.

The EPQ case in brief

Health care in Sweden is provided by public organisations financed mainly from taxes. Each county has its own health care organisation. This case study concerns Västerbotten, which is one of the 24 counties of Sweden. Like other public organisations, health care has experienced financial problems during the 1990s, with an increasing demand for reduction in costs and increased productivity. In

1992, Västerbotten County Council decided to implement the EPQ project in order to cut spending, making the organisation more effective without lowering quality. This project was launched in parallel with a major organisational reform in which a buyer–provider organisation replaced an earlier functional organisational structure.

A number of activities were fulfilled as part of the EPQ project. A new accounting system was designed. This comprised a new method of measuring 'production' at clinics as well as new routines for distributing financial resources from the council to hospitals and further down to clinics and new budgeting, planning and reporting procedures. During the first years after the project launch in 1992 the focus was on productivity. The changes were initially designed by special taskforces, but there were no specific project groups active during implementation. Instead, implementation was made the responsibility of the line, i.e. the clinic heads and the managers at different levels in the hierarchy.

Different medical specialties responded differently to the EPQ subprojects. Some clinics, e.g. surgery, accepted and made use of the new systems quite quickly, whereas others, e.g. psychiatry, had problems implementing the new 'product-oriented' philosophy of measuring production. Also, as clinic doctors and clinic heads had the ultimate responsibility for implementing the changes, implementation was slow in some clinics or hospitals and faster in others because of differences in managerial priorities.

As the project focused on productivity issues, it was generally held that quality development and quality assurance had been neglected. Therefore, a second 'wave' of renewal was started in 1995 in the form of a TQM subproject. All employees received quality training and a new set of techniques for measuring and improving quality was adopted. Other measures taken included the appointment of 'quality coaches' within all medical clinics.

Many of the initial routines, procedures and systems that were implemented during the first year were later revised in response to a number of problems. It turned out to be very difficult to measure 'production' and to use such measurements for resource allocation; the buyer–provider organisation did not work as intended; and the independence given to clinics as part of the new accounting system was not entirely successful in all clinics. On the other hand, efficiency, in terms of number of patients treated in relation to the money spent, increased in almost all areas, total spending went down and 'more' health care could be provided to the inhabitants. Managers in the organisation were generally given better instruments for decision making.

The project was a typical renewal project in that methods for renewal were unknown or only vaguely known initially and success was dependent on many individuals throughout the organisation. In the final stages of the projects, a number of renewal goals had to be revised or abandoned while others were added.

Group 2: projects concerning part-organisation renewal in a flow-process context

Projects in this group involve transformation, by senior managers, of a regular, recurring product development project into a renewal project. The cases are as follows:

Project	Host Organisation
'JAS 39 Gripen'	Saab Military Aircraft
'Saab 2000'	Saab Aircraft
'Volvo 850'	Volvo Car Group

Projects JAS 39 Gripen (undertaken by Saab Military Aircraft), Saab 2000 (Saab Aircraft) and Volvo 850 (Volvo) are different from the all-embracing enterprise renewal undertakings described above in that they involved only part of the organisation and focused specifically on the product produced (and, in the case of Saab Military Aircraft, on only part of the product). They are all unique, once-only product development ventures (Lindbergh and Sandström 1994; Lundin *et al.* 1995) and are in fact among the largest projects of the kind undertaken recently in Sweden. Thus, they focus on the qualities of a new version or model of the main product, to be produced in the future. The issue is one of radical change in the design of an extremely complex product: technical sophistication, superior performance and outstanding cost-effectiveness are expected to be the hallmark of the new creation.

The approach used in product renewal is characterised by an emphasis on supplying project team members with essential new knowledge. Considerable resources are released and free scope is allowed for creative thinking and learning. However, the prerequisites of focusing on the final product as well as the strict time constraints mean that severe conflicts in the project team have to be avoided, and thus members with a similar professional background have to be recruited. These projects have a great impact on the future organisation of production and business operations. This is because there exists a continuous exchange of ideas and work assignments between the project organisation and the more permanent base organisation. Being exceptional endeavours, the chances of obtaining commitment to the project are high. Two of these projects will be described here, Saab 2000 and Volvo 850. As the JAS 37 Gripen project was studied as part of another context, its main features are described in the section on group 5 projects.

'Saab 2000' – Saab Aircraft

Saab Aircraft is a division within Saab-Scania that develops and manufactures aircraft and components for other aircraft manufacturers. In the late 1990s, Saab-Scania markets three aircraft: two propeller-driven passenger aircraft, Saab 340 and 2000, and one military aircraft, JAS 39 Gripen.

In 1984, Saab Aircraft launched its passenger plane, Saab 340, on the market. The 340 aircraft carries 34 passengers in its standard version. Almost immediately after completing the development of 340, it was decided to develop another passenger aircraft with better performance and more seats. Initial studies were begun in 1985, and by 1988 the specification for the new aircraft was decided upon. According to this specification, the new Saab 2000 aircraft was to be a turbo-prop aircraft, capable of high speed and long range, high rates of climb, better economic performance than conventional regional turbo-props and jets, and with 58 seats. It opened up a new market for long-range regional aircraft when it was introduced on the market in 1994 after certification procedures.

The Saab 2000 case in brief

Saab 2000 is a turbo-prop regional aircraft, serving as a regional aircraft. The project took five years (1989–1994) from the formal decision to carry out the project until certification of the aircraft. Important dates are:

1985	Planning for the development of a second regional aircraft starts
1988	Specifications for Saab 2000
May 1989	Formal decision to conduct the Saab 2000 project
February 1990	Production of three prototypes
December 1991	'Roll-out', i.e. prototype leaves factory and is showed to the general public
March 1992	First test flights
March 1994	Saab 2000 is certified and ready for service

The project management group consisted of a project manager, a controller and a coordinator. This relatively small group had the responsibility for five different units: engineering, flight operations, quality and flying qualities, production, and purchasing. The sponsoring permanent organisation was reorganised during the project, and this meant that the workload for those involved in the project changed, although this did not directly affect the formal organisation of the project.

The development of the aircraft was initially divided into 45 different 'arbetspaket' or tasks. Most tasks involved production of parts of the aircraft (e.g. wings) or specific subsystems (e.g. the fuel system), but equally important were tasks involving analyses or testing. All 45 tasks were defined according to scope, design criteria, input needed from other task groups, output delivered to other task groups, time frames, budget, etc. A computerised system (ARTEMIS) was used to keep track of the different tasks and of the project as a whole.

ARTEMIS could also be used to analyse the performance of individual organisational units (e.g. those doing carrying out work on different tasks) or the progress of general activities such as testing (consisting of the work of several task groups).

Each task group was headed by a so-called monitor (who could be responsible for more than one group). The monitors helped to determine the role and goals of each task group and were responsible for the delivery of the group's output. There was a kind of contractual agreement between the project manager/ management and the various monitors, who had to sign an agreement when accepting the role. Some tasks were mainly performed by companies other than Saab. For example, the wings were developed by a Spanish company. However, in all cases monitors were employed by Saab in order to guarantee Saab influence and to facilitate project management contacts with different units in the project.

An important task for the project, as a whole, was to guarantee a short lead time from order to delivery once the aircraft was certified. Since Saab receives a down-payment when an order is placed and final payment after delivery, a short manufacturing time reduces the need for capital for both Saab and the customer. The first Saab 2000 took around 200 days to manufacture, but this time was reduced to around 100 days after the first year. To achieve this, Saab subcontracted technology and processes.

'Volvo 850' – Volvo Car Group

Volvo is, by international standards, a small but independent car manufacturer. The Volvo 850 was a new car model released in 1991. It was the first car developed by Volvo to be built around a front-wheel-drive technology. The Volvo 850 was the result of a systematic search for new car models that was initiated in the 1970s. From 1978 to 1981 a development team experimented with different types of new car with formal development of the 850 taking place between 1986 and 1991. In 1991, the Volvo 850 was launched as 'a dynamic car with four world-sensational breakthroughs'. These four features were: transverse five-cylinder engine driving the front wheels; a delta-link rear axle that combined the dynamics of independent suspension with the security of a live rear axle; SIPS (integrated side-impact protection system); and, finally, a self-adjusting front seat belt mechanism.

The project also included the planning and development of factories and production processes. As the Volvo 800 series was different from earlier Volvo models, marketing efforts and market research paralleled the development project at some times.

The Volvo 850 case in brief

Project work started with the evaluation of different alternatives in the late 1970s, conceptual work continued until 1986 and car development was undertaken between 1986 and 1991, following which the car was presented to the markets. It was, to Volvo, a huge project in which almost US$3bn was invested.

When the project was initiated (in the mid-1980s), the intention was to avoid the independent and sequential development organisation that had been characteristic of previous development projects. That meant that the project had to be more interactive and interorganisational to guarantee that, for example, production engineers were involved in construction and vice versa.

The project was headed by a project management group comprising a variety of representatives from engineering, purchasing, production, aftersales, marketing, quality and finance. The management group also headed a concept group, a product technology group and a premarketing group, each of which in turn headed different, more specific, development efforts. For each component area or subsystem, a component head was appointed. Component areas included the interior, engine, transmission, electricity, climate and body. A component head was responsible for the whole family of products. A specific 'cross-organisational component area management group' and a 'preparation group' were formed for each component or system area. These groups were initiated to ensure communication between different parts of the organisation and between different development efforts. A 'product technology group' was formed to deal with any adjustment necessary within the specific development project.

Consequently, the project was managed (i) as a project with traditional project management functions, (ii) as a cross-organisational effort with various ways of dealing with project–permanent organisation issues and (iii) as a cross-technology effort with different methods of linking similar technology development efforts in different parts of the company and different development efforts within the same project.

To this overall organisational structure was added a time plan, with new projects passing through the stages of preparatory studies, system design, prestudy (when a specific car project is designed) and product project (the development of the car). The aim is that when a new car project is launched it should be possible to make use of project development efforts or system designs carried out previously, in other words to 'repackage' parts of the car wherever possible.

Group 3: projects concerning total organisation renewal in a projectised context

Projects in this group are total organisation renewal projects instituted by senior managers. The projects and the organisations concerned are as follows:

Project	Host organisation
'3T' Total Time Thinking	Skanska Construction Group
'Cultural Renewal'	Diös Construction Group
'Let's Rebuild!'	Diös Construction Östra
'The Challenge'	Kullenberg Construction Stockholm
'Retraining of Operators'	Ericsson Östersund
'Reorientation of Business'	Digital Equipment Sweden
'Theatre Group Renewal'	Young Klara at the Stockholm City Theatre

'3T' – Skanska Construction Group

The Total Time Thinking project (3T) in Skanska (Ekstedt and Wirdenius 1995) is, like the T50 project in ABB described above, a radical attempt by corporate management to renew the traditional way of running construction projects. In terms of it scope it is like a combination of a one-off and piecemeal approach with the aim of bringing about a short-term as well as a long-term transformation of activities. Moreover, the prime target of renewal is the work behaviour of all organisation members in order to increase the quality of the buildings delivered and the service rendered at reduced cost and in less time, and thus increasing customer satisfaction. 3T is different from T50 in that it focused not only on organisational work behaviour in general, but also specifically and primarily on the behaviour of all actors involved in the construction project process.

The main feature of the approach is its focus on training in a new way of thinking (the '3T working model' for construction projects). This was combined with targets for the reduction of production times and defects at final inspection, as well as some modifications of work roles. Corporate management made use of and integrated external and internal expertise in the endeavour, as well as the experiences gained by ABB in its T50 project. Acceptance and commitment varied between local units, but on the whole corporate goals seem to have been achieved. Two construction projects in different regions, Skanska Stockholm and Skanska Norrland, have been investigated specifically. The 3T initiative has triggered off action in both cases, as will be illustrated in group 4 below.

The 3T case in brief

The renewal endeavour launched by senior managers in Skanska was called 3T (Total Time Thinking). This refers to the well-known fact that the construction industry is undergoing dramatic change. The structure of the market is changing and business opportunities have been drastically reduced (as a result of increasing competition and new customer demands). In order to develop in a positive direction and be more competitive the corporation had to become more efficient and better functioning. This was to be accomplished by using time as a directive instrument. Senior management envisaged dramatically shortened production times while maintaining acceptable quality and at reduced costs for customers, combined with heightened motivation and commitment in the organisation. Satisfied customers were the basic objective of 3T.

The top management renewal manifesto stressed the following aspects of Total Time Thinking:

- 3T is the start of a process of continuous development in which *all* members should participate.
- Work is to be carried out in a smarter way, not faster, by means of a new Total Time Thinking working model.
- A new work organisation is to be formed at the building site.
- The aims are a radical reduction in production times and the number of defects detected at final inspection.

All members of the organisation were expected to engage in a radical change effort through the application of Total Time Thinking. Corporate management pushed and supported the renewal activities by appointing 3T project managers at corporate, company and department levels. The 3T project managers chosen were among the most highly qualified employees in the organisation, emphasising the importance attached to the project.

Three types of measures were taken: *structural, operational* and *supporting.* Structural action at the corporate level set the stage and conditions for production. Operational steps focused on the preparation and planning procedures. The supporting measures primarily concerned training, information, marketing and quality certification. Training in the application of the 3T working model was given to everyone in the organisation. It demonstrated the relationship between shorter time and lower costs, as well as between shorter time and increased quality.

The new basic model of work organisation implied a refinement of the leadership roles and more distinct areas of responsibility at the building site. Preparatory and production roles were separated.

A primary objective of the renewal endeavour was the reduction of production times by one-third within two years. Costs were also to be lowered considerably, and zero defects are to be demonstrated at final inspection. (For a more detailed description of the 3T project, see Wirdenius 1994.)

'Cultural Renewal' – Diös Construction Group

The project that was the subject of the Diös case study, which was named Cultural Renewal (Lundin and Wirdenius 1989; Wirdenius 1991; Ekstedt *et al.*, 1992, 1993), is also an example of a venture aiming at radical change of operations primarily within subsidiary companies, and in a situation where these were facing serious problems. It was an approach by the new CEO characterised by more or less dramatic changes introduced successively over time. His chief target of change was work behaviour at senior management level (including managing directors of subsidiaries) with a view to transforming the hitherto tradition-bound family firm into a modern construction business. The approach included profitability targets for subsidiaries, radical reorganisations and the purchase of consultancy services. However, the old family culture withstood the changes, and acceptance and commitment were not achieved.

The Cultural Renewal case in brief

The Diös Construction Group case study is an example of process-oriented renewal effort in a projectised production context. This group of companies had faced a difficult market situation and had hired a new CEO, recruited from outside the firm. He was expected to reverse the negative financial trend and to revitalise the tradition-bound family business.

Over a two-year period, the CEO took a wide range of resolute steps to realign the organisation. At general meetings he informed all staff about the emerging financial crisis and concluded by setting profitability targets for the future. He reorganised the subsidiary companies, appointed new managing directors and streamlined the headquarter organisation. A number of external consultants were engaged to conduct investigations and analyses with a view to producing a basis for strategic decisions.

The steps taken involved various types of initiatives, but they were obviously not based on a comprehensive conception or vision of the future, except possibly reflecting an underlying idea of rationality. Certainly, the CEO attempted to create a general awareness of the financial crisis, but he did not communicate a new attractive image or identity of the firm or present a well-thought-out change strategy. The message he transmitted was a detailed and complex one, not easily understood. It lacked any clear view of the future and was not seen as a coherent entity. He applied an incremental or piecemeal approach to the change process.

It is not surprising, therefore, that he met with opposition from many key actors, including a number of subsidiary managing directors. He failed to obtain necessary support and commitment to the change process. The new corporate CEO served for two years, but in a dramatic week he was asked by the owners (the grandchildren of the founder) to leave, along with half the board of directors (including the chairman).

'Let's Rebuild' – Diös Construction Östra

A completely different course of events could be observed in Diös Östra, a subsidiary of the Diös Construction Group. The managing director, who had long service in the company, made the renewal endeavour analogous to a building project (with the slogan 'Let's rebuild!'). The programme involved a one-off effort to change work behaviour both generally in the organisation and specifically in the construction-project process. The stated objective, transition 'from a production organisation to a business organisation', implied action with a concern for customer demands. The approach was to a certain extent inspired by external consultants and included the following actions: by way of introduction, a study of customer relations and expectations was carried out; profitability targets were laid down; in order to involve all staff and generate new knowledge, company-wide organisation development work groups were set up; company and team spirit was cultivated by regular meetings with top management, for example. In this case, general commitment was achieved.

The Let's rebuild case in brief

The renewal initiative in the Diös Östra subsidiary company forms a contrast to the one undertaken in the mother organisation described above. In this case, the managing director took a completely different approach. He organised the effort as a distinct project, 'Let's rebuild!', with himself as project leader. The programme was undertaken against a background of gradually declining profitability and a recent large loss. The managing director had been with the company for a long time with regular promotions and thus had a thorough knowledge of company operations and of the long-tenure staff. The action he took had the following basic features:

- At a general meeting he informed all staff about the financial crisis facing the company – a unique event.
- He stated clearly at the outset that no one would be laid off as a result of the project.
- Objectives were set in profitability terms and a contrasting vision was presented ('from a production organisation to a business organisation').
- Every staff member was engaged in the various phases of the renewal process.
- He assumed the role of driving force, making himself visible, penetrating the whole organisation and personifying the ideas of the project.
- The new mode of operation was stated in concrete form ('Six ways for us to do better business').

- Every six months he met with all staff to inform them of the (improving) financial situation.
- The change process was programmed and short with a fixed termination point (a gathering with all staff and their families).

Commitment was strong at all levels of the company and the radical initiatives initiated by the managing director were appreciated and complimented. The profitability goals were reached, albeit possibly with some help from improving markets.

'The Challenge' – Kullenberg Construction Stockholm

The Kullenberg Stockholm project (or rather programme), termed 'The Challenge', extended over the lifetime of a CEO, a period of about eight years. We had the opportunity to study this endeavour from beginning to end by participant observation. The basis for the research was a verbal agreement with top management that we would have complete access to all company activities (senior management meetings, customer contacts, development projects, seminars, training sessions, etc.), and that we were to report back at intervals on our observations. Later we expanded this approach into 'the interactive research approach', a method characterised by the drawing up of a research contract, visiting, withdrawal from and revisiting the research site, with the aim of understanding the system under study as well as the changes brought about by the interactive aspects of the research, and trying to do this by 'distant reflection' (Lundin and Wirdenius 1990).

This investigation was our first serious investigation into the renewal problems face by organisations, and the renewal paradox in particular (so representative of the construction sector). It gave us low-level experience of the variety of problems facing many project-organised companies when they try to evade this paradox.

Like the Diös Construction Group described above, the Kullenberg Stockholm case study is an example of enterprise renewal in which a new managing director makes efforts to turn around a company facing serious problems using a long-range, piecemeal approach (Wirdenius 1991). The prime target of renewal was the general work behaviour of all members of the organisation (from top managers to construction workers) with the aim of restoring customers' trust in a company with a poor reputation on the market. Later the focus shifted to the adaptation of work behaviour to a changing and dwindling market under the slogan 'The Challenge'. In a special investigation of a construction project (described below in group 4) we observed that particular efforts also were made in targeting the work behaviour in the construction project process and product qualities specifically. In this way, the company tried to ensure customer satisfaction, especially in complex building projects.

The renewal approach taken was mainly to recruit new staff, to reorganise operations and to start company-wide organisation development work groups. However, the old company culture was a hindrance to seniors managers in their striving for general engagement in these endeavours. And their efforts to integrate the old and the new culture met with resistance, and support for the process sought from a variety of external specialists made little difference.

'Retraining of Operators' – Ericsson Östersund

The case of Ericsson in Östersund is an illustration of the transformation dilemma in a nutshell. It is an example of how some parts of a single factory try to handle the transformation from traditional industrial production to knowledge-intensive, project-organised service production. In the renewal project, which we have named Retraining of Operators, an entirely new activity was started with the existing workforce as a basis: employees engaged in production of articles were retrained as independent programmers. Thus, this case is an example of a radical effort to change business operations in one go. To accomplish this required a change in work behaviour, and the main strategy used for this was massive individual training.

The transformation from flow-process production to project-organised production entailed abandonment of detailed, rule-directed work, which was replaced by a goal and problem-directed work. Simple, repetitive routine work was pushed into the background and the development of problem-solving capability was encouraged. Also, even in ordinary activity a culture of continuous learning was developed. Experience-based know-how was supplemented by continual reflection, i.e. individual team members were required to acquire the capacity for independent analysis.

This solution to the transformation dilemma was achieved after a rather long search process. The idea of retraining employees as programmers of security systems within the Ericsson Corporation evolved at a late stage. It was achieved by committing a great deal of resources on the part of the company and the surrounding society. There was also strong commitment from firebrands in the project management team and among those who participated in the transformation process (Ekstedt 1991).

'Reorientation of Business' – Digital Equipment Sweden

The Digital Equipment case study, termed 'Reorientation of Business', is an example of renewal attempts in a knowledge-intensive organisation that wants to change its operations from a technological to a market orientation by means of a continuous transformation process (De Geer and Ekstedt 1991). This renewal effort was a combination of a once-only and piecemeal approach to bring about both a long-term and a short-term transformation. The long-term transformation was an attempt to reduce hardware dependence and become more service oriented. The short-term renewal work aimed at increasing sensitivity to customers' needs and wishes in designing projects.

The chief target of renewal was the work behaviour of all company staff: they were expected to satisfy customers by sensing and understanding their needs and by acting in close cooperation with them; in this way, both the quality and features of the 'products' (computer systems) and services delivered would be assured. The renewal approach used partly involved recruitment of persons with varying background, but the main emphasis was on extensive individual training programmes (directed at both staff and customers).

'Theatre Group Renewal' – Young Klara

The theatre Young Klara, operating under the auspices of the Stockholm City Theatre, has a 20-year long history of continuous development and renewal. Its fiery founder and art director personifies the theatre and acts as its driving force. Her ambition is to produce performances of exceptional quality intended for young people and novelty-minded adults. The Young Klara ensemble can be seen as a combination of a free group and an institutional theatre. It in fact functions as 'an anti-institution within the institution of the Stockholm City Theatre' and as 'a laboratory for theatrical investigations about style of acting and dramaturgic expression' (Sparby 1986). Thus, the emphasis is on the creation of favourable institutional and organisational conditions for experimental, creative work.

Over the years the art director has developed a unique model of project management under the motto of 'we are to do the impossible every time, create things that are new, do the untested, dare to express what we feel is important, and have fun at the same time' (Sparby 1986). The approach is based on participation of all members of the theatre – and the audience – as well as teamwork, seminars, educational exercises, creative assignments and improvisation sessions in the ensemble group. Thus, the prime target of renewal is the behaviour of actors with a view to accomplishing innovative performances.

This case study, named Theatre Group Renewal, is an example of successful organisational renewal in a projectised context. A small organisation, a limited number of productions, a strong rule system, a focus on new knowledge and learning, combined with an active direction, has made it possible to create a new way of producing theatre plays.

Group 4: projects concerning part-organisation renewal in a projectised context

In this group senior managers transform a regular, recurring production project into a renewal project. The cases belonging to this group are as follows:

Project	Host organisation
'*Lolita*'	Royal Opera
'*Money*'	Young Klara at the Stockholm City Theatre
'Block Gångaren'	Skanska Construction Stockholm
'Expressway Söder'	Skanska Construction Norrland
'Södertälje Hospital'	Kullenberg Construction Stockholm

'Lolita' – *Royal Opera and 'Money', Young Klara*

Two projects in this group derive from the world of theatre. In this field, the production is decidedly organised in the form of recurring projects, albeit characterised by varying complexity and uniqueness. Both projects are in fact regular production projects treated as unique projects for renewal. The participating institutions are the Royal Opera and the Young Klara ensemble within the Stockholm City Theatre (Lundin and Wirdenius 1995).

The project from the Royal Opera (the new opera *Lolita*) is to a great extent a radical renewal undertaking in one go, and this is in some measure true also of the Young Klara case (the new play *Money*). Both teams/casts target the qualities of their main 'product', try to create performances that will attract, affect and satisfy the people in the audience (and of course please themselves as artists as well). The Young Klara ensemble – thanks to its art director – has for a long time focused on the work behaviour of actors in the project process; this in an endeavour to produce a performance of the highest possible quality. The approach used in this kind of 'product development' has the underlying aim of renewing the repertoire of the organisation in the long term. The project approach is characterised by an emphasis on the physical facilities and the institutional conditions. In Young Klara, for example, all actors receive special attention by the thorough education and training arranged in connection with the new production.

These two projects will probably have a renewal effect on the future production programme of the theatres, particularly in the case of Royal Opera, the new programme diverging markedly from the regular offerings. In both cases, the commitment of actors has been extremely high. However, negative reactions were voiced in some quarters because of the diverging character of the opera production. The regular customers were used to being offered a classical repertoire rather than this new opera with modern, 'incomprehensible' music (12-tone music), and this special production consumed much more resources than other productions.

The Lolita *case in brief*

Producing an opera in the Royal Opera in Stockholm is generally a very tradition-bound procedure developed over many years, and is also the one used in the project *Lolita* (see Kungliga Teatern 1986). Typical of this particular case was the formation of a core project team, comprising the director, the set designer, the conductor and the composer, with the general director as a strong supporter.

A leading Russian composer offered the general director the chance of producing his new opera *Lolita* and of having its world premier at the Royal Opera in Stockholm. The opera was based on the English-language novel written in the 1960s and was difficult to produce. The text had to be adapted to both the Russian and the American conceptual worlds. This, in turn, meant that the role of the set designer was crucial. The theatre's principal art director was chosen to direct the project in cooperation with a well-known American set designer.

The art director started by studying the piece in detail. The *Lolita* story is on one level fairly straightforward, but it also contains an allegory with many possible interpretations. In the end, it is the interpretation of the art director (and the ensemble) that counts. In this case, the art director attempted to include many possible interpretations in the work. The production concept had to be developed and be more clearly defined for the actors involved. At an early stage, therefore, the art director entered into close collaboration with the set designer in order to create a stage model reflecting her conception.

The implementation phase involved casting, exploratory rehearsals, the accumulation of potential props, costume design, construction work, auditions, publicity design and many other things. A primary task for the art director during this phase was to instil energy into the project, to transmit her enthusiasm to the various groups of professional actors. Together with the set designer and the assistant producer, she discussed the sketches of décor, costumes, wigs and masks. With the conductor, the choirmaster and the leader of singing rehearsals, she discussed how to bring to fruition her vision of the opera. She conferred with the choreographer regarding the dancing performances.

The leading actors were chosen by the art director in consultation with the conductor. A critical stage in the process was the collaboration with the artists, which took place less than two months before the premiere. On that occasion the art director conveyed her vision of the piece. Naturally, she wanted to have complete freedom to interpret the opera, which can sometimes be a problem when, as in this case, the composer is still alive. However, the collaboration worked quite well.

Once all the elements were complete, the stage rehearsals started. The assistant art director worked side by side with the art director to ensure that all steps taken, agreements and decisions made by the art director were well documented and explained for future use. The final, full rehearsals with the orchestra were scheduled to take place only two weeks before the first performance.

The press conferences were then arranged accompanied by special campaigns to target groups.

On the whole, the performance was commended by the critics. The production and the stage design were seen as praiseworthy, the singers' contributions likewise. However, the music was regarded as static and monotonous and there was some very strong negative (and unexpected) criticism of the content. The piece was conceived 'as insidious propaganda for sex with children'. On the other hand, likewise unexpectedly, there were no open objections by the critics to the provocative and explicit sex scenes, unusual in the opera context.

The Money *case in brief*

The Young Klara group has developed a unique culture, combining the values of a free group and an institution theatre. It is creative and yet characterised by orderliness. The intellectual level is high, as is morale, and the demand for participation presents an opportunity for learning. This culture, developed over many years by the art director, reflects the company's aim of relating to current events and topical issues of public debate. The group wants to be creative, do the untested, always try a new approach. As a consequence, the company prefers to perform new plays and has a playwright in residence. In other words, the aim is to put on first performances. It is felt that new texts are good for the group as this makes everybody a creative designer of the play and constantly provides new parts for the regular actors.

Often the art director will select the play. But she will also listen to ideas and suggestions from actors and technical staff. In the case of *Money* it was the dramatist who discovered the play and recommended it. However, the final decision rests with the art director and depends on whether she believes that it will earn the support and enthusiasm of the group. The mood of the time and the entertainment aspect are also important, as is the aim of provoking the audience.

An introductory reading of the first draft of the play took place as soon as the art director had put a cast together. At this stage, the play was subjected to a bombardment of creative ideas by the art director, the set designer and the actors. This was then followed by 'folk high-school' an idea of the art director: a week-long seminar of films, lectures, improvisation rounds involving the whole group (including technical staff, administrative staff and designer), discussions of objectives, and exercises for the actors. In other words, all actors are sent to school for a thorough investigation of how to bring the play to life and how to narrate it in an artistic way.

During the implementation phase, the production team was engaged in exploratory rehearsals, collecting props, costume design, construction work, auditions, casting, publicity design and more. A preliminary model of the stage was built. Actors for the play were selected by the art director. More young, new actors were cast than before. Rehearsals began.

To begin with the rehearsals took the form of improvisations, readings and 'play'. The art director let the actors become creative once she had conveyed her own analysis of the play to the group, its mental process and its 'message'. As the actors come to feel secure in the situation they dare to take greater risks in acting. Gradually the art director started to exercise increasingly tighter control of the development procedure. A typical feature of Young Klara is long rehearsal times.

The performance was well received by the critics. They noted that the production was a daring mixture of styles and modes of expression. New scenic solutions were introduced and the choreography expressed incessant movement. The actors' performance was also praised, However, the play was generally felt to be too long.

'Block Gångaren' – Skanska Construction Stockholm

This case is related to the Skanska 3T effort alluded to above. The major rebuilding project Block Gångaren, carried out by Skanska Stockholm, was a total contract (in which the builder also takes responsibility for the project work) (Ekstedt and Wirdenius 1995). The production schedule was very tight, and, as in any construction project, it was important to meet the completion date. The resources allocated to the project were greater than normal. A 3T man in the division was specifically assigned to act as a supporter in the project. Moreover, the project manager placed great stress on bringing about an incentive agreement, motivating the builder as well as the client.

It seems to us that the thinking of 3T took root and started to grow, especially among salaried employees. The renewal project was still at such an early stage that it was difficult to determine whether the skilled workers were really active in the 3T work. Several members of the salaried staff perceived the 3T message to be vague at first, perhaps during the whole of the first year. 'It mostly seemed to be a lot of fine words.' Later, having grasped the concept, they become inspired to achieve its aims. However, inspiration was provided not only by the information given and training programmes set up by top management but perhaps also by the decline in the construction industry, which may have increased their awareness of the need for change.

The projecting and planning stages were stressed in the renewal efforts. The cost of preparatory work is relatively low compared with production work, as it amounts only to the salaries of a few people. A reduced production time is profitable, if only because of the associated reduction in credit costs. Furthermore, it is in the planning stage that the major changes have to be made and really could make a difference. One problem identified, however, was that subcontractors had also to be influenced by the 3T spirit in order to make a contribution.

The importance of computer support for time scheduling was pointed out. Another crucial condition for renewal work that was continually emphasised was the need for competence development in parallel with such work.

'Expressway Söder' – Skanska Construction Norrland

The large-scale road construction project Expressway Söder, carried out by Skanska Norrland, is a total contract (Ekstedt and Wirdenius 1995). The project manager had been involved in the development of 3T for the division and was now trying to apply the ideas to this project. Thus, he allocated extra resources to projecting, planning and production control in particular. He regarded this assignment as an opportunity to create a model for the design, planning and management of similar projects in the future.

An inquiry within the division showed that about one-third of the staff were working with 3T to the full, some of them partially, and the others not at all. Again, it appeared that the dissemination of 3T had primarily affected the salaried employees. This was mainly because the skilled workers received their training later. However, site managers expressed the opinion that the prospects for 3T being accepted among skilled workers were very good. They were to become more involved, to get more responsibility and to be spared from supervisory control. Direction towards distinct objectives would be the common way of work.

3T thus implies that much more stress is given to planning. An activity plan, with an articulated vision and strategy and distinct objectives, was devised. Even to articulate the future in words required much reflection and analysis. What was done previously in accordance with more or less clearly stated routines was thus recorded. This, of course, made progress evaluation much easier than previously, particularly as one man had been assigned the job of following up the project. The higher costs associated with better planning were seen as insignificant compared with the possible savings at the production stage.

Secondly, goal direction became central in the design of the project. Time, costs and quality targets were identified in line with the general objective of 3T. It is also important to point out that a concrete time schedule was made up with monthly statements of cost accounts. It became possible, therefore, to evaluate the project in detail during its progress, and consequently to make successive improvements.

Thirdly, the division of responsibility among the various actors became more distinct. Everyone signed a statement of responsibility, whether or not they held the principal responsibility for an area. Objectives and procedures were much more clearly defined.

'Södertälje Hospital' – Kullenberg Stockholm

Senior managers in Kullenberg Stockholm undertook a unique initiative when carrying out a major complex construction project, Södertälje Hospital (Wirdenius 1991). They transformed it into a renewal project by taking action to improve the management approach in running the construction process. It was a radical endeavour to demonstrate to the market that the company had the necessary qualifications to carry out complex projects of this kind. And this construction project was intended to become a model for effective project management within the firm in the future. Examples of special actions taken are: very early involvement of the various actors in the planning process; well-planned, regular planning and follow-up meetings with members of the project team and other actors involved, as well as special problem-solving meetings off site; frequent study visits to other construction sites to acquire fresh knowledge; activities and meetings after working hours to develop a team spirit and a sense of challenge in facing the project. Afterwards the project was described as successful by all parties concerned.

Group 5: projects concerning societal–interorganisational renewal in a projectised context

The projects in this group are exemplified by a singular renewal project initiated by senior managers of a consortium of interested organisations in society. Cases belonging to this group are as follows:

Project	*Host organisations*
'Arlandastad'	Sigtuna local authority
	Board of Civil Aviation
	BPA Construction
	Skanska Construction Group
'Sophia Antipolis'	Côte d'Azure Economic
	Development Company (CAD)
	École de Mines – Nice Prefecture
	Nice Chamber of Commerce
	Nice Regional Council
	Nice University
'Uminova stad'	Skanska Real Estate Norrland

	Umeå local authority
	AP Fund
'JAS 39 Gripen'	Supreme Commander of the Armed Forces (ÖB)
	The Air Force (FV)
	Defence Material Administration (FMV)
	Industrial Group JAS (I G JAS)

'Arlandastad', 'Uminova stad' and 'Sophia Antipolis' projects

We have studied three megaprojects geared to urban development with a view to creating a new research and business town or park: Arlandastad, Uminova stad (Lundin *et al.* 1992), and Sophia Antipolis (Wirdenius 1992).

The cases are large societal endeavours sponsored by a group of interested parties from society and industry which act as host organisations for the project. They mainly represent long-term renewal ventures. They are directed towards the qualities of the final 'product' (the design and functioning of the town) and can be regarded as unique, singular projects.

Massive efforts have been made in both Arlandastad and Sophia Antipolis to avoid conflict and try to gain acceptance and commitment of the ideas among the many parties and persons concerned. Temperamental individuals have played a crucial part in the initiation and planning stages and as project managers and action-oriented entrepreneurs and commitment builders in the implementation stage. In the Arlandastad case, for example, experienced people from different professional cultures were invited to assist in the idea creation process, and by producing a unique product could secure general support. This is a case of knowledge formation by combination and integration of knowledge from widely differing sources. The progress of the project was set back by the recent crisis on the real estate market, but one construction stage is finished, another is about to start and a few related subprojects have been achieved or are currently under way. The Sophia Antipolis High-Tec Park is completed and occupied, and a similar large spin-off project in the neighbourhood is in progress.

The Uminova stad undertaking is characterised by inertia and lack of action. The project manager had been commissioned to administer an undeveloped project idea and handle the negotiations between the interested parties. He was put under strong pressure by the developer to carry out the project quickly. Agreement was not reached and so the project has come to a standstill.

'JAS 39 Gripen' Project

JAS 39 Gripen is a renewal venture directed towards a societal object. It was initiated by the Swedish defence authorities to increase the effectiveness of the Swedish Air Force. It is managed by the Defence Material Administration (FMV) in collaboration with the Industrial Group JAS (I G JAS), a holding company owned by four industrial partners, headed by Saab Military Aircraft. The degree of difficulty is exceptional, as much of the knowledge required to carry out the project did not exist at the start but had to be generated. The project managers had to rely on expert partners abroad to do this, and it became apparent that they faced problems in succeeding. It is a project of extremely long duration, lasting over the whole period that the plane will be in operation. In previous aeroplane development projects, most of the steering has been assigned to the military authority and the minor part to industry. In this case, the tables are turned, the military authority acting as project managers is focusing on function and performance of the aircraft, and industry is taking on the responsibility for a development contract. However, later it became necessary to change the distribution of steering and control between the two partners.

The JAS 39 Gripen case in brief

The JAS 39 Gripen project is the greatest military project ever undertaken in Sweden, involving the development of a new aeroplane, a combined fighter, fighter–bomber and scouting plane. It is a project (or rather a programme containing several subprojects) of extremely long duration, covering the whole period that the plane and its support system will be in operation, that is for 20–40 years. It differs from earlier projects in several important respects: it is based on a fixed-price deal with industry and has a different distribution of work between the military and the industrial partners. In earlier aeroplane development projects, the major part of the steering was assigned to the military authority and the minor part to industry. In this case, the tables are turned, the military authority initially acting as project managers focusing on function and performance of the aircraft, and industry taking responsibility for a development contract. However, it has since become necessary to change the distribution of steering and control between the two partners.

The industrial partner is a holding company, I G JAS, owned by four companies, with Saab Military Aircraft as the central producer. This particular project involves an extremely complex task, not least technologically. The cost is fixed to half the usual price, and this is to be achieved by making the plane half the weight of a regular plane but still capable of performing three different tasks. As the plane is designed to be less stable and thus more manoeuvrable, it requires more computer processors to steer it, a difficult technology that has yet to be developed. It is a high-risk project, as both the volume of work that will be required and the knowledge demanded are unknown. Thus, external development resources and knowledge of subsystems are utilised to a greater extent than previously, with the associated problem of suppliers having different philosophies of running projects. This is particularly critical in this case as the aircraft industry has little previous experience of subcontractor purchasing.

A major problem for the industrial partners in this case is how to deal with the inevitable time-lag between recurring megaprojects of this nature. It entails a great risk of loss of knowledge, and this is what happened in the JAS project. Thus, lack of qualified staff (engineers) and knowledge contributed to delays early in the project, delays that have remained all along. Two crashes caused by deficiencies in the steering system led to interruptions in the test programme and further delay. The subcontractor involved obviously did not manage to make the system work. Overall, the project has broadly complied with the specifications of time, technique and economy, showing only a moderate overdraft of time and cost. However, the industrial partners have sustained heavy losses.

Some concluding remarks

The case studies presented in this chapter cover a wide range of organisational contexts, renewal contents and situations. Descriptions are rather brief, but they nevertheless present the core of each project and the major renewal issues that have arisen in the different projects. Some aspects of the projects have been highlighted, such as context, scope, pace and target. It is obvious that the projects presented are different because of differences in, for example, their targets. Developing a jet fighter is something completely different from implementing a new organisational structure. Nevertheless, discussion of the context, scope, pace and target is a way of demonstrating how action and knowledge elements are defined and dealt with in the projects. And, in doing so, it is evident that all projects in one way or another have to deal with action and knowledge issues. Getting things done (i.e. action) and improving or developing new knowledge are perhaps the most prominent features of renewal in general and of renewal projects in particular.

Basically, action and knowledge, and the organising issues associated with them, are at the core of the remaining chapters of the book. First, action and knowledge will be alluded to in the next two chapters, in which some of the theoretical foundations of the concepts will be provided. Having done that, the cases will be revisited in Chapter 7. Chapter 7 concentrates on how the 'marriage' between action and knowledge formation has led to renewal, and in what ways this is dealt with as a part, or as a consequence, of the organising efforts.

5 Action formation in temporary and permanent organisations

It is hardly revolutionary to suggest that action is necessary to get something done. This means that intuitively there is an element of resoluteness in the concept. The action concept at the level of the individual is at times contrasted with the concept of behaviour (see, for example, Norén 1995: 142–3), and the difference is often described as the presence or absence of explicit purposiveness. We will very briefly touch upon this in the following, but otherwise we will more or less leave the level of the individual and concentrate on organised action. Again, however, we focus on action as getting something done. In that particular respect there is also no difference between temporary and permanent organisations. The difference is to be found in the kinds of actions involved and in how these actions can be understood in their own contexts. The demand for focused action is certainly more prominent in temporary organisations in which time is limited and the task in general is defined in a specific and measurable way. If the label 'project' is used for the temporary organisation, the demand for focus is even more prevalent. In fact, focused action means that only actions specifically related to the particular task at hand are considered to be relevant or even permissible in a project (or a temporary organisation) context.

In permanent organisations, on the other hand, most action – at least action directly related to the *raison d'être* of the organisation – is of a routinised type and part of the ongoing stream of actions taken more or less by habit or at least without too much explicit elaboration. On a very general level one might even say that in permanent organisations most actions belong to a continuous flow of actions, whereas actions in temporary organisations mostly are (meant to be) of a discontinuous type, even in some cases signalling something of a break with the past. In this chapter the importance and the significance of action in temporary as well as in permanent settings will be elaborated upon as well as defined along a variety of lines in order to provide a basis for a more developed theoretical understanding of neo-industrial organising and renewal.

Social action and action contexts

Action is a fundamental concept within a number of fields, e.g. philosophy, psychology and sociology. Much effort has been spent on classifications of action on a philosophical level, e.g. by discussing whether intention precedes action, whether or not human action is 'free' and what the relation between action, interpretation and reflection might be (see von Wright 1967). One classical division is between determinism (or fatalism, particularism, reductionism) and voluntarism (or intentionalism, indeterminism). The former standpoint argues that action is determined exogenously and that individual free will is in fact an illusion, whereas the latter position holds that individual acts are guided by the individual's own will only.

In their pure (or simplified) forms the two standpoints, voluntarism and determinism, are both unacceptable not only on the level of the individual but also as explanations for the integration of the individual into a wider social context. Behaviouristic cause–effect relationships of a deterministic type are difficult to establish empirically except in very extreme situations (if the stove is hot you withdraw your fingers instantly), and the absolute voluntaristic position that free will is without conditions and absolutely free would mean that no action to be considered is in fact related to any other actions (past, present or future). For logical reasons the absolute voluntaristic position might be regarded as impossible. In their pure forms, voluntarism and determinism do not exist, but the continuum in between does. Since there is almost always freedom of choice between at least two action alternatives, it is impossible to regard action as strictly depending on or contingent upon one particular cause. On the other hand, practical and other limitations of freedom of choice make it difficult to regard actions as completely free and independent of everything else (see Østerberg 1986).

For the reasons suggested above, thinking about action in terms of voluntarism and determinism is not very useful when it comes to analysing action formation in temporary and permanent organisations. In these cases, action formation is not only part of a social context, but also part of special social contexts denoted temporary and permanent organisations. Permanency or temporality carries implications for how action formation might be perceived. Action in social settings (organisations being one type of social setting) can be considered both free and unfree according to Giddens (1976). Structures (e.g. organisational structures) are shaped by human beings, and human beings could also be said to be a product of the established structures. Each new generation is exposed to a process of socialisation whereby values, norms and attitudes are transmitted to the newcomers from the older generations (see Berger and Luckman 1966). This transmission process is facilitated by various organisations: churches, schools, work place, sports clubs, etc. In other words, action has a social base and is socially dependent. Moreover, action is always social or it has important social dimensions to it. One way to describe the main message or content of the present chapter is to say that it represents an attempt to specify the meaning of the theory of structuration (Giddens 1976) for the neo-industrial organising environment.

Society offers a multitude of social contexts, of which some were mentioned above. In practising religion a certain set of norms is important for an individual. Other norms are central when the individual becomes a student or attends a trade union meeting. Such social contexts provide meanings for the actions taken. The action and the actor are included in a context, given an identity in that context and are acknowledged by the social sphere of people who 'understand' the action and the actor provided that the action is correctly taken and in accordance with that particular context. For our purposes, action should be taken as different from behaviour. When called upon, the actor is expected to provide his reasons for taking action. Behaviour in this context should be regarded as a way to adapt to the social context at hand, whereas action is related to a task, implicitly or explicitly. This kind of reasoning leads us to the conclusion that actions are interpreted by others. Actions are always related to a context and are provided with a meaning in accordance with that context. Such a construction of meaning is a necessity for facilitating social interaction and social intercourse. Thus, it is important that we can understand other persons and their actions as something meaningful [see also Weber (1968) on social action and Mead (1934) on social interactionism and 'lines of action'].

There are two implications of this. Firstly, action is dependent upon rules in such a way that different social situations provide expectations that actions will look in a special way. As soon as the social situation is defined, the mere definition gives rise to a special type of interaction between the actors involved. A board meeting gives rise to a special type of interaction, and so does a demonstration, a church service or a visit to the local shop [cf. Winch (1958) and Lyttkens (1981) concerning rules of inference]. Secondly, the rules are also related to the role that a person has in a particular situation. The clergyman has a different role from the congregation, and this defines what the persons involved are expected to do. Thus, the anarchist, the monk and the CEO all have very special and particular actions to take in the different social situations that might develop. They follow different 'codes' for their role behaviours.

So far, the following conclusions can be drawn:

1   Action has to be understood in a social setting and in a physical context, i.e. action is primarily social. Actions are comprehensible only if they are related to a particular context. Contexts can be of various kinds. Organisations are one context and among organisations a number of different organised contexts can be defined. Churches, government

agencies, multinational corporations and small manufacturing firms can be expected to show different context characteristics.

2   Actors have to be understood in terms of systems of interacting actors rather than single individuals. As individuals relate themselves to social settings it is important to link the understanding of action to other actors and actions in that particular setting. Roles and patterns of interaction are thus more interesting than solitary actors.

3   As a corollary of 1 and 2, observable action is generally interpreted in a social context. Either the action serves to reinforce the customs of the social setting or the action is perceived as something that is in some ways at odds with the customary and the expected. In this way, expectations might ascribe different meanings to action (even though there usually is a social pressure to converge on meaning) at the same time as the actor may or may not have special intentions with actions ventured. This leads us to the notion of action embeddedness.

Action embeddedness

Modes of action embeddedness

The concluding summary in the previous section indicates that action is always contextually embedded. This embedded character of action can be categorised into some major contextual aspects. In the following we will distinguish between action embedded in (i) physical and technical systems, i.e. physically induced action; (ii) institutional rules and traditions, i.e. institutionally induced action (North 1990; Putnam 1993); (iii) the organisational level, i.e. locally conditioned action; and (iv) the individual level, i.e. individual or entrepreneurial action.

The differences between these can be illustrated by comparing business operations with sports activity (Ekstedt and Wirdenius 1995). For example, in football, the structural level – structure being determined by physical and technical systems – corresponds to the playing ground or playing equipment being used. The chances of a good game will increase with a fine pitch and suitable boots. As long as all the players have access to equally good equipment the structural conditions will not influence the result of the game. However, if only one team has studded boots when playing on wet grass, that team will have an advantage over the other. New equipment could in many cases entirely change the conditions of the game. In other sports, for example skiing, the equipment has even more decisive importance. Action can therefore be induced by *physical* or *structural* characteristics.

One can influence the structure of the organisation by purchasing technology (or internal technological development). Purchased technology principally implies an adaptation to the general technical level. Technology developed within the company, on the other hand, could be more competitive. Both externally and internally developed technology will in many cases force new actions on company actors. This could, in turn, have an effect on the attitudes and conceptions that develop. In other words, structural changes are often imperative, and generally have a great influence on the development and performance of the organisation. In capital-intensive operations, for example the forestry or steel industries, technology dominates the organisational design and, thus, has a major impact on actions taken.

If we pursue the football metaphor, the institutional level, representing rules and traditions, corresponds to the rules of play and the way of playing. New rules would inevitably change the game, for example a new rule saying that the goal-keeper is not allowed to handle a back-passed ball would undoubtedly liven up the game. In addition, the way of playing affects the result and the motivation of the players. This can be illustrated by the differences between the lively and entertaining type of football developed in South America over a long period of time and the more tactical and defensive style of the European teams. During the 1998 World Cup, the most successful teams seemed to combine the lively South American technique with the tactical playing culture developed in some parts of Europe.

The institutional conditions for the company could be both external and internal. All enterprises work under a given set of general rules. They could be rules drawn up by external bodies, for example the parliament or government, but they could also be implied or tacit rules. Laws as well as tradition govern the organisations' actions in a market. Quite often companies try to influence the general rule system through organisations working as their representatives (e.g. trade associations). Organisations are also very dependent upon the professional tradition that develops over time. This could concern anything from the terms of collaboration between different actors to the design of occupational training for persons being recruited. All these institutional conditions mean that action can be *institutionally induced.*

In recent years the predominant, traditional tayloristic work organisation has been questioned and loosened. New, more flexible organisation forms are spreading. The division of work is becoming less rigid, organisation members are increasing in all-round competence and work tasks are becoming more challenging. This is a consequence of new demands from customers as well as from workers. The conditions for acting reflect all these trends. The ability to work in teams, to communicate, to support and criticise one another (with ensuing synergy effects) is increasingly emphasised. Modern structures with small, flexible machines (computers) also contribute to new organisational solutions. The new institutional and technical set-up provides a wide potential to find new ways of acting and organising.

In football, the organisational level corresponds to the team line-up.

The rules of the game (that is the institutional level) stipulate the number of players. The coach or trainer and the team are then free to organise the players as they wish. The principal task of some is to attack, whereas the function of others is to defend. Traditionally, some players act as defenders, others midfielders and others again act as forwards. Within this (institutional) tradition a number of playing systems have flourished. The much older system with completely fixed positions has been replaced by a more flexible organisation (increasingly players are assigned different tasks depending on the situation). The selection of players is also undertaken at the organisational level. The composition of the team is undoubtedly of importance for both teamwork and the distribution of tasks.

As we have seen from the example of football, institutional conditions (both rules and traditions) have great influence on the design of the organisation, not least because organisation members have been trained in a system that presupposes a certain work division. In addition, the structural level (e.g. some heavy machines) restricts senior managers' capacity to design the organisation. However, each organisation has its specific mixture of external ingredients. Possible actions become conditioned. Senior managers can try to influence internal conditions. They can lay down targets for co-workers to achieve, or they can try to introduce a certain company culture, that is try to inculcate a particular way of thinking and acting. In the first case, incentives or threats of sanctions can force a change in behaviour in the hope that an attitude change will ensue (compare with structural change). In the second case, top management tries to exert an influence on attitudes in the belief that this will change behaviour. Action is therefore not only institutionally and physically induced, but also *locally conditioned/organisation induced* as a result of local solutions, organisational designs, task formations, etc.

At the individual level is, obviously, the individual football player. However, as already pointed out, individual performances often start from a well-functioning environment. Thus, great specific demands are placed on individuals provided that they receive the necessary support in terms of good facilities (structures), traditions (institutions) and the club or the team (organisation). They must know their specific task but they also have to understand the whole in order to be able to contribute to the final result. They have to develop their ability to cooperate with others. To reach the top level in sports a demanding programme of training and practice for each individual is required. Players must improve their technique but also their ability to understand tactics and solve certain problems quickly. Creativity is also an important ingredient at the individual level. To do what is not expected or immediately foreseen is often a result of individual creativity and ability. This fourth embeddedness aspect of action is therefore *individually premeditated*.

Table 5.1 summarises the different levels of action and action embeddedness.

Table 5.1 Action embeddedness and corresponding metaphors

Action embeddedness	Metaphor
Structural level (physical system, technology)	Playing field/playing equipment
Institutional level (rules, tradition)	Rules of the game/playing technique
Organisational level	Team line-up/selection of players
Individual level	Players

Obviously, actions are interrelated. Changing a physical setting can change conditioned action within an organisation in the same way that new playing equipment might change the way in which a game is organised. However, for analytical reasons, different types of action will first be discussed one by one and in a later section their inter-relatedness will be more clearly addressed.

A few tricky questions have been only briefly touched upon this far. What is an action? How can action be distinguished from inaction? These questions are particularly important when the acting party is an organisation. Towards the end of the chapter we will return to these questions in summary form. However, one of the important points made earlier in this chapter is that an action is viewed in relation to the context in which it has been taken. An action assumes meaning only from its context. More often than not the context should be taken to be a sequence of actions and of the rhetoric that might go along with the action, rather than general circumstances in the direct vicinity of the actor and the action. Certainly, this is usually true of actions emanating from an organisation. One should rather speak of a sequence of actions and the rhetorics rather than the action *per se* as an isolated or discernible entity. It is the whole sequence that constitutes the action and that provides the meaning for it. Consider, for example, a man stepping into his car. If we know that he is going abroad, the total trip conveys more interesting information than the fact that we have seen him getting into the car.

In everyday language action also implies something unexpected and resolute. In general, the performance of routines, whatever their origin, is not discerned as 'real' action. Such action is regarded as anonymous and not worthy of attention. However, when something unexpected is done, that action is deemed to attract much more attention. So if you are given the information that the man stepping into the car is going not on one of his many trips to one of several European countries but to Asia, that information gives you a hint that something special is going to happen (the company will be opening new business connections in Singapore for instance). The 'real action' content of the event is further strengthened if some policy changes are announced at the same time. The rhetoric supports the notions of importance attached to the unexpected trip.

The discussion on embeddedness issues could – in line with what was said above about 'real action' – be interpreted as if action is determined by different structural or organisational properties of the context. That is, however, incorrect. The bottom line is that action can be more or less determined by where and how it is embedded, but it does not matter whether action is completely voluntaristic or determined. Actions are always carried out in a context, and it is important to understand that context in order to understand action formation. Emphasising embeddedness should therefore not be understood as a way of denying voluntaristic aspects of action.

Different action types due to embeddedness

The first action embeddedness category refers to the structural level: the *structurally* or *physically induced action*. Although easy to understand in general terms, it might be difficult to determine whether or not a specific action is physically induced. The reason for including physically induced action in this discussion is because changes in physical conditions are one way of promoting changed action by those involved. New equipment (e.g. computerisation) can be used to induce new behaviour, as in the case of CSN. The investments made in new technology in CSN also meant that behaviours had to change since the new computer system 'demanded' that people changed. Under such circumstances new action is more or less 'given', although it is not certain that new action that comes around will be successfully carried out or that the change is simple or without difficulties. New production technology and rearrangement of workshop facilities can also, as in Sunds Defibrator, be used to change work behaviour among employees. In that case, the physical environment was changed and thus action in that environment had to change.

Institutionally induced actions, the second category – related to the institutional level – might be regarded as a stabilised form of social action and interaction in which roles, rules and norms are recurrent and change very slowly if at all, and in which expectations are confined to a fairly narrowly defined set of alternatives. Institutionalised action pertains to individuals as well as to organisations of various types and to decisions about how to design organisations or work tasks (see, for example, Scott 1995). In other words, both individuals and organisations can be described as demonstrating institutionalised actions. Moreover, institutionalised action has two sides to it. On the one side there is the acting party performing the action – implicitly or explicitly ascribing a special meaning to it – and on the other the observing party, which ascribes meanings to the actions or to the activities being observed. In both cases, prescriptions as to what actions are legitimate are normally at work. The party performing the action obviously regards the action taken as appropriate (or it would have been avoided) and timed correctly (or different timing would have been chosen), but it is by no means true that the observing party shares that opinion even though institutional rules are at work for the observer as well. In fact, the action taken might be contested by the observing party ascribing some kind of illegitimacy or inappropriateness to what is being done. And the observing party might also have the view that action was timed incorrectly.

The determinism content of institutionalised action says that the notion of what is regarded as legitimate (appropriate) or otherwise is at the heart of the institutions. Essentially, one might say that if a field is heavily institutionalised the range of actions considered to be appropriate by the sending party will be relatively small, as will be the range considered to be appropriate by the observer (see Jepperson 1991). In that sense, the sending party is more constrained than the observing party, who always has the opportunity to contest actions taken. Thus, the observing party (or, rather, observing parties as a one-to-many relationship is more usual) functions as an extra constraint for the acting party. Not only does the acting party have specific ideas about what is appropriate or not in a general sense, but the imagined or real expectations of potential observers add several other dimensions. The idea of observers acting like watchdogs is thus part of the notion of institutionalised actions. So institutionally oriented action is not only constrained by the thinking or the imagination of the actor, but should also be seen as constrained by the immediate environment, that is by the observing party. If acting and observing parties have different views about what is appropriate, the observing party might impose sanctions on the actor. It should go without saying that inappropriate behaviour is not the same thing as unexpected behaviour. Unexpected behaviour might very well be labelled 'brilliant' by the observer, but such an epithet would never be used for something regarded as inappropriate.

In more general terms, institutionalisation as an action embeddedness category works in several ways. Legislation is perhaps the most obvious director of rule-following actions, but institutionalisation could also operate in more sophisticated ways. In the construction industry, there are firm conceptions on how to negotiate and come to terms with contractors and how to relate to different collaborating companies during a construction project. These ways of relating to each other are not negotiated every time. Instead, they are institutionalised and thereby form an expected action pattern, e.g. when different negotiating companies meet. In Skanska and the 3T project, the management tried to change this institutionalised behaviour by introducing new ways of planning and conducting construction site work. Also, in ABB, T50 was a way of questioning and changing traditional action principles long institutionalised in the company. The ABB subsidiary in Poland, ABB ZWUS, is perhaps the most obvious example of a renewal project targeting institutionalised actions as 'change object'. In this case the aim was to change the management style by 'importing' a new style (and new 'rules') from the West.

The third category is *organisationally conditioned action*, meaning action that is conditioned by local organisation features or circumstances. Actions are meant to be conditioned in the sense that they are standardised and bureaucratised responses to stimuli evoked from the environment or generated from within the organisation. The fact that they are conditioned implies that they are in principle to be regarded as automatic responses to stimuli belonging to a group of stimuli well known to the individual involved. They have developed more or less into routines. This conditioned aspect of action is particularly evident in mass production industrial organisations but routinised actions that are organisation specific also occur within a project-organised environment.

Conditioning of action is a crucial aspect of the organising activities that organisations have been through over time. Conditioning is at the heart of investment activities and standardisation in industrial activities. Conditioning might even be thought of as an investment *per se* (even though the results of such activities cannot be found on the official balance sheet). Successful conditioning leads to efficient production according to the beliefs promoted in traditional industrial circles. In fact, it was (and is) believed that conditioning enables the abolition of unnecessary premeditation in production activities. Thus, conditioning is concerned with standardisation and routinisation of the results of problem solving. In accordance with popular industrial belief, problems related to production are solved once and for all as part of the organising activities so that the organisation members can be free from tasks other than acting as measurable parts of the production system. The need for premeditation is thus reduced to a minimum. However, for the sake of efficiency, conditioning of action has to be a success.

Conditioned action is viewed as organisation specific in the discussion above. Some actions in permanent organisations might seem to be standardised and inflexible, even though they are certainly not organisation specific. In this case, the standardisation is not confined within the borders of the particular organisation. Standardisation might cover the entire industry or at least a wider organisational field. Under those circumstances, it might be accurate to use the term institutionalised action.

Institutionalised action and conditioned actions have many traits in common. In both cases, for example, the appropriate action in response to a stimulus is prescribed in some way. Thus, it is also evident to the individual that actions should be taken. The difference between institutionalised action and conditioned actions is that conditioned actions are supposedly confined to a particular organisation. Thus, prescriptions concerning both institutionalised and organisationally conditioned action are to be found in organisation handbooks. Prescriptions related to institutionalised action are also widespread in educational material and are to be found in publications from professional associations (e.g. pmbok guide 1996). Notions of institutionalised action are promoted from within the trades not from within the organisation or from the leadership of any particular company. Institutionalised action is regarded as an appropriate behaviour connected with the individual and it is further believed to be organisationally neutral (whereas conditioned action might be regarded as organisation specific and as authorised behaviour, i.e. authorised by the leadership of the particular organisation).

The differences between institutionalised actions and conditioned actions might not be very easy to perceive. Both of them are prescriptive and have at least one component in common, that is stressing action as necessary. Moreover, not just any action will do; rather a particular stream of activities would seem to be necessary. In addition, individuals may feel obliged to act in a specific way in accordance with the expectations associated with their current role. Thus, notions of both conditioned and institutionalised action solve the problem of what an individual should actually do. They present themselves as natural under the circumstances in which they are applied. However, those same notions also solve a problem for the managers in the sense that managers also know what to expect. Managerial work in a context regulated by institutionalised action or conditioned action is reduced to managing disturbances and deviations from expectations. In any case, we believe that it is fruitful under the present circumstances to distinguish the differences in origins of these two types of standardised actions. We will return to this issue later.

The fourth category presented in Table 5.1 (individual level) is *individually premeditated action*, and this represents actions taken as a result of individual premeditation. This type of action is consequently more a result of capacities and abilities held by the individual and interpretations made by him or her. A true entrepreneur acts out of his premeditation without regard to surrounding institutional or organisational demands. Thus, pure individually premeditated action is difficult to foresee or plan since it is more of an outcome of creative processes.

Premeditated actions can be of various kinds. When individuals encounter situations that are unknown they have to act out of their own premeditation. In other situations, in which known and appropriate behaviour could be used (in accordance with institutional rules or organisational conditions), an individual can choose to act out of premeditation if, for example, such an action sequence appears likely to be more successful or 'better' in some way.

Most of the time premeditation takes on the form of talk, i.e. finding words and describing what the action should be about and why it is needed. When managers try to influence the actions of subordinates they tend to use rhetorical aids to do so in an effort to persuade. Perceived thus, at the individual level action is very closely related to decisions (even though the individual might not conceive of what is happening as decisions). However, as should be obvious from the discussion on various levels of embeddedness above, one alternative route to instigate action would be to work on other levels and to resort to other forms of influence.

Obviously, as indicated above, the four embeddedness categories presented in this section are not working in isolation relative to actions taken in organised contexts. Different embeddedness categories can have impact on actions taken at the same time. When analysing actions in an organised setting, it is possible to find institutional or organisational explanations alongside individual or physical explanations. During the development of Volvo cars or Saab aircraft, both institutionally induced actions (e.g. as learnt by engineers) and organisationally conditioned actions (e.g. means for adjusting development work to plant facilities) are at work at the same time. Also, premeditated action is also taking place since many of the necessary inventions are made as a result of individual's creativity. In the Royal Opera case, the director and producer acted as they were supposed to do according to standard procedures within theatres around the world (institutional) and those specific conditions at the Royal Opera House in Stockholm (organisational), but there was also room for some creative individually premeditated actions on the part of the director, and at the same time something new was being tried out in the opera house.

Renewal efforts can similarly be directed towards one or more of the different action embeddedness categories. The outcome of a renewal project is therefore dependent on the whole approach, and an ideal model for action should integrate all four levels. In practice, however, it is not easy to coordinate action at different levels when it comes to timing, sequence and content. The capacity of senior managers to exert influence and to implement changes also varies greatly between levels. The institutional level is probably particularly difficult to influence. Rule systems develop from an interplay between internal and external conditions. They involves spheres of power only partly or indirectly influenced by top management. The possibilities of changing traditions quickly are not great either. It is hardly feasible to implement at a given point of time a company culture that is capable of fundamentally changing traditional ways of thinking and acting. It might be easier to influence some internal rules and restrictions.

Our case studies include numerous examples of combining efforts at different levels simultaneously. When renewing ABB by introducing T50 both institutional rules and organisational conditions were meant to be renewed. The same is true for the renewal of construction projects carried out within Skanska. There an attempt was made to change the general way of planning and organising construction projects in order to change all embeddedness categories except the physical one. Take another example from a totally different environment, health care: the EPQ project essentially was launched as subprojects on all four levels, but, as the measures taken were found to be inconsistent in practical work, the measures had to be adapted over time to factual behaviour outcomes of the effort. The relative success in accomplishing renewal may be due to the combined effort. In any case, the four categories of action embedded-ness are perhaps best considered as overlapping and interdependent.

Action in permanent and temporary organisations

It has been noted that action of the interesting kind is a sequence of actions performed by an individual or by a group of individuals (see discussion in the first section of this chapter on Social action and action context). In the preceding section, different embeddedness categories were introduced, and we now turn to different organisational contexts. In this section we will continue that taxonomy/typology approach to the notions of organised action.

There are two main ways or rather broad categories of organising action, depending on context: (i) continuous action in permanent organisations and (ii) discontinuous action in temporary organisations. They can both be further analysed in terms of the embeddedness categories discussed previously.

Continuous action in permanent organisations

Permanent organisations are dependent on routines, procedures and standards. Basically, routines are designed to ensure that similar situations will be met with similar actions over time. For example, production should continue to be performed in the same way tomorrow as it was yesterday. Machinery and other production equipment are a guarantee that actions will be standardised over time. Standardisation of actions is also a path to company benefits from the learning curve. Hence, much effort is directed towards the design and maintenance of standardisation of actions within the company.

Quality guarantee systems are another example since they are implemented in order to achieve a consistent way of dealing with certain situations. The introduction of authorisations for quality-verifying systems further emphasises this. Also, accounting systems have similar characteristics. Such systems are supposed to measure economic performance in the same way, regardless of time and actions that might be triggered by such systems. Continuity is the aim and measurements will be similar over time.

Action in the context described above is continuous, meaning that there is no visible or easily detected beginning or end to the sequence that includes single actions. Implementation of a new production system means that actions change as a consequence, but it does not mean that the start of the new actions is considered to be important for how actions are organised and, furthermore, there is no defined and important end to the new actions even though everybody knows that any new system will be replaced in due course. In other words, beginnings and endings are of no importance for organising actions in the permanent organisation. Consequently, actions are considered to be continuous.

This has a number of implications. First, time assumes less importance as it has no limit, as it does in projects. Time is therefore primarily divided into periods (months, years, etc.) and each period is given some attention in the systems themselves (e.g. production statistics or financial statements). Second, continuity fosters incremental changes in action rather than leaps. As actions are repeated (and often formalised) it requires an immense effort to change them. Minor difficulties can be resolved by minor changes, e.g. incrementalism, but such changes do not necessarily affect routines. Major changes will most likely have to be dealt with as projects. Third, continuous action will, over time, rest more and more heavily upon institutional and conditioned embeddedness and less on individual premeditation. Initially, when new employees enter the organisation they have to premeditate, but when they have learnt how things are done, premeditation will be less important to them.

Action and different types of temporary organisations

Whereas routinised action (e.g. forms of conditioned and institutionalised action) dominates the activities of the rank and file employees of many permanent organisations, premeditated action is more important for the temporary organisation, which is regarded as unique, and in particular for the management of that temporary organisation. The kind of premeditation involved concerns more often the effectiveness of the organisation than efficiency. Thus, the motives for forming a temporary organisation are always to be formulated explicitly, at least in our hemisphere of the world. By comparison, the *raison d'être* of a permanent organisation is subjected to scrutiny quite rarely. One reason for this might be that organising for stability in permanent organisations also implies organising in order to avoid such scrutiny.

Creating a temporary organisation relies not only on the explicit formulation of a task to be fulfilled by that organisation (or at least on a tentative formulation of such a task) but also on a notion of the limited time that the temporary organisation has at its disposal to fulfil the task. It includes the selection of people to be involved in the effort and the design of an appropriate control system to be used. Depending on the task, premeditated activities may soon develop into institutionalised behaviours. Once the temporary organisation is defined as belonging to a recurring type, premeditated behaviours are designed accordingly. This typically happens when managerial work involved becomes professionalised. And in certain trades – in particular trades whose products are tangible – managers appointed to handle temporary organisations more often than not become professionalised with stabilised beliefs as to how to work with temporary organisations and the particular tools that should be applied in this context. In that process they promote efficiency. At the same time renewal paradox mechanisms might start working.

A temporary organisation can be established for a wide variety of reasons. One such reason is to renew in some way a permanent organisation. In this case, renewal is the action purpose, which by definition cannot be a standard task and thus can hardly be standardised. In this way, a special relationship is created between the permanent organisation and the temporary one. The establishment of a temporary organisation certainly also involves premeditation on the part of the management of the permanent organisation. Managers are expected to handle problems and threats by establishing some kind of temporary organisation. For instance, if efficiency of the production apparatus is of explicit concern for the permanent organisation's management, a temporary organisation might be created to resolve the problem. In this way managers focus on a problem that they believe exists. It is also evident that some kind of non-standard action has to be taken.

By explicitly defining such a task and by allocating resources to the task, management of the permanent organisation has introduced extraordinary action into the permanent organisation. The definition of the task sends a message to the members of the permanent organisation that something that might affect them in the long term is in the making. It further sends a message to those responsible for the temporary organisation that results are expected within a predetermined time limit.

The premeditation on the part of those responsible for the operation of the temporary organisation is different. Their responsibility is for the temporary organisation as such, so their range of activities is greatly restricted compared with the range of activities open to the general management of the permanent organisation. The scope of their activities is defined by the task and by the resources at hand. But they have to find a path of activities that leads from the present state of affairs to the desired state. Such a pattern of renewal activities cannot be determined by performing routinised activities but must be considered as genuinely different from the current situation.

The emphasis on premeditation, allocation of specific resources (including time) and institutionalised ways of commencing and terminating the effort implies that project action is discontinuous. Action is rearranged and reorganised when a new project is initiated and, despite the fact that some projects are recurrent, action is therefore discontinuous. There is an end to the sequence of action that is planned and organised as a project.

Next we analyse in more detail action and, even more importantly, the significance of action in temporary organisations in the two forms: recurring and unique. The main reason for doing this is that the system for interaction is very special in temporary organisations, making them action prone. One definition to be clarified before going into an analysis of action in different types of projects is the notion of recurring versus unique. Those who subscribe to the generic idea of a social construction of reality (Berger and Luckman 1966) will realise that a project *per se* can never be recurring or unique and the correct terminology should be that a project is *perceived* to be recurring or unique. Furthermore, one should realise that the dichotomy recurring/unique is not a generalised form of the phenomenon at hand. As suggested by Gioia and Poole (1984), one might prefer a continuum describing the typicality of the situation (ranging from low to high), where a novel situation is accompanied by unscripted behaviours and actions and high typicality is associated with a stereotypical situation. In the latter case, actions will follow a strong protoscript and will be performed almost mindlessly. The benefit of a continuum compared with the dichotomy is that combination variants of the two extreme positions are allowed for.

However, to return to the main line of reasoning and sticking to the dichotomy, an individual's behaviour (action) is dependent on his (selective) perceptions and interpretations of the total situation rather than particular manifest elements in it. (Basically, however, all projects are unique in the sense that conditions vary from one project situation to another as regards physical and human elements.) Therefore, it should be up to the project participant or the project observer to decide whether a project is to be unique or not. And different participants in the same project might have quite divergent opinions as to whether the project is recurring or unique. Consider a company's reorganisation effort for instance. Such an effort is apt to be labelled unique by the company people involved, but for the organisation consultant hired explicitly to facilitate the reorganisation effort, the project is likely to be one in a series of similar efforts. Much of what he does might very well be standardised response to stimuli present in the reorganisation context.

Even so, there is usually agreement as to whether a project is predominantly recurring or whether it is unique. This is mostly the case in the opening phases of a project, when the group involved actually defines the project as unique or recurring. If they define it as recurring they are likely to construct brackets around it, thereby protecting it or even isolating it from disturbances from what is regarded to be (or defined to be) the environment. If the project is regarded as unique, the group will tend to keep the project/environment borderline more open to prevent premature isolation of the project. With hindsight, the project participants might convince themselves that their project was in fact one in a series of similar projects, but that redefinition is related less to how they actually treated the project and more to how they prefer to rewrite history *ex post facto*. We have found the distinction between recurring and unique useful, especially when it comes to how action is treated and regarded, so it will be applied in the analyses below.

Table 5.2 Differences between recurring and unique projects

Recurring projects	Unique projects
Designed for action by time, task, team and transition	Action is an ultimate goal, but not extremely important because of uncertainties and ambiguities. Rhetoric important
Isolation from environmental disturbances (e.g. host organisation)	Openness towards environment
Run by project professionals	Run by non-project professionals
Easy evaluation	Difficult evaluation

The distinction between recurring and unique projects made here is based on the perceptions of the individuals and groups involved. The differences between the two concepts as discussed above and below are summarised in Table 5.2.

Table 5.2 illustrates that the action context is quite different in recurring and unique projects. In the next two sections we will exploit that difference.

Discontinuous action in recurrent projects

Projects perceived as recurring usually take place within the realm of one particular host organisation. This means that actions are taken as well as judged with that fact taken into consideration. Looked at from the inside, actions taken within a recurrent project are subject to two kinds of constraints: constraints emanating from the host organisation and constraints emanating from the fact that the project is of the recurring type. Judged from the outside, the appropriateness of actions could be subjected to the same constraints: one type emanating from the particular host organisation involved in the project and the other attributable to the fact that the project is recurring. In recurring projects or, rather, projects in environments that are used to regarding them as recurring, the inside/outside views are probably not very different as there appear to be such strong suppositions and expectations governing the field. Probably the differences are more pronounced on the part of the host organisation as some of the premeditation factors involved in project handling and appropriate project procedures are less obvious to outsiders from the host organisation than to outsiders from the same professional field.

In the case of recurring projects, the demarcation between the project and its environment, for instance its host organisation, is very clear and free from ambiguities for the actors involved. It is as if the actors agree that the boundary between the project and its environment should be kept clear for the benefit of efficiency or for other reasons. In the example of the theatre case study and the play *Money*, it was explicitly clear from the very beginning of the project when the first performance would take place and who the crucial members of the team would be. The selection of the play was made a combined effort (with some restrictions caused by the theatre itself) and the director seemed to develop a clear view of how the 'product' could be developed almost as soon as work began. In this way the transition problem had at least a tentative solution at the start of the project, at least concerning the procedure to be applied in developing the end product, the play. And that procedure was very much the same as for work with previous plays. However, overall, the *Money* project was clearly something special in the life of the theatre and was viewed as an entity in its own right with its own budget. The same reasoning can be applied to the Royal Opera's *Lolita*, the Volvo 850 and the Saab JAS projects.

These examples indicate that, as far as projects regarded as recurring are concerned, there are a few common traits. All of those traits seem to be very much in line with the idea that action, and not any action but very particular action, is to be promoted. Action is at the fore in recurring projects. The basic concepts in determining action seem to be (Lundin and Söderholm 1995) time, task, team and transition, the so-called 4Ts. The task describes what should be accomplished in very precise and unambiguous terms. In the case just described, the task was to perform the play *Money* for the theatre audience. The time concept describes the time limitations that the project team has, for reasons of efficiency, been allotted to fulfil the task. In this case, the date of the opening night was decided well in advance and in terms of project work was almost as important as the play itself. And that procedure that was followed was essentially the same as the procedure prescribed for previous work. In accordance with the director's philosophy, the procedure included ample time at the beginning of the project for artistic freedom to understand the play and determine the messages to be transmitted to the audience. This serves to illustrate that in a recurring environment even concepts such as artistic freedom have to be well planned.

The project is defined and decoupled from its environment so as to make it a clearly discernible entity. It is given explicit boundaries in relation to its host organisations, and the host organisation lets this happen in the expectation that action will result. In fact, all planning within the project is concentrated on the fulfilment of the task. One type of failure in recurring projects is extremely conspicuous, the failure to meet the deadline: when the building is not completed in time, when the opening night at the theatre has to be postponed or when the customer does not receive the merchandise at the time previously agreed upon. Action in accordance with the task is what counts. It should be added that premeditated actions occur during recurring projects and so do institutionalised and conditioned behaviours.

This means that evaluating a recurring project is in one sense very easy. The measure of success is whether the task was fulfilled under the applied resource constraints such as the team and the time. In this respect, the project cannot be separated from its host organisation. The moment of truth for the relation between the project and its host organisation comes when the project result is due. And in that moment of truth only appropriate action counts. So, as far as recurring projects are concerned, one might say that they have been designed and are used for one thing only, and that is for action.

Discontinuous action in unique projects

In the case of unique projects, action is less self-evident and is not so outstandingly important as to be totally dominant as is the case for recurring projects. Even though unique projects are labelled in terms of problems to be solved or actions needed to be taken, doing nothing or refraining from action is still an option in most projects of that kind, at least in their initial phases. This means that unique projects are not, at least not initially, explicitly or even intentionally action oriented. This might be because of the different kinds of uncertainties that most people seem to associate with unique projects.

Since unique projects are not recurring in the sense described above, the immediate expectation is that they do not have a clearly distinguishable task, nor a team, a time limitation or a clear transition path along which one would expect the project to be carried over time. However, most of the time, the 4Ts mentioned above also serve in a unique project as reminders of how to run projects. Thus, the label 'project' is powerful as it outlines a procedure that finds support also in an environment of this kind. And the label 'project' is undoubtedly associated with many implications for how the work is to be handled, e.g. some type of action to alleviate the tension that generally has been built up is required.

Whereas recurring projects are run by (or in fact controlled by) professionals in the area of the project work (such as architects, engineers or construction experts), unique projects are seldom the responsibility of this type of professional. Unique projects are usually controlled by senior managers, for example, but they often rely on consultants who are professionals in running such projects (and who possibly perceive them as 'recurring' projects). Thus, the enterprise renewal endeavours in ABB, Skanska, Diös and Kullenberg relied on international consulting expertise. At the very least, knowledge of how to run projects in the 'correct' way does not usually play a prominent role in the education or training of senior managers. Of course, the participants in a unique project might well be professionals, but in this case their professionalism is not directly related to the project. This means that what happens inside the project takes on a different character. The restrictions regarding how to run the project and what happens in the project are, if not fewer, at least different. In general, one would expect the degrees of freedom felt by project participants to be greater and the procedure for running the project to be less constrained.

In addition, in a unique project the expectation is that the project process is much less linear than in the case of recurring projects. This means that the notion of different project phases is relatively weak in unique projects. The models used to describe project work along the 'recurring' lines are phase models [see, for instance, the descriptions provided in the pmbok guide (1996) or Lundin and Söderholm (1995)]. One way to build models for the unique case might be to utilise the same kind of models as used in recurring projects but to provide them with a feedback mechanism so as to allow recycling in the project process. One other possibility might be to determine the kind of roles that different project actors might take over the project period. To our knowledge, such a model has yet to be put forward. In any case, the reasoning serves to illustrate that the notion of action really is different for the two cases. In the unique case, premeditation plays the major role in the pre-project phase and the project appears to evolve rather than follow project plans set up initially and once and for all. The unique case not only handles a unique kind of problem, but is also treated in a unique way.

In order to illustrate the various forms that action might take in a unique project, we will describe and analyse a unique project in order to highlight the action elements. The example we will use is the health care reform project, EPQ, described previously. This case study can be described as a renewal project involving the general conditions for health care and the introduction of market factors in the resource allocation process of the health care association of one county in Sweden. Similar renewal work was introduced in all Swedish counties at the time, so one might say that, according to the reasoning presented above, the project includes a strong institutional element. However, at the same time it was made clear by the managers of the health care association of the county that the particular form of renewal that they had in mind was quite unique and was not a generic solution to be applied to all counties. There was obviously quite a strong incentive to label the renewal work as unique (which seems also to be the case in other counties from which information is available).

The renewal process essentially coincided with the arrival of a new top civil servant in the organisation. He was hired explicitly to work on renewal in the county and he latched on to the idea of introducing markets into the health care organisation. Simultaneously, he latched on to some other renewal investigations finalised before his arrival and launched the notion of the 'radical renewal' of the county. At the time 'introducing markets into the health care system' was described as the major purpose of the radical renewal. This task label is fairly vague and not in line with the recurring project notion that the task should be unambiguous and easy to evaluate. Rather, the label seems to have been chosen for its rhetorical effect. Radical renewal seems to imply a complete break with the previous system, not only in terms of resource allocation. The radical connotations of the label had the effect of making all employees look out for the new and appreciate the idea that something special was happening.

Not only was the task somewhat vague, but so was the time allotted to the renewal effort. Rather than specifying when the radical renewal was to be completed, the time element was chosen by taking the annual budgeting cycle and the general election periods into account. This also meant that the general task of radical renewal was described differently over time in the different kinds of documents produced. The verbal rhetoric was also altered over time as various efforts related to the general radical renewal task were described.

In fact, one might say that the entire scheme was planned and executed in accordance with the time restrictions involved. The entire abstract, radical renewal project was sequentially defined and made concrete in a number of minor projects and efforts – the concept of 'strategic projects' has been used elsewhere (Lundin and Söderholm 1997) – and those efforts were handled much more like recurring projects in that they were given a definite task within the radical renewal framework, a time limit adjusted to the timing requirements alluded to above, a team that was made responsible for the action in total, and with a plan designed by the leadership of the county. The strategic projects were of a variety of types, from introducing new economic control systems to leadership training for the managers in charge of various parts of the organisation. The projects seemed to be chosen sequentially and adapted in response to experiences from other projects. Moreover, projects and their accompanying rhetoric appeared to be mutually dependent, at least it was in general impossible to determine which came first, the rhetoric or the project. One might say that rhetoric at each point in time appeared to play a role as an integrator of the totality of the projects rather than as a prerequisite for the projects themselves.

The radical renewal team fluctuated, although it did not change completely, over the course of the project. The top civil servant should be regarded as the main architect of the radical renewal, and he was involved during the whole lifetime of the radical renewal, as were the politicians. However, other senior civil servants did not necessarily remain in the same capacity throughout the project. On the contrary, it appeared to be a management principle to reshuffle regularly the senior managers in the headquarters of the organisation. What is important is that the team notion, which is so prominent in recurring projects, was not apparent.

In this particular case, it might be conjectured that the parallel development of strategic projects and rhetoric functioned as a vehicle for premeditation. In the present context premeditation developed not as a discernible phase in the project work but as an extended activity. Premeditation was, in effect, an active ingredient during the entire life of the radical renewal in the sense that radical renewal, from the beginning, was never given a definite end point, a time horizon for when the project should be accomplished. And, in fact, the end point has to this day not been announced even though most actors would agree that radical renewal, is no longer on the agenda. Thus, one might say that the overall project never ended but rather that it 'faded away'. One reason for this 'fading away' is to be found in a new set of general political ideas that arose during the 1995 elections, by which time the market method of handling scarce resources had fallen into disrepute. One way to evaluate the whole effort would be to say that the notion of introducing markets into health care was never accomplished in practice, although one could say that the introduction of 'bureaucratic markets', a very regulated variant of a free market, was achieved.

This last point might give the reader the impression that not too much was accomplished in the radical renewal effort. Such a conclusion would be entirely wrong. On the contrary, many different strategic projects were completed, and some of the projects are still being carried out as proof of the ambitions and accomplishments of the county's leadership. And some of the reforms, e.g. reforms of the economic control system, will certainly be around for years to come as evidence of these accomplishments (see Blomquist and Packendorff 1998). This serves to show that the evaluation of unique projects and recurring projects can take different forms. In the case of unique projects, the task to be fulfilled and the time limitations are not explicitly defined at the beginning of the project. This means that it is not possible to compare the project outcome with some initial formulation of the task, but that the entire process has to be taken into consideration. This might be one reason why most unique projects are rarely regarded as a complete success (in fact we have still to find a unique type of project judged to be a success). To generalise then, unique projects differ from the recurring kind only in that the task was never specified in its entirety at the beginning of the project, and so there is essentially no way of evaluating the project results in traditional project terms.

Other unique projects included in Chapter 4 can be described in similar terms. ABB's T50 project had a clear aim, to reduce throughput times, but it also had vague descriptions of what actions should be taken to achieve that aim. The project was more of a starting point for action in a number of different directions throughout the company. Most of them would have been difficult to predict in advance. Officially the project had an end date but action continued in various ways afterwards. Those that had been successful in achieving the T50 goals wanted to continue improving their operations. The project faded away rather than being terminated, although the emphasis remained on a 50 per cent reduction in throughput times, and action was organised around this goal. Consequently, the major T50 project gave legitimacy to a number of projects within the company, each one organised as discontinuous action. When the JAS 37 Gripen jetfighter development project was formed it was genuinely unclear how to perform the task. The project description included the use of material and technical equipment not available at that time. Even though it was a traditional project dominated by engineers, they had to work under a major uncertainty during some phases of the project. This does not mean that they could be more relaxed concerning the action part, but it was not possible to foresee or plan action in a traditional 'project-effective' way.

The implication of this is that it appears fair to say that projects of the unique type are also devoted to action. However, since there are so many uncertainties involved, there are also multiple ways of instigating inaction and stalling the project. One mechanism might be to question the formulation of the task and suggest that the general premises for the projects are all wrong. Another way might be to indicate that the bracketing of the project is not well done, for instance by indicating that resources set aside for the project be reallocated to other projects in greater need of them, etc. Compared with the means to halt action in a recurring project, it could be said that a recurring project is like a train – once it has been set in motion, it is difficult to stop – whereas the inherent properties of a unique project allow several opportunities to stall a project temporarily or to halt it altogether.

Differences between discontinuous action in recurrent and unique projects will now be summarised. Table 5.3 shows some basic differences that have an impact on action (see Ekstedt *et al.* 1993).

Table 5.3 shows that action can be of different kinds depending on the type of project. The last two columns show that in permanent organisations action is discontinuous and continuous in recurrent and unique projects respectively.

Action embeddedness and contexts – a summary of notions

Action is a fundamental concept for all sorts of human endeavours and social life in an organisational context. One might even maintain that action is a basic aspect of human life. However, not all kinds of action are relevant in the present context. Thus, we have confined ourselves to action and action formation as they seem to pertain to permanent and temporary organisations. These organisational settings provide different contexts for action. Action in permanent organisations is continuous (no clear beginning or end), whereas action in temporary organisations is discontinuous (organised between beginnings and endings). Action is also embedded at different levels of the organisation. It can be either structurally or institutionally induced, organisationally conditioned or individually premeditated. In other words, actions taken can be guided by or related to different levels of embeddedness.

Taken together, contexts and embeddedness categories explain how action and action formation have quite different meanings in permanent and temporary organisations. Combined, the two dimensions can be used to analyse this relation further.

Table 5.3 Differences between recurrent and unique projects

Variables/characteristics	Recurrent project	Unique project
Situation	Relatively static	Relatively dynamic
Uniqueness of task	Varying	Unique task
Complexity of task	Varying	Complex task
Delimitation of time	Fixed termination point	Flexible termination point
Delimitation of scope	Clearly defined	Diffuse limits
'Owner' of project	Project manager (PM)	Chief executive officer
Statement of goal	Concrete, specified	Abstract, visionary, complex
Actors involved	Project group + business partners	Many organisation members (+ business partners)
Direction/steering	Programmed steering by results	Idea based steering by process
Leadership/motivation	By PM leadership	By CEO leadership + attraction of vision
Degree of uncertainty	Simple uncertainty, known alternatives	Problematic uncertainty, unknown alternatives
Know Why	In project description	Requires renewal pressure + crisis experience
Know What	In project description	Requires search process for alternatives
Know How	In organisation and individuals (tacit knowledge)	Requires search process for alternatives
Competence demands	Experience	Creativity, flexibility, readiness to learn
Competence formation/ learning	Experience, refinement	Reference knowledge, alternative-seeing learning
Development process	Physical, reversible	Mental, irreversible
Evaluation	Result oriented, objective evaluation of goal achievement	Utility oriented, subjective evaluation of goal achievement

Table 5.4 provides examples of what happens when a specific context is combined with a specific embeddedness category. The examples are much more numerous than shown, but the table at least hints at some possible and quite usual aspects of the different combinations. It should be observed that the middle category of the action contexts is much more open than the other two contexts. In fact, one might argue that merely selecting the 'uniqueness' label frees the project from some of its constraints or exogenous impact.

It can be concluded that both permanent and temporary organisations rely on conditions for action that are either outside the control of company management or very difficult to change. In the continuous action context, the difficulties associated with change are especially prominent since there

Table 5.4 Contexts and embeddedness combined

Action contexts	Action embeddedness			
	Structurally given	Institutionally ruled	Organisationally conditioned	Individually premeditated
Recurrent projects/ temporary organisations: discontinuous action context	Project site and technical equipment	Project management methods and tools, client demands, societal regulations	Company-specific routines for project management	Required of project managers, e.g. planning projects ahead, acting upon project's current state of affairs, disturbance handling
Unique projects/ temporary organisations: discontinuous action context	Weak	Through consultants etc., but generally weak	Weak	Individual action required and important
Permanent organisations: continuous action context	Production facilities	Rules of the industry, official requirements	Company routines and procedures for action	Entrepreneurial action within the company, e.g. by incremental innovativeness

is no clear end to the line of action taken. When organising action discontinuously and possibly changing the structural setting and individuals involved it might be easier to renew operations. A major difference between discontinuously and continuously organised action is that the former includes a number of beginnings and ends over time (project start-ups and project terminations). This in turn provides managers (and others) with a window of opportunity (Tyre and Orlikowski 1994) in which premeditation is more natural and can have a greater impact than in the continuous action context.

Moreover, in the case of projects it is correct to say that the notion of action is almost part of the very definition of a project, consisting of project task, time delimitation for the project, allocation of resources, e.g. in the form of a team, and transition (in terms of project progression). These four basic concepts of a project – time, task, team, and transition – appear in fact to be constructed in order to demarcate for action. The other side of the same coin is that there is almost an action imperative in the work of projects and project participants. Projects exist to serve the sole purpose of getting things done and the participants are there to ensure just that.

In permanent organisations, action usually means institutionalised and conditioned action. In fact, permanent organisations are almost exclusively set up in order to produce an output in a steady-state fashion. In this way they promote efficiency and productivity. As a side-effect much of what happens in a permanent organisation becomes routine. This implies, almost by definition, that permanent organisations are slow-moving entities when it comes to action of a non-routine character. Thus, it is necessary to establish a temporary organisation to carry out the non-routine task. Instead, action in permanent organisations generally consists of the following rules or norms. The organisation has been conditioned to promote certain acts.

Institutional and conditioned action can also be present in temporary organisations, and there is ample evidence of institutionalised behaviours in project-oriented firms (in recurring projects). However, in contrast to permanent organisations, in projects institutional behaviour is intended to increase efficiency. Acts and actions can only be understood in relation to the context in which they take place. Whereas actions in permanent organisations should be viewed as a consequence of the history of these organisations, action in temporary organisations might be seen as moulded by expectation about the future. Thus, all in all, temporary organisations have a distinct comparative advantage over permanent organisations when it comes to action.

The explicit relationship between action and renewal as seen through the concept of action as presented here is that action can be taken on different levels affecting not only that level but also future actions taken on that same level as well as on other levels. Thus, embeddedness functions to exert constraints on actions. However, embeddedness is also the key to affecting future actions of various kinds since embeddedness itself can be the target of action. This means that the renewal part of the 'equation' is in a sense a result of restructuration in the Giddens meaning of the word (Giddens 1984). However, from a renewal point of view, it is not sufficient with any kind of action. Change *per se* is of only limited interest in the present context. Renewal requires knowledge formation too and not merely 'blind' and resolute action. This is where the notions of knowledge formation come in – to be treated in the next chapter. Knowledge is linked to the spheres of action embeddedness, as will be demonstrated.

6 Knowledge formation in permanent and temporary organisations

Knowledge is essential for informed action in virtually every context. In fact, action without a firm basis in knowledge could be regarded not as intentional but as a reflex involving neither the human nor the 'organisational' mind. Thus, for informed action knowledge and/or beliefs are crucial. This means that a discussion of knowledge and knowledge formation is of fundamental importance for neo-industrial organising. By using the concept 'knowledge formation' rather than the traditional word 'learning', the intention is to stress the fact that knowledge formation covers a whole range of phenomena related to various forms of knowledge acquisition and handling and to variants of knowledge embeddedness. In other words, there is more to knowledge acquisition than individual learning, as will be demonstrated below.

In this chapter we will allude to forms of knowledge and learning in permanent and temporary organisations respectively. Conceptually, knowledge and learning are different in temporary and permanent organisations. One of the main differences lies in the method of handling knowledge and learning. Knowledge has different qualities, it is linked to the organisation in different ways, and it is utilised, developed and combined differently. The differences directly influence the capability of and the potential for renewal of the functioning of organisations. The transition from a traditional industrial organisation to an economic set-up in which temporary organisations are more important affects the conditions for knowledge formation. This is associated with the transformation dilemma mentioned previously, implying a questioning of existing institutions with their traditional, incremental knowledge processes. In order to understand and be able to develop strategies for renewal of neo-industrial organisations, it is thus necessary to obtain insights into the variety of paths to knowledge formation in permanent as well as temporary organisations and into the relations between them.

Little attention has been paid to the conditions for knowledge formation in an activity with a substantial element of project organisation. However, on logical and empirical grounds one can maintain that they should differ from those of traditional industry. For instance, new models for knowledge formation are required to handle the pitfall denoted the renewal paradox that projectised activities often seem to lead to. Projects may contain great capacity for knowledge formation and renewal in them, but the difficulty lies in releasing this potential and transmitting the outcome of that activity to future projects. Some related topics will be discussed here, and this chapter will conclude with a discussion about promoting and arranging such an activation, while the question of knowledge transmission will be addressed in Chapter 8.

Approaches to knowledge formation

Learning and knowledge are central concepts in many organisation theory approaches to organisational change, renewal or development. The first term, learning, is a particular favourite of many organisation theorists. Traditionally, learning is associated with individual learning and with the mental capacities of the individual, developed within the frameworks of the sciences of pedagogy and psychology. In behaviourism, for instance, learning means that individuals come to respond in a particular way to a certain stimulus or set of stimuli (cf. Pavlov's dogs). According to this line of thinking, learning is connected to behaviour in a direct sense. The human mind is transformed into a black box of no or little interest (see Harré and Gillett 1994) for the behaviourist. However, learning is also important in cognitive theories, according to which individuals have, or make, cognitive maps or schemes when approaching and interpreting the outside world (Louis 1981). Cognitive maps affect learning, but they also change in response to learning, i.e. when a certain scheme, or part of a scheme, proves to be 'outdated' or 'wrong' some changes are made and thus behaviour is changed. Recent developments at the individual level (cognitive psychology) include the role of discourse (Harré and Gillett 1994).

Learning is not only an individual matter, and changing focus from individuals to groups and organisations means that social or cultural contexts have to be included more deliberately. Learning is affected by human interaction, implicit and explicit norms for the interaction as well as behavioural rules. This also implies that individual and organisational learning are two different issues even though organisational learning is normally also considered to include a change in behaviour as a result of new knowledge (see, for example, Argyris and Schön 1978; Lant and Mezias 1990; Senge 1990b). The authors mentioned deal with different levels of learning and thus differentiate between a problem-oriented type of learning (single-loop learning, adaptive learning, etc.) and a more reflective type of learning (double-loop learning, generative learning, etc.). Following this line of thought, learning can be described as more or less radical. New knowledge or different knowledge included in the learning that occurs can be contrasted with a previous level or stock of knowledge in a variety of ways. Many of the differences can be accounted for by using the social or cultural context as an explanation for the type of learning that occurs and the kind of limitations to learning that affects learning processes and knowledge acquisition. Knowledge formation takes place in a context and the concept has to be contextualised accordingly.

Another basic issue that has to be included when changing focus from individuals to organisations is the fact that learning is not only an intra-individual process (see Cohen and Sproull 1996). If it is accepted that learning is linked to knowledge, it might be argued that results from learning processes or knowledge formation processes can be 'stored' in different ways. Cognitive schemes are only one way of storing knowledge and of making use of it. Organisations have a number of other different methods of dealing with knowledge. Most obvious is physical equipment, such as machines and other production facilities. Less obvious but of considerable importance are routines and procedures maintained within the organisations. These forms of knowledge systems have to be included in an analysis of organisational learning and will be introduced more fully in a later section. Next, a scheme for how one might conceive of learning mechanisms at the organisational level will be described.

Forms of knowledge and learning in organisations

Economic organisations are good at different things. Some are good at producing long series of products or services quickly and of a reasonable quality, whereas others are good at solving complex and unique problems. One prerequisite for success in both cases is access to relevant knowledge. Another prerequisite concerns the capability of using and developing knowledge in relation to the organisation. Knowledge is thus made up of a *stock* somehow linked to the organisation. However, organisations also have the potential to process knowledge. Through an almost organic process knowledge of different kinds can come to be generated, diffused, used and phased out (Ekstedt 1988; Nonaka and Takeuchi 1995). This *flow* – which may be considered as a learning mechanism at the organisational level – can be initiated by external as well as internal circumstances: externally mostly through influences from the market, internally through the development of technology and individuals. To understand the renewal capacity of an organisation it is thus necessary to consider both the organisation's stock of knowledge and its knowledge process.

One rationale behind distinguishing between knowledge and learning – that is between the stock and flow of knowledge – becomes particularly evident in a comparison between temporary and permanent organisations. In a temporary organisation individuals and other resources are brought together with a view to using their different abilities in a joint effort during a predetermined period of time and for a particular task. Renewal of knowledge, for instance in terms of genuine learning for the project members, can no doubt take place during the project, but the essential condition is that the resources brought together already possess certain knowledge profiles. Combining knowledge profiles is regarded as one of the most important tasks in project management. In a permanent organisation, the perspective is different. Permanent organisations have ways of gradually adding new knowledge to the stock of old knowledge. Institutional arrangements (e.g. for investments) secure, at least normally, that there is a gradual update of technology and individual knowledge. As a general conclusion at this point it can be said that temporary organisations develop knowledge for the task at hand through a process encompassing locating and combining different stocks of knowledge, whereas permanent organisations normally renew knowledge through an incremental process or approach.

Thus far we have regarded the concepts of knowledge and learning as something all-embracing but unitary. However, at times there might be a need also to differentiate between various forms of knowledge and to be more precise. One might distinguish between the degrees of reflection and conceive of three types of knowledge: skill, know-how and competence (Rolf 1991; Rolf *et al*. 1993). Such a differentiated discussion is too detailed for our purposes. The mention of it, however, serves to illustrate that we will have to omit much theoretical and empirical work on knowledge and learning.

One particular distinction needs to be elaborated upon though. As already mentioned, we concur with researchers who argue that it is fruitful to distinguish between incremental and radical organisational learning (Miner and Mezias 1996). This distinction can also – with some difficulty – be applied to our primary empirical base, the 25 radical renewal projects studied. They include both gradual renewal and renewal in one go. The renewal can target behaviour and products, as well as the formation of knowledge. We take this as our starting point and will designate the gradual renewal of knowledge that generally takes place in flow-process production (in ABB Control and Ericsson for example) and in recurrent projects production (in Skanska, Kullenberg and Digital for example) *refinement*. We will term the dramatic renewal and shift of perspective that evolves in radical overall renewal projects (the ABB T50, JAS 39 Gripen and *Lolita* projects for example) *alternative seeing* (Ekstedt 1988). It is conceivable that gradual refinement is possible within the scope of the built-in norms, rules and roles of an organisation, but that a situation finally will develop in which the existing way of thinking has to be reconsidered for further progress; new alternative solutions have to be sought. These alternatives are usually to be found outside one's own organisation, in organisations and individuals with different ways of thinking and other experiences. Quite often these alternative ideas are transmitted by consultants who have broad contacts with companies and research. One good example of a situation in which the limits of an existing organisation model was reached can be found in ABB, where line production was abandoned in favour of goal-directed groups.

Thus, we propose that one should draw a distinction between different forms of knowledge and learning. And we also distinguish between knowledge as *stock* and knowledge change as *flow*. The flow-process of knowledge, *learning*, can evolve through gradual refinement (single-loop learning) or develop through alternative seeing (double-loop learning). In the second case, the traditional way of thinking is questioned and put in a new context (second-order knowledge). When it comes to the conception of knowledge as stock, the notions of embeddedness (Ekstedt 1988) are important since this is where permanent and temporary organisations differ.

Knowledge embeddedness

In the section above, a variety of knowledge-related concepts were discussed. Here, an attempt is made to reach some tentative conclusions on knowledge formation in organisations, and knowledge will be considered in relation to different forms or modes of embeddedness. The notion of embeddedness was introduced in the previous chapter as a way of discussing action focus. Considering knowledge and embeddedness, instead, the following terms will be used:

* (real) capital-embedded knowledge
* institution-embedded knowledge
* organisation-embedded knowledge
* individual-embedded knowledge

Institution- and organisation-embedded knowledge combined will be denoted:

* system-embedded knowledge.

As for action, the notion of embeddedness helps to broaden the perspective of organisational renewal and to avoid too narrow a focus on individuals and their capacities. Consequently, our point of departure is that knowledge described as being embedded introduces important organisational and non-individual elements into the understanding of knowledge formation.

We argue that the knowledge that is embedded in the individual develops (and can be exploited) in combination with the knowledge that is embedded in real capital (physical facilities) and in institutions (rule systems and the traditions/culture), not least in the rules and traditions connected with the specific work organisation/system. Being able to grasp the concept that knowledge embedded in individuals has different qualities from knowledge embedded in machinery is particularly important in any comparison between temporary and permanent organisations. Many permanent organisations are built around a large-scale and stable assembly of machinery, whereas temporary ones generally have to rely on human resources as their most important element. Sunds Defibrator and the Central Study Support Committee (CSN), for example belong to the first category, and the projectised construction companies and theatres to the second.

Modes of embeddedness

Capital-embedded knowledge refers to knowledge associated with technology, tools and machines used. The knowledge of generations is ploughed back into the tools and machines used in an organisation. Although technological inventions and scientific achievements are put to work at the company level, the tools and machines in fact represent artefacts that are the combined products of learning and thinking and use over decades. The scientific, technical and practical conceptions of different groups and individuals contribute to their current design. The way in which the tool is used is generally closely associated with social practice. The tools of the industrial society have in most cases been developed from basic principles within the field of mechanics. This development has generally been able to take place without the engineers or practitioners involved having been capable of fully expressing or understanding the underlying principles. However, knowledge of the functioning of various tools has become a natural element of everyday life for many people. Individuals today can usually drive a car, and even a small child knows how to choose channels on a TV set. It will probably take some time (another generation) until the principles and applications of computer technology and biotechnology become as deeply rooted in our society as mechanics. The same thing can be said about modern information technology, since the new applications are so different from the original ones (such as the fax or phone).

A considerable part of the knowledge used in organisations carries a number of more or less explicit rules or roles, in other words an organisation uses *institution-embedded knowledge*. These rules and roles are a vehicle for transferring feelings, thoughts and actions from one generation to the next. To some extent, they represent our way of performing work, and at the same time they convey what people in an organisation feel and think of it and of one another. The concept of *tradition* is therefore closely related to the concept of *culture*. Cultures are generally conveyed by traditions, and traditions often convey cultural expressions. Traditions and conceptions in working life manifest themselves as work culture and company culture. These two concepts reflect different perspectives of social phenomena, both of which are prevalent. Work culture chiefly refers to conditions in the production process, and could thus bear upon several different organisations, companies and lines of business. Company culture hints at a particular company (organisation) and its image. Work culture mainly concerns employee relations, whereas company culture is a concept often linked to a management perspective (Rolf *et al.* 1993) and to prescriptions for managing.

Cultures are not a neutral store of methods and patterns that can sort our thoughts, feelings, decisions and actions. They chiefly embody some kind of identity: a 'we feeling'. Anyone wanting to be included in a 'we' must be seen as one of us; the rules of intellectual fellowship become a *sine qua non*. If you do not understand these rules of language, actions and thinking you become incomprehensible or unnoticeable, and if you violate them you will be excluded. The rules of social interaction are a common store of knowledge, developed over generations. It is true that they are modifiable and negotiable. But both rules and roles represent continuity; for practical reasons it is impossible at any moment to negotiate everything. However, most social changes, and negotiations, take place in a social context (Rolf *et al.* 1993; Polanyi 1958).

One task of formal institutions is to reduce the transaction costs, that is the costs of searching for, negotiating and monitoring agreements. These institutions are also of great importance for the design and activity of organisations. Special accounting systems, central stock exchanges and established forms for setting up companies are examples that exist in most countries. Thus, the modern entrepreneur has to consider legislation on bookkeeping, company formation, taxes and the labour market, among a great number of other things. The work division of organisations is directly influenced by the need for companies to employ specially trained individuals, e.g. legal experts and economic advisers, if they are to operate in the institution-dense environment. Institutions and rules consequently give rise to special work roles in the labour market (Coase 1988; Williamson 1983).

It is probable, however, that the formal institutions, rules and roles alluded to above are the results of traditions developed in a social interaction over a long period. In recent years, therefore, the importance of the informal institutions for political as well as economic development has received increasing attention (Putnam 1993). The ability to resolve conflicts (like the prisoners' dilemma for example) and to counteract destructive opportunism is dependent on a broad social interaction. Soft solutions, e.g. voluntary cooperation, are easier to bring about in societies with a stock of social capital developed by tradition (Bates 1989). The somewhat diffuse concept of social capital refers to a state of affairs in which norms, relations and networks are based on a high degree of mutual trust among the members of society. In a social organisation characterised by a high level of trust among its members, efficiency can be improved as a result of the increased ease with which activities can be coordinated. Safeguarding is minimised.

It could be argued that the prevalence of opportunism, fraud and evasion increases as societies become more complex. Thus, the importance of social capital increases with continued economic development. The question is 'what kind of rule systems develop in a particular society – or in a particular organisation?'. Is there a tradition of collective action and trust or is there one that emphasises dependence and hierarchies? It is the historical development that determines which one of these usually very stable solutions will characterise a given organisation and society. The inertia is not a result of history sorting out or encouraging collective irrationality. Nor can it be attributed to individual irrationality. On the contrary, individuals respond to the social context in which they live. There their actions are rational. In this way individuals strengthen the well-worn social paths. This path dependency is self-reinforcing although ineffective from a societal point of view (North 1990).

In addition to institutions, organisations also matter. In an idealised organisation model, managers would have the option of combining fairly freely capital-, institution- and individual-embedded knowledge and of bringing them together and forming different kinds of technology, rules, roles and individuals into a work organisational community. In reality, it is often necessary to understand the knowledge that is embedded in the *work organisation* to be able to influence the logistics of internal and external operations. For actors to be able to function in an organisation – that is to communicate, handle and activate contacts – they must understand and be capable of retrieving and applying the *organisation-embedded knowledge*. Often, it can be difficult in practice to separate organisation from institution when it comes to determining how and where knowledge is embedded. What appears to be an organisational decision could sometimes be best explained as determined by environmental rules (i.e. institutions). Decisions on how to organise locally can be made in accordance with long-established rules in that industry. Investment procedures can be a result of demands originating from the financial sector, for example, and vice versa. A distinct demarcation between institution-embedded knowledge and organisation-embedded knowledge cannot therefore be drawn. This is the major reason for introducing *system-embedded knowledge* when referring to both organisation and institution embeddedness and when the differences between them are of less importance. However, differences between organisational and institutional embeddedness are also obvious. When institutionally embedded rules are changed in one organisation it is likely that inertia will be experienced not only in that organisation but also, for instance, in the environment. We will therefore make use of the difference between organisational and institutional embeddedness in such lines of arguments.

Individuals are obviously central, and as actors they are of great importance for the organisation in which they work with special reference to knowledge as *individual embedded*. They possess thinking, feeling and acting patterns, which can be developed and transformed. Both knowledge and motivational aspects are woven into these patterns. Sometimes there are strong similarities between patterns. At times individuals are believed to hold cognitive maps that could come to characterise companies and even whole industries (Bower and Hildegard 1981). This is not to say that individuals cannot play a crucial part in the development of organisations. There are several examples of strong personalities owning unique ideas who have carried through changes that very few other people believed in initially (Philips 1988).

In our empirical cases taken from the entertainment world, individual directors and actors no doubt play a very important part. They put their stamp on the performances. But they do not act in a vacuum. Their knowledge is integrated within a very special environment. Our point is that individuals also exist in a knowledge context. They live in and are shaped by their environment with its specific rules and special role sets, and with access to various technical resources.

Knowledge embeddedness in different types of companies

There are many possible methods of creating and accumulating knowledge in various types of companies (Ekstedt 1988). Recruitment, internal training, external training, on-the-job training, internal R&D, purchase of technology, public R&D and on-the-job development are some examples. In process industries, such as forestry and steel, a considerable amount of knowledge is embedded in real capital. The mode of working of the organisation, its logistics, is to a great extent dependent on the technical knowledge that is stored in machinery. It sets limits to and alternatives for staff action. It is also the basis for the capacity of the organisation to continue its operations for a long period of time. The renewal of the organisation is strongly dependent upon technological development. Among our case studies, Sunds Defibrator is the one most closely related to this type of organisation. This engineering factory furnishes the forestry industry with heavy machinery. It should be noted, however, that regular manufacturing is increasingly tinged with elements of project organising. The ordering, manufacture and delivery of a machine can be seen (and is seen by management) as something extraordinary, as a separate project. In pure process industries, however, for example the paper and pulp and steel industries, the permanent organisation remains completely dominant.

In construction companies, knowledge is embedded differently. Real capital plays a relatively insignificant role. Knowledge seems first and foremost to be embedded in a firm tradition, containing both the know-how of the trade and the logistics of the construction process. Individuals cannot gain access to this knowledge unless they have been members of the organisation for several years. Only then they will know how the various parts of the construction process are related, and only then will they be fully accepted by the other participants. They become bearers of the construction culture. The combination of institution- and organisation-embedded knowledge (termed system-embedded knowledge) plays a decisive part in many of our case studies. This is particularly evident in the construction companies and the entertainment business. However, this knowledge undoubtedly also has a strong influence in engineering companies and in the medical field.

In computer companies, knowledge is embedded in the computers and in the software available, but principally knowledge is embedded in the individuals. This means that the companies are rather weak organisations, which in turn means that they have to make themselves attractive to their employees in order to retain them, i.e. the knowledge capital. This is mostly because an important part of the knowledge formation is taking place outside the company. The people involved are well-educated individuals who are continuing their self-development through their work with different customers. Thus, they are people who could easily take their knowledge to other organisations and projects. Knowing a special trade is more important than working for a particular company (Ekstedt 1988). This scenario appears to be true for the computer company we looked at, Digital Equipment, but individual-embedded knowledge can also be a decisive factor in other advanced activities, in stage plays for example.

In practice, organisations naturally use many different combinations of approaches to knowledge and knowledge embeddedness. However, the clarity of the empirical observations facilitates the connection with a broader theoretical perspective. There is no doubt that the range of *physical equipment* exerts an influence on the organisational design and the way of working. Certain technical inventions have had a revolutionary influence to say the least. The industrial revolution, which introduced a completely new division and organisation of work, was closely related to technical knowledge and development. Technological invention evolving into innovations with diffusion to many different activities was one of the most important incentives to transformation. Some of the major innovations were important for the organisation of society as a whole. The invention of electricity (together with a number of innovations based on electricity) had, and is still having, slightly more than a hundred years later, significant consequences for the organisation of companies and factories and for the planning of work as well as leisure time.

Computers and information technology have made it feasible, in principle, to transmit information instantly (texts, pictures and control signals) anywhere on Earth. The operations that are linked do not need to be under the same roof or even in the same country. The geography of organisations takes on a new, partly unknown, face. However, it is also becoming easier to bring individuals and companies with special competence together for temporary commitments. Projects are becoming a more common organisational form of work as a result of the development of computers and information technology. The physical structure thus influences both the time-bound and geographic dimensions of organisations. Modern computer techniques allow for a multitude of variations of organisational design compared with the stationary machinery of the traditional industry (Ekstedt 1988; Gareis 1990; Ekstedt and Wirdenius 1995).

Knowledge in temporary and permanent organisations

In economic activities and exchanges in general, and in renewal endeavours in particular, a permanent part of the organisation is usually combined with a temporary part. In some spheres, the permanent organisation is entirely dominant (e.g. in the paper and pulp industry). In other industries, it is the other way around: the temporary parts are dominant (a classical example being the construction industry). However, despite these manifest differences in the two types of organisation, it is with the permanent organisation that we associate activity (as discussed previously). A construction worker is identified with the company for which he works, rather than with the projects he has participated in. He is, for example, a 'Skanska man' in spite of the fact that his colleagues may be more likely to be actors from other organisations than from the permanent Skanska organisation. This is not that odd considering the importance of recognition for permanent organisations in reaching long-term goals. The name of the permanent organisation is associated with certain qualities, e.g. it may conjure up an image of high quality. And for the individuals who are on the permanent staff of the company, professional identity is supplemented by something tangible, the company image, which is a source of energy to rely on and to return to.

In traditional industrial enterprises and in public services, a major part of the activity is permanent. Traditional industry, based on a capital-intensive, stationary machinery of production, must become long term by necessity. However, the legal system, the education system and the transport system, having law and order, knowledge formation and ways of communication as spheres of activity, respectively, are also of a standardised and recurring nature. In all three cases, therefore, permanent, bureaucratic forms of organisation are the rule.

The knowledge of people working in industry is closely related to the knowledge stored in the machines. Skill and know-how develop through interaction between humans and machines. Long ago the worker in a pulp mill learned how to judge the state of the process by means of his senses. Changes in smell and noise levels were indicators of disturbances in the process (Ekstedt 1988; Zuboff 1988). However, in modern industrial enterprises individual closeness to the process seems to be reduced.

Processes are controlled by computers, and supervision is through the medium of the computer display unit. This transition changes the knowledge required in a very tangible way. Analytical and abstract abilities rather than judgements based on physical perceptions are demanded to an ever-increasing extent. Know-how receives a reflective element.

Essentially, a major element of capital-embedded knowledge in an organisation is indeed of a permanent nature. This is illustrated in some of the renewal ventures we have studied. In ABB ZWUS Signal, Sunds Defibrator, ABB Control and the CSN, capital-embedded knowledge plays a prominent part. In ZWUS we observed that the arrangement and logistics of the machines were much the same as when the Communist regime took over more than half a century ago. At that time the company was a subsidiary of the Swedish LM Ericsson. The Ericsson way of organising had been transferred to Poland, to be cemented there. In the renewal work now under way with ABB as an investor the aim is to develop new, modern forms of organising machine utilisation, among other things. In Sunds, the physical rearrangement of machines was a means of reinforcing new forms of working. A new logistical system was developed, resulting in the need for new levels of cooperation. In CSN, rapid technological progress in the field of computing necessitated new organisational solutions. All local offices in the country are linked to a shared information system; distances are reduced. In capital-intensive activities, capital-embedded knowledge plays an important part in organisational design and renewal. Permanent organisations dominate over temporary ones. In permanent flow-process production it is customary for renewal work to be institutionalised. Special departments for the development of technology (R&D) and education and training are created. However, the use of projects to undertake technical development work can also be observed to a marked extent. The Saab 2000, Volvo 850 and CSN STIS 2000 projects serve to illustrate this.

It is not only technological development that influences the design of the industrial organisation. More well-informed and demanding customers often require that the products should be specially designed or supplied in combination with services (maintenance, training). This leads to increased projectisation, an observation made in ABB companies producing large complex products, among others. In modern industrial enterprises, therefore, temporary arrangements increase at the expense of permanent ones.

In many of our cases the combination of institution- and organisation-embedded knowledge (system-embedded knowledge) is a salient feature. In the construction sector, in the theatre world and in the health care field institutionalised ideas are particularly evident. In all three of these spheres professional training plays a prominent part. What is required is a combination of formal training and experience-based acquisition of knowledge. In the construction and theatre fields, experience-based knowledge carries most weight, whereas in the health care sphere, for example, medical training encompasses both study and practical work in a systematic way. Many of our renewal projects involve a combination of permanent and temporary organisations. Examples are Skanska Stockholm's 'Gångaren' project and the production of the play *Lolita* by the Stockholm Royal Opera. The permanent parts, that is Skanska Stockholm and the Royal Opera, are dominated by institution-embedded knowledge, whereas the temporary parts, the Gångaren and *Lolita* projects, rely on a mixture of institution-embedded knowledge in the form of professional roles and specific individual-embedded knowledge. In the *Lolita* venture the unique performance of the singers attracts attention.

To summarise our discussion of knowledge in temporary and permanent organisations, we conclude that the permanent or temporary nature of the economic activities is related to the dominating mode of embedding knowledge. Roughly we can see the following pattern. *When capital-embedded knowledge is dominant the organisation form is primarily permanent.* Temporary organisations, such as committees and development projects, may be seen as additions. *When the knowledge in an economic activity is strongly embedded in institutions or in the organisation, permanent and temporary parts are combined.* The activity is organised as an interplay between different roles. In the construction sector we distinguish between the company and the project, in the entertainment sphere between the theatre and the play, and in the legal system between the court and the criminal investigation. There are reasons to return to the problem of how the work division between the permanent and temporary parts is carried out or should be carried. *Activities dominated by individual-embedded knowledge usually take on a temporary character.* However, they are safeguarded by certain supporting functions. Authors have difficulties in asserting themselves without a publisher. Painters/artists need an art gallery in which to exhibit, and a consultant needs marketing through some kind of company establishment of a permanent type.

Renewal of (or acquiring) knowledge in permanent and temporary organisations – learning processes vs. combinatorics

Forms of knowledge and the way in which knowledge is embedded differ decisively between permanent and temporary organisations. This difference is even more apparent when the renewal of knowledge is taken into consideration. Permanent organisations, with their long-term perspective, increasingly exhibit a tendency to build into their activity functional entities that are assigned the task of utilising, developing and diffusing knowledge. One of the principal tasks of personnel departments with training functions, R&D departments and senior managers is to promote the development of knowledge. Close contacts with well-informed and demanding customers tend to be useful for developing knowledge for future activities. Essentially, the result of these efforts is a gradual development of knowledge, which can be the basis of incremental change in organisations and products.

In temporary organisations there is less scope for setting up institutions for the development of knowledge. Who is to utilise the knowledge that has made its contribution as soon as the task of the temporary organisation is fulfilled? Instead, people and other resources with a certain potential are combined to produce a specific product or service. The end product can actually have a great content of knowledge – it can be, for example, an advanced product such as JAS 39 Gripen or the result of a research project. Those who join the project are expected to be able to contribute to it and to finish it, and their ability in this respect will no doubt increase in the course of the work. But the crucial problem is how this knowledge is to be retrieved. The odds are that the individual who participated has become more able and experienced but that this will have no future effects on the particular organisation. This can be illustrated by the ever-lasting discussion on the difficulties of diffusing knowledge in the construction sector. One explanation of this problem – besides the dispersed and changing working sites – is that it is in the interest of the individuals to keep their acquired knowledge to themselves in order to become more attractive for recruitment to the next project. Not only is there no vocabulary for dispersing knowledge, but it is not in the individual's interest to articulate his knowledge, and this also makes diffusion of it more difficult.

Thus the dynamics of temporary organisations, as far as knowledge is concerned, is primarily developed during the design of projects. We will return to this matter later in this chapter, but first we will discuss the renewal mechanisms in permanent organisations in order to better grasp the problems that arise when capital-embedded knowledge has a lesser influence on the development of the organisation. This, among other things, is of course what happens when the temporary part of the economic activity becomes more important and has greater influence, which is what happens when we are passing into a neo-industrial economy.

Learning processes in permanent organisations – promoting incremental (or constrained) change

Permanent organisations are dependent upon the existing set-up of knowledge and its embeddedness. This means that permanent organisations in general have invested heavily in that existing set-up, which in turn makes them apt to prefer 'constrained change' in an incremental manner.

In the conceptual discussion earlier in this chapter it was argued that knowledge can be described as *stock*, which means that it is stored in various forms within a company or a public office: capital-embedded knowledge, the combination of institution- and organisation-embedded knowledge, and individual-embedded knowledge. Learning, on the other hand, is a process concept, which implies a *flow* – a change of knowledge in some form. For the sake of simplicity, we conceive of learning as processes taking place in stages over an imagined life cycle: from generation to diffusion and storing and, finally, phase-out. In large permanent organisations, we can think of all stages as being represented. In practice, there are no distinct boundaries between the stages. They are closely linked by both content and time overlapping. Learning occurs with respect to some given special knowledge somewhere in its life cycle. The mutual relations between the two concepts (knowledge as a stock and learning as a flow process) will be discussed below and provided with a meaning in relation to one another.

Capital-embedded knowledge is thus such knowledge that is linked to investments in machines, production equipment, tools or capital-intensive products such as houses and aeroplanes. This type of knowledge is a basis for the activity of the traditional industrial organisation, and innovations within this form of knowledge, among other things, paved the way for the industrial revolution. Change in capital-embedded knowledge can take place in organisations in a number of different ways. In some cases, new technical solutions have emerged in a more or less haphazard way, but there also exist institutionalised procedures, which lead to changes in capital-embedded knowledge.

First, in many countries tax legislation encourages a continuous change in the capital-embedded knowledge concurrent with writing off investments that have reached the end of their economic life. In other words, there are established forms, formal institutions if you wish, for the phasing out of capital-embedded knowledge and for the search for new investments – usually more effective machines – as replacements for the old ones. The system encourages gradual refinement by speeding up the diffusion of technological knowledge.

Second, large companies in general have some form of established R&D unit or activity whose objective is to develop new products and/or production processes. The activity run by these permanent organisations usually results in gradual changes. This is particularly true for the process field.

Third, within several spheres of technology a number of societal institutions (e.g. Nutek in Sweden, Sintef in Norway, often funded publicly as well as privately) assist in, for example, diffusing new techniques or in transferring new technological advances from universities to industry. Sometimes such undertakings are supported by financial backing.

The methods described above promote change in capital-embedded knowledge. It is not likely, however, that these institutionalised methods will lead to radical renewal. More often, the methods lead to marginal changes in existing techniques. In terms of the total production system, each new investment represents only a minor part of that system. Radical renewal in fact calls for a change from one type of system to another. Regarding radical renewal in this way implies that it does not occur very often in practice.

There are many ways to diffuse and maintain an established capital-embedded basis of knowledge internally. Standardisation of manufacturing processes, for example, makes it easier to transfer techniques, staff and production between different production plants. Maintenance and continuous marginal changes are also means to try to maintain an established basis of knowledge within the organisation. In addition, in the case of mass- or process-manufacturing companies, changes are often complex and difficult to carry out without interruptions in production, and therefore it is natural to try to retain an established capital-embedded knowledge as long as possible. In companies relying on piece or batch production and close customer contacts, there may exist entirely different conditions for carrying out relatively large-scale changes in the final product or the production process. In such cases, market pressure is the basis for renewal or change of knowledge.

There also exist established forms for the generation and phasing out of individual-embedded knowledge. Procedures for reducing and increasing the workforce are well known and, although difficult to implement, both these functions are usually firmly established in the organisation. Recruitment procedures are often associated with introduction, training and education in various forms in order to make sure that the new staff members will be capable of shouldering new or altered occupational roles. In the case of existing staff, various types of competence development programmes are normally arranged, in the form of training, job rotation or introduction of self-directed groups, for example. Such efforts are usually combined with expectations of learning taking place more naturally in daily work. Retirement procedures are usually well established, and a fall-off in demand or changes in operations necessitating redundancy are usually also well documented. Society facilitates the execution of new recruitment and phasing out of company staff, e.g. through a variety of employment policies.

Although recruitment of new personnel may result in an inflow of knowledge via new individuals, this will not necessarily result in renewal. New staff are often chosen, educated and trained in order to fit into the prevailing, established organisation. This reduces their chances of acting as catalysts for renewal. New managerial staff – a new CEO for example – may initiate a radical transformation of the activity, particularly if the reason for their recruitment was contingent upon previous problems in the organisation. Likewise, the recruitment of new staff can be made with the explicit aim of contributing to the build-up of a new activity, in which case the introductory training must be different. No matter what result the new recruitment eventually will produce, there are forms of recruitment, employment, introduction and phasing out of staff that make it possible to renew, maintain or phase out individual-embedded knowledge.

The form of knowledge consisting of a combination of institution- and organisation-embedded knowledge, which we have termed system-embedded knowledge, consists of knowledge that is linked to organisation structure and established bureaucratic systems for controlling activity. Such knowledge differs from capital- and individual-embedded knowledge in that institutionalised forms of renewal are to a large extent deficient in this area. On the contrary, bureaucratic control systems, work organisation and organisational rules have a strong element of self-preservation and are often designed in such a way that they promote their own survival. Bureaucratic solutions are developed with the explicit intention of making them permanent, and efforts to change the systems often remain partial. The preserving forces are thus strong. This is partly a consequence of the fact that system-embedded knowledge is in many respects defined by circumstances beyond the control of the individual organisation. Education and training systems, industry-specific knowledge, forms of work organisation, communication systems, standardisation principles, etc. are influenced, for example, by trade associations, national or international laws, rules and agreements, as well as by education and training systems.

Changes in system-embedded knowledge do not take place naturally, and there are few institutionalised ways to promote renewal. There are instead a number of circumstances that lead to the diffusion and maintenance of established knowledge within the organisation. The bureaucratic control systems are in this respect the most important form for maintaining present knowledge by formalised organisation structures and the established systems for communication, information and reporting. Systems of this sort are designed to be stable, that is they have the explicit aim of remaining invariable and not changing through their own power. This is what usually is termed 'the inherent incapacity of bureaucracy for learning from its own mistakes'. Representatives of bureaucratic systems, however, might consider stability as a means of handling the organisation, its activity and employees in a uniform way over time, and thus increase manageability.

Other circumstances that have a stabilising or conserving effect include the existence of certification and accreditation within certain lines of business or fields of action. Quality certifications or professional authorisations often require that a certain type of certified system is maintained. Professional occupational groups, with mandatory working licences, for example, also demand that the organisation of the activity matches up to certain stable norms.

In such a situation, change and renewal almost becomes an anomaly, an unnatural situation to be avoided. The renewal that nevertheless takes place is usually the result of active renewal efforts in the form of projects aiming at the implementation of new, or at least changed, bureaucratic control systems. In other words, the renewal is based on the argument that one type of stable control system should be replaced by another type of stable system. The principle stating that system-embedded knowledge should be firmly established in structure and system is very seldom, if ever, abandoned. In other words, the learning process – generating, maintaining and phasing out knowledge – is more difficult to sustain when it comes to this form of knowledge. This, in turn, is due to the lack of fixed institutionalised forms for generation or phase-out of knowledge and to the strong preserving forces that are maintaining established beliefs and knowledge.

It should be noted that so-called 'learning organisations' are often associated with individual learning in organisations (see, for example, Senge 1990a). Discussions on learning organisations thus tend to overlook the importance of organisationally or institutionally embedded knowledge that is a relevant environment or frame for individual learning. The notion of learning organisations is therefore a quest for incremental learning within the frames provided by, for example, organisationally and institutionally embedded knowledge, and hence not sufficient to promote or understand organisational renewal issues. This is not to say that scholars involved in theorising around learning organisations have gone wrong. Rather we would like to draw attention to one important limitation in the learning organisation concept.

Thus, organisational changes suggested by Senge (1990a: 139–), for example, as necessary for building a learning organisation involve a change in the individual's modes of perception, mental models and visions. This is, of course, important in order to reveal other modes of knowledge embeddedness discussed in this chapter, but it provides few insights into what kind of organisation is needed or how larger organisational systems should or could be designed.

The discussion this far is summarised in Table 6.1, which shows different forms of knowledge and their relation to the three phases of learning. Each cell contains examples illustrating how different forms of knowledge develop through the three phases, from generation of (new) knowledge to phase-out of obsolete knowledge.

Table 6.1 illustrates different forms of knowledge and learning in organisations and shows a number of elements of a 'learning theory' for organisations. In the case of capital- and individual-embedded knowledge in permanent organisations, there are forms for generation and phase-out, and, even if this in itself does not necessarily lead to renewal, there are readily available procedures which can be developed and refined with the aim of reaching a substantial renewal effect. The text in italics in Table 6.1 shows the phases and types of knowledge with relatively few institutionalised forms for generation and phase-out of knowledge

Table 6.1 Methods for the development of knowledge in different phases of learning

Phase of learning	Form of knowledge embeddedness		
	Capital	*System*	*Individual*
Generation	Physical restructuring Purchase of technology R&D ventures/ R&D departments New investments	*New organisation/ reorganisation projects Organisational fads or trends Issuing of new rules, new standards Introduction of new 'cultures' in the organisation and/or new management*	Recruitment procedures On-the-job training Job rotation Education/training
Diffusion and storing	Company-wide technical training Technical maintenance Standardisation Continuous updating	Bureaucratic systems for control, reporting, information and communication Certification systems (e.g. ISO) Cultivation of 'guilds'	Job rotation Education/training Mentor system Recurrent training
Phase-out	Scrapping Writing off Innovations make current technology outdated	*Outdated rules 'Peer' pressure Legitimisation problems*	Dismissal/transfer Retirement Unlearning

respectively. This leads to the conclusion – as far as system-embedded knowledge is concerned – that there is a special need for renewal and initiatives to bring about renewal, since natural forms for this are missing.

The transformation dilemma – obstacles for renewal in neo-industrial organising

The neo-industrial organisation has a different and probably also a more complex character than traditional industrial organisations. The greater frequency of temporary undertakings implies that the formalised renewal processes of capital-embedded knowledge have less influence on the renewal of the organisation. There is a transformation dilemma: the traditional tools and institutions for change no longer work so well. In the search for solutions to this deficiency, many industrial and public renewal projects are started, as illustrated in Chapter 4. Most of these projects have the aim of changing the system (the way of working and thinking), in other words they are acting on institutional- and organisation-embedded knowledge. Whereas investments in technology and changes in staffing are in many cases matters of routine or routine projects, renewal ventures within an organisation or system are usually projects with a great element of non-routine action. The unique or unusual feature of these endeavours is accentuated. At the same time, projects aiming at changing system-embedded knowledge are among the most difficult to bring to a successful conclusion. Whereas new machinery, new buildings and new staff fall readily in place, it seems to be much more difficult to exchange established bureaucratic systems or organisational structures for new creations. There are a number of reasons for this. First, machines, establishments and staff are tangible whereas, for example, communication and reporting systems are relatively abstract. Second, changes in capital- and individual-embedded knowledge are often directly linked to the activity, whereas changes in system-embedded knowledge generally take place in two stages: the company is reorganised, which then has an influence on the current activity (makes it more effective). In other words, it is not possible to observe directly the effects of such a reorganisation project. Third, as has been noted previously, the lack of institutionalised change procedures within the category of organisation-embedded knowledge implies that the renewal process as such is more difficult to handle and control.

This discussion has considered the different forms of knowledge and the different phases of learning as separate. This is a simplification however. Conditions and changes within one form of knowledge influence the conditions for the other forms of knowledge in various ways. For example, investments in new technology can lead to changes in organisation-embedded knowledge. Conversely, established technology will undoubtedly have a restraining effect on renewal initiatives within other forms of knowledge. Similar relations exist between all forms of knowledge, and these can both hamper and stimulate learning.

The relative importance of the different forms of knowledge in an organisation is dependent upon the activity and the traditional organisational form that characterises the company or the public office. The traditional, industrial firm (with mass production and much capital invested in machinery) will be dominated by capital-embedded knowledge. This implies, among other things, that the other forms of knowledge are more likely to be influenced by capital-embedded knowledge than the other way round. The same applies to those activities in which capital-embedded knowledge is manifested in the final product, e.g. in construction companies. Recruitment needs, hierarchic structure and the demands for competence in the staff will in this case be governed by requirements defined by the production facilities or by the final product.

A typical knowledge-intensive firm is dependent on the individuals employed in the activity, and thus will be dominated by individual-embedded knowledge. Law, accountancy and consultancy firms fall into this category. In these companies, individual-embedded knowledge determines the organisational structure and the appropriate capital investments. In a similar way, activities in which coordination and organisation dominate, for example in the so-called professional bureaucracies or diversified companies, are above all dependent on system-embedded knowledge. To this category also belong companies with some kind of diversified or multifarious activity, as well as organisations with strongly regulated activity (many public organisations, for example).

A few examples of how different forms of knowledge can hamper or support changes within the other forms of knowledge are presented in Table 6.2. The table is by no means complete, but it demonstrates a variety of possible interdependencies in different types of activities.

One conclusion is that renewal is often driven by the dominating form of knowledge. On the one hand, this implies that renewal endeavours in an organisation that is dominated by capital-embedded knowledge will have their basis in demands and conditions within this form of knowledge and in connection with capital investments. This, in turn, implies that engineers are likely to have a great influence on this process. On the other hand, it also means that renewal of the other forms of knowledge can come to be subordinate to capital-embedded knowledge. An analogous condition applies to organisations dominated by individual- and system-embedded knowledge. Although in practice many renewal efforts tend to concentrate on the rhetorical aspects of the renewal efforts (i.e. renewal efforts as persuasion), it is in fact the dominant form of knowledge that reveals the best means for renewal in any particular case.

However, many organisations are complex and complicated in many respects. An organisation can run several different activities, include different professional spheres of knowledge and be dependent upon both specific technologies and specific occupational categories with the associated coordination and control problems. Given the discussion in this chapter, the complexity can be understood as a consequence of the fact that the company or the public office is dependent upon each one of the three forms of knowledge for its development and survival, i.e. the activity is not dominated by any one of the forms of knowledge.

For the complex organisation, therefore, learning processes and forms of knowledge and their interdependencies are not obvious and predictable. Different forms of knowledge can dominate certain parts of the organisation, at certain times or specific issues but without dominating the whole activity. Health and medical care is one example of such an activity. It is characterised by advanced technology, professional

Table 6.2 Interdependence between different forms of knowledge embeddedness: hampering and supporting conditions for renewal

	Influenced		
Influencing	Capital	System	Individual
Capital		Technology demands certain organisational systems	Capital-embedded knowledge guides training programmes
		New technology promotes organisational changes	New technology, new products demands new sets of individual knowledge
System	Organisational system is unable to handle certain types of technology or new products innovations		Established systems define individual roles and recruitment needs
	Bureaucratic systems define lifespan of technology and products		Bureaucratic programmes for training improve individuals' knowledge
Individual	Individuals' knowledge limits areas for capital renewal	Individuals' attitudes and mental awareness hinder organisational renewal	
	Innovative individuals foster development of capital-embedded knowledge	Individuals' firm actions 'reveal' organisational problems and their solutions	

occupational groups with strong identities, as well as a great number of internal links between different subactivities, which require well-developed systems for coordination, direction and control. Companies that concurrently carry out advanced research and commercialisation of dissimilar products belong to the same category. In addition, traditional industries, which have in many cases been transformed into customer-oriented businesses, implemented temporary assignments and self-directed groups within production, and introduced continuous product development, will become more and more complex in future. It is important to point out that complexity is not something that characterises only large organisations (large in terms of the number of employees or annual turnover), relatively small organisations can also demonstrate complex features whereby each one of the different forms of knowledge is essential for the long-term development of the activity.

The neo-industrial organisation is thus influenced by the circumstance that more and more organisations are increasing in complexity, and permanent activities increasingly are mixed with temporary ones. Capital-embedded knowledge, representing physical production, is losing its unique position as a driving force for renewal. More and more organisations are finding that they need to renew all forms of knowledge, possibly also in one go, and in this respect renewal of system-embedded knowledge will become the most crucial challenge, since this is where the greatest difficulties lie.

Combinatorics of temporary organisations – to be caught in the renewal paradox or to promote radical change?

The knowledge processes that develop during the lifetime of a project are difficult to grasp. In project work, knowledge formation is not one of the main priorities and knowledge gained is difficult to pass on. In activities dominated by recurrent projects, as in construction companies for example, the problem of how to make use of experiences gained and the diffusion of knowledge is often pointed out as traditional. The opportunity to renew knowledge in relation to earlier projects primarily exists when new projects are set up and designed. How different resources and knowledge should be combined and coordinated comes to the forefront during the initial phases of a project. The knowledge processes of permanent organisations, in terms of learning organisations for example, are almost non-existent. Instead, formation of knowledge takes the form of recruiting and combining people with particular special knowledge who will work under the supervision of people with certain institution-embedded knowledge, such as project management knowledge, e.g. theatre directors or other professional project leaders.

But how should people and resources be combined in projects? How is this process to be controlled? Is a firm tradition being followed or could strong actors form new ways of combining people and resources? And how does the combination influence the formation of knowledge and the renewal of the organisation?

In neo-industrial organisations a strategy has to be devised so that the activities, e.g. knowledge-intensive and problem-solving activities, can be combined and so that the openness called for by various customers can be preserved at the same time as efficiency is promoted. These circumstances can be illustrated by organisational changes within enterprises. The majority of Swedish ABB companies have changed from a traditional line production to an organisation dominated by goal-directed groups. The group members have direct contact with suppliers as well as customers. In the traditional organisation these contacts were handled by people with special functions (Ekstedt and Wirdenius 1995).

Some project-intensive companies have created systems to manage combinatorics in an efficient way. One of the major IT companies, Cap Gemini, continuously updates a file – a worldwide data bank – of the knowledge and experience profiles of all employees. When forming a new project the company is thus able to use the file to choose the most suitable combination of employees for that particular project in order to maximise experience and professional skills. On a less systematic scale, theatre and film producers as well as builders are known to hold similar files.

As an overall principle one can argue that a temporary organisation could be built either on combinations of people from a uniform culture or on combinations of people from a diversity of cultures. An organisation with a uniform culture is dominated by norms, values and rules of conduct that derive their origin from a common history, e.g. the same professional training. In an organisation with great cultural variety, several cultures exert influence on perceptions and work behaviour. The first strategy could be named *homogenising* and the second *pluralistic integration* (Ekstedt *et al.* 1994). These concepts are related to ideas of assimilation and integration, but are more closely connected to knowledge formation (Berry 1983).

The homogenising strategy aims to create a uniform culture. People with similar experiences and professional training are brought together in the temporary organisation. A replica of a system with familiar kinds of embedded knowledge is created. Pluralistic integration, on the other hand, is an ideal type that recognises diversity as well as openness. The term could in part be interpreted as a contradiction. Pluralism stands for diversity, whereas integration indicates unity. The combination, however, points to the fact that pluralism seldom can manifest itself without a comprehensive and integrating system of general norms or rules, maintained by bodies and institutions of power. The absence of such a system would probably lead to chaos and anarchy. The openness is, in other words, restricted by some norms and rules of action accepted by the actors.

Handling the combinations of different resources, such as professional knowledge, is naturally closely connected with the existing institutions, in other words with the historical set-up of internal and external traditions, rules and roles. Whether there is really a choice of strategies is therefore open to question. The central issue is not this however, but rather how organisational renewal and development is influenced by contemplated homogenising and pluralistic integration strategies. The uncertainty created by the transition from a traditional industrial to a neo-industrial organisation leaves more room for exploring something new. This is an indication that real choices can and should be made.

The homogenising strategy

The homogenising strategy is likely to dominate organisations striving for cohesion and stability. In recurring projects, which are common in the construction sector, for example, this striving is natural. The stability that is in-built in the stationary machine equipment of the traditional permanent flow-production is lacking almost entirely. Persons and companies are brought together in similar role constellations again and again. Consecutive projects are often handled by the same (or almost the same) team. This makes it possible to solve tasks that are in the given fields of experience in a quick and efficient way. One way to derive advantages from experiences is to develop routines and programmes. They have the same function in organisations as grammar has in the everyday use of language. Routines are usually followed without question in every situation or even without knowing when and why they were established. They consist to a great extent of tacit knowledge. An even and high standard of services and products can be achieved. Employees from different professions know what is expected of them, and customers feel secure when it comes to deliveries. Common programmes and routines simplify communication between different units and mistakes are avoided (Rolf *et al*. 1993). Short-term efficiency is improved. At the same time, the culture is strengthened by the shared routines and practices. If successful, it will prolong the organisation's life and result in a long series of similar successes. This stability is also a guarantee of a certain degree of efficiency. Established norms and routines build up an institution-embedded knowledge that guides the action of individuals (Ekstedt 1988). However, major changes in opposition to well-established ways of work have difficulty in gaining acceptance. The renewal that takes place occurs gradually by refinement of the existing methods of working. Cultural homogenisation tolerates only incremental change.

There is much evidence to suggest that in the short term the homogenising strategy contributes to efficiency. The advantage from a top management perspective is that uncertainty is reduced; by using knowledge of one's own the result can be predicted. More and more stress is laid upon economic control and project management. System-embedded knowledge will play a prominent part. It is possible to carry out refinements of the working routines. However, in the long run this certainty can be turned into uncertainty. The strategy will increase group cohesion and resistance to new ideas. In these kinds of temporary organisations expected goals can be achieved, but revolutionary thinking is rare. The venture might become trapped into a renewal paradox mechanism.

In organisations that are heavily dependent on temporary activities, such as the construction sector, there exist obvious renewal problems. Familiar actors carry through a more or less recurring project. The participating actors have learned their roles through experience. These roles, in a sense, replace the stabilising function of real capital in the industrial process. There is an important difference however. Renewal institutions in organisations dominated by flow-production are almost non-existent. Companies in the construction sector have separate R&D departments only to a limited extent. There is a paradox. The great flexibility shown in the daily activity does not seem to leave a deep impression on the long-term renewal (Ekstedt *et al.* 1992).

Pluralistic integration strategy

Is it possible to avoid the mechanisms of the renewal paradox? Could short-term flexibility be transformed into more fundamental and long-term renewal capacity? Pluralistic integration might be the answer. The combinatorics approach may well develop into a truly dynamic force. A more open view of the possibilities of utilising alternative knowledge might produce energy. However, energy is rarely released without friction, although, through interplay between permanent and temporary organisations, it might be possible to control friction in such a way that knowledge and experience from different spheres in society can be utilised and developed in the projects. This interplay has also to be systematised, so that knowledge developed in the projects can be retrieved to be used in future activities. The latter question – of retrieval – will be dealt with in Chapter 8. Here we will focus on the problem of creating dynamics for renewal.

In the pluralistic integration strategy, contacts and interchange between people and organisations with different knowledge and cultural background are furthered. It differs from the homogenising strategy in that cultural characteristics are used to advantage and utilised as motors for development. However, the pluralistic integration strategy is difficult to organise. A pluralistic organisation is open to other cultures in its environment and indeed contains several cultures. Integration is a system that respects other cultures in a striving for certain common goals and attitudes. Forms of integration that allow cultural differences not only to remain but to flourish and live side by side under controlled friction are sought. In other words, the project needs an environment that can tolerate 'creative tension' (Hampden Turner 1990). This calls for institutions and rules of action, e.g. ethical rules with broad acceptance which allow high tolerance (Brytting *et al.* 1993).

The question is whether rules with such a strong claim on the organisation will develop without a long historical testing. It should be obvious that pluralistic integration is difficult to bring about in strong, hierarchical organisations. Too strong ties can thus hamper economic development (Granovetter 1973). This is most evident in cultures in which companies are managed by family members rather than professional managers (Fukuyama 1995). Weak ties between equal and independent actors make it possible to combine ideas and action patterns of different origins. As a consequence, this ideal model requires great awareness and understanding of the functioning of different cultures (Laine-Sveiby 1991)

The homogenising strategy aims to reduce cultural friction, whereas the pluralistic integration strategy endeavours to control it at a certain level. In the latter case, the idea is that the friction will generate energy for a continuing renewal process. Through openness as well as diversity of ways of thinking and acting, new combinations of ideas will develop. American studies show that building teams with ethnic diversity is a fruitful way of promoting renewal in companies (Skog 1996). Some people argue that the success of Astra, a pharmaceutical company, is due to its active and deliberate policy of recruiting people with mixed backgrounds. Their cultural mix consists of well-educated people of different nationality and gender. Challenging and stimulating workplaces are created (Sundin 1996). In a multicultural environment, the old working methods are questioned and new alternatives are offered. This is, for example, the ambition when international corporations try to connect the R&D activity of subsidiaries. This approach is termed 'coexistence as a world strategy' by the Japanese Canon Corporation. The idea is not primarily to create a uniform research activity in the corporation but to promote cross-fertilisation between different research traditions and competencies in various parts of the world (Norgren 1989). Another element in such a strategy is that the various subsidiaries are permitted to develop in different directions but in constant confrontation with each other. There is not one but several valid visions, applied simultaneously. An important task of senior management is to create systems that further confrontation between different cultures, that is to utilise the greater openness associated with the changed nature of internationalisation (Ekstedt *et al.* 1994).

There are three principal reasons why controlled cultural friction in pluralistic integrated organisations could contribute to renewal. First, there is a greater chance that among a multitude of cultures there are renewal-furthering elements that could be utilised. The broader selection facilitates the renewal search process. Second, the number of possible combinations is increased. Knowledge developed in one cultural context can be combined with knowledge acquired in another context. A more effective constellation can be formed. Third, confrontation with other cultures can increase awareness of the significance of one's own culture. Critical and constructive knowledge processes can be catalysed.

As to the *first argument*, a number of researchers have in recent years pointed to the fact that there are traditions that further the development of certain solutions and that there are also traditions that are obstructive (Putnam 1993; Fukuyama 1995). Thus, both supporting and hindering conditions could be found in different cultures. In his extensive studies of variations in national character, Hofstede (1980, 1993) proposed some variables (individualism-collectivism, power distance, uncertainty avoidance, and masculinity–femininity) that describe fundamental aspects of a culture. An important characteristic is the way its members look upon other cultures. It is conceivable, therefore, that some of these variables are directly related to tolerance and the ability to adapt to other cultures. It is likely, for example, that a culture that tolerates uncertainty will have fewer problems in taking in elements from other cultures.

Neo-industrial features no doubt increase the chances of carrying out broad cultural search processes. Close contacts with customers in many activities can make it easier to accept multiplicity of thinking and acting. In addition, the spread of information technology and the changed nature of internationalisation with increased presence in foreign countries indicate that it is possible to benefit by broad experiences. The town development renewal project Arlandastad, for example, was initiated with a broad search process. Project managers invited actors from many spheres of society for discussions in order to bring a multitude of ideas into the design phase. Large permanent organisations, industrial enterprises, were supplemented and combined with small, temporary organisations. A great deal of the concrete economic activity was carried out in projects with a time limit, whereas the overall coordination and development of the activity was handled by companies, industrial groups and various kinds of authorities. This search process was also repeated later on in the project. Ideas with a different cultural/organisational basis were continuously inspiring the project. Project management was made responsible for the coordination of ideas and the action involved.

The *second argument* implies a striving to take advantage of the competence and cultural characteristics of people of different professions, age, sex, education and training, religion and ethnic affiliation, and to change the organisation with this new competence as an input. The diversity increases the number of alternative combinations. Project organising is an ideal opportunity to work in this way. In bringing together people and roles it is important to break up ingrained lines of action and take the risk of designing new combinations. A diversity-oriented strategy could also be pursued in the composition of goal-directed groups. The various characteristics that we have attributed to the neo-industrial organisation seem to facilitate pluralistic integration.

Experience shows, however, that in many cases the potential of project organisation is not fully exploited. This applies particularly to some types of industry, e.g. the construction industry, in which project members, be they engineers, technicians or construction workers, are almost exclusively men (Ekstedt *et al*. 1992). It also appears as if the ideas about pluralistic integration go beyond general project management techniques, as described by the pmbok guide (1996) for example. The pmbok guide is internationally seen as the principal source of knowledge about project management. It claims to describe 'all those topics, subject areas and intellectual processes which are involved in the application of sound management principles'. It is also evident that this source views renewal via projects as a successive, incremental process (Engwall 1995; Ekstedt and Wirdenius 1994a).

The construction industry approach is quite different from the approach taken by the Young Klara theatre group. In creating the play *Money* the art director invited all participants from different professions actively to contribute their ideas in an introductory phase. The cooperative phase began with an almost chaotic but creative period. As time went on the direction and design became increasingly tighter. Ideas originating from different professional traditions were included in the final product. In addition, this way of working has the advantage of making all members feel that they participate in the final product, in this case part of the play.

A *third argument* is that confrontation with other cultures can increase awareness of one's own culture. In working and business life much thinking and acting is tacit. Manners and customs survive without question or challenge. This becomes evident in the encounter with other customs. In some cases, these cultural clashes can of course lead to open conflicts, while in others they can cause people to reconsider obsolete solutions. Sometimes it can even be a matter of articulating and elucidating a conduct one has not reflected upon before (Rolf 1991). The conditions for constructive self-reflection are probably most favourable for people standing on a stable and conscious ground. A strong identity reduces the uncertainty and accordingly increases the openness towards the unknown (Laine-Sveiby 1991).

In the ABB ZWUS Signal case one can discern a clear indication that the cultural confrontation triggered reflective processes. Managers from Poland's planned economy period were faced with entirely new ideas both with respect to the market and the internal organisation. These ideas were further developed in training programmes and in manifest action during cooperation with individuals brought up in traditions of Western large-scale enterprise. However, the Swedish consultants facilitating in the renewal process were also confronted with new ways of thinking. They developed new knowledge that may be of great use in future activities in other environments.

Cultural diversity can thus contribute to the introduction of constructive knowledge processes among members of temporary organisations. Know-how linked to different working traditions can be compared, evaluated, debated and reconsidered. Wider frames of reference and increasing insight into one's own knowledge gives feedback, and one's own ideas of know-how can change (Rolf *et al*. 1993). Profound renewal processes can thus be catalysed by cultural friction, which in turn can be handled and fuelled by a conscious pluralistic integration strategy. In many respects, though, these processes are associated with the individuals who participate in temporary projects. However, the processes are often long term and therefore not always quite so easy to utilise in the ongoing project. Again, the question of the transfer of knowledge from the temporary to the permanent part of the activity becomes important.

Knowledge embeddedness and renewal – a summary of conclusions

Together with action, knowledge formation is the chief prerequisite for renewal of economic activity. The knowledge involved can be stored in the real capital of the organisation, in its individuals, in the rules laid down by the organisation or in external rules that influence the organisation. The knowledge of the organisation can be changed by different types of knowledge processes, that is by learning, but also by combining different stocks of knowledge in various ways.

In most large permanent organisations there are well-developed institutions for the knowledge process. Skills and know-how are developed in education and training programmes, among other things, in R&D departments, on the job, and in close contacts with the market. The stock of knowledge can be improved by purchasing new, more advanced machines or by recruiting capable staff. Also, by designing a 'learning organisation', a more efficient incremental knowledge development process can be initiated (Senge 1990a). However, as indicated previously, the 'learning organisation' approach does not solve the knowledge problem for projectised activities. Combinatorics is needed.

In temporary organisations, knowledge processes also exist, but the most important thing in the design of a project is the combination of project members and the resources allotted to the project, that is relying on the combinatorics of different stocks of knowledge. The system-embedded knowledge that is used in a project cannot, of course, have been stored there, but has to be retrieved from the permanent organisation and from societal institutions. Temporary organisations often utilise professional knowledge, codes of knowledge developed in certain occupations, in the Project Management Institute or similar organisations, for example. The outcomes of the knowledge processes that take place in the projects are difficult to feed back to the permanent organisations. The organisation-embedded knowledge of the project organisation therefore easily becomes rigid and old-fashioned. However, the projects can very well develop skill, know-how and competence of individual members.

In many permanent organisations there exist institutionalised models

Table 6.3 Characteristics of the two ideal ways of combining knowledge

Homogenising	Pluralistic integration
Uniform culture	Diversity of cultures
Stable routines	Controlled cultural friction
Short-run efficiency	Search process
Incremental change	Fundamental change or failure
System-embedded knowledge	Knowledge from different cultures
The renewal paradox in action	Problems of knowledge transfer

for generation, diffusion, retrieval and phase-out of knowledge. The methods are particularly well developed in organisations in which capital-embedded knowledge carries great weight. In organisations in which the main emphasis is on organisation- and individual-embedded knowledge, the in-built renewal models work less well.

Thus, it is when the renewal mechanisms of the real-capital-intensive industry are tottering – in other words when the transformation dilemma appears – that the focus will shift to the renewal potential of the temporary organisations. How could this be utilised for the long-term development of all economic activity? How could knowledge generated in unique product development projects be transferred to future products, and how could the knowledge combinatorics of projects be designed to become instrumental in the development of permanent organisations?

Finally, we have discussed two main principles for combining knowledge in projects: homogenising and pluralistic integration (Table 6.3). In the homogenising strategy, actors with similar conceptions, professions and organisation cultures are combined. An effective organisation, with a minimum of negotiation costs is formed, and has good prospects of incremental change. Pluralistic integration implies greater uncertainty. But alternative knowledge, which is the basis for radical renewal, can develop because a broader combination of knowledge is utilised, new combinations of knowledge are formed and increased self-reflection is started in actors when they are confronted with other ideas.

To conclude this discussion, one can say that the neo-industrial renewal challenge consists of finding ways to design projects so as to catalyse fundamental renewal activity and then make it possible for permanent organisations to transfer results to future activities. In this chapter, we have constrained ourselves to the first part of the challenge, how to activate knowledge formation. In Chapter 8 we will return to the empirical basis and discuss general roles of permanent and temporary organisations in the renewal of economic activity. One important issue is the role of permanent organisations when it comes to transfer of knowledge from one project to another.

7 Marrying action and knowledge formation in 25 renewal projects

Keeping in mind the discussion in Chapters 5 and 6 about action and knowledge formation respectively, we will now return to the 25 renewal projects from various industries presented in Chapter 4. What can we learn from these cases about action and knowledge formation? How were the efforts organised and what were the relationships between permanent and temporary organisation, and, more generally, how can the cases be analysed so that we can understand the transformation of traditional organisations into neo-industrial ventures? What are the main ingredients of that transformation process and of neo-industrial organising?

This chapter thus deals primarily with the first of the two fundamental problems that organisations have to cope with in the emerging neo-industrial economy, namely the transformation dilemma (see Chapter 1). We will discuss how a number of organisations have approached this dilemma or, more precisely, how they have endeavoured to realise organisational renewal by combining action and knowledge formation in setting up a unique temporary organisation, a renewal project. Moreover, we will examine the interaction between the permanent and the temporary organisation, as well as the roles played by them in the change process.

Renewal problems brought to the fore

During the 1990s various sources reported that many organisations had been experiencing renewal problems and thus were instituting special efforts – renewal projects – to handle the problems (Wikman *et al.* 1998). The cases we have been working with are all evidence of renewal projects. Before delving into the different cases we might want to ask ourselves why renewal problems came to receive so much attention in the early 1990s. Where did all the renewal efforts stem from? There are no simple or unambiguous answers to this question, but there seems to have been many serious problems in several industries at the time, and these problems were accentuated by the general economic situation, which was less of a slowdown or a minor recession and more of a structural problem of an it-will-not-go-away-by-itself character. The integration of Europe was intensified and 'globalisation' became a buzzword among the corporate giants of the world. Thus, the impetus for special efforts was everywhere. Some renewal efforts were no doubt also related to the growth of the consulting business, with consultants offering efficient and quick direct solutions for change. However, our main contention is that these circumstances only contributed by speeding up the process – renewal problems are in fact much more profound and are of a qualitative nature. To be slightly more precise, we contend that renewal efforts are primarily associated with the organisational changes and reforms that mark the change from a traditional industrial society to a new industrial society – the neo-industrial society. They are therefore, to a great extent, efforts to handle the transformation dilemma.

In the traditional industrial society, much of the renewal was forced by inventions and by technical progress supported by institutions such as educational systems, institutes of technology, R&D departments, tax rules, etc. Renewal was also supported through a long series of production runs and through production for storage rather than for immediate sale or consumption. It was possible to carry out production runs and to try gradual change and renewal in the form of refinement on a grand scale. In this way, rigid, bureaucratic organisations were able to handle continuous action and renewal as a flow, although some of the technological advancements occasioned a gradual automatisation of the economy on a large scale.

However, the trend towards individualisation and customer adaptation and the prospects for flexibility that modern technology offers have resulted in less stress on production *per se*, leaving more employees free to work with knowledge-intensive tasks, often in projects, rather than with physical production. This means that many of the traditional institutions of industrialism, including ways of thinking, have become obsolete. They appear to have become a hindrance to continuous change and renewal. Radical projects for renewal – signalling discontinuity – offer one way for the organisations to get a fresh start on renewal. And, if the projects are well planned and well received, there is hope for a future characterised by a new level of continuous renewal.

Radical renewal efforts can usually be described as consisting of two steps. The first step is an initial and radical phase aimed at unlearning established, ancient ways of working and thinking about how the organisation is to work. The second step involves creating a new climate for the organisation (including permanent as well as temporary elements) that makes continuous renewal not only feasible, but also a reality. This might be one reason why some CEOs and general managers prefer not to use terms such as 'project' to describe renewal work. By definition, a project has a time limit, and some managers consider that their renewals efforts have no specified end point. Rather, they think of the renewal work as being the beginning of something completely new. In this chapter we will describe how some of the companies (and other organisations) we studied carried out these two steps. In the next chapter we will attempt to describe an organisational model for renewal in a neo-industrial economy using an organisational structure characterised by coexistence and cooperation between temporary and permanent entities.

Based on the case material, we argue that traditional permanent organisations generally have the potential for continuous refinement of their operations in incremental steps. They usually opt for 'constrained change'. When it comes to radical renewal, however, a special effort, a *unique temporary organisation*, is needed. However, in regular, recurring production projects (temporary organisations) sponsored by the permanent organisation, piecemeal refinement (in small steps, if any) is also the rule. In such cases, radical renewal may require a change of perspective, a transformation of a specially selected project into an *'imagined renewal project'*. In other words, renewal elements are incorporated into the ordinary production project, and this is perceived by those involved as a unique, special and yet informal effort designed to renew the implementation of such projects. The same holds true for regular recurring product development projects. Sometimes such projects receive special status as a vehicle for total organisational renewal. Thus, in addition to the targeted renewal (that is the work behaviour of the actors involved and/or the qualities of the specific product concerned), they also sometimes come to incorporate elements of radical renewal of strategic importance to the firm.

Renewal – a close relation between action and knowledge formation

Our case studies reveal that organisational renewal appears to require both knowledge formation and action: they have to be joined in a marriage. In particular, this means that action is needed to secure a supply of new knowledge by developing learning processes within the organisation or by procuring knowledge developed elsewhere, *as well as* action to utilise this knowledge, e.g. by motivating or even forcing people to put it into practice and to pursue the effort. Neither new knowledge nor action alone can bring about renewal of an organisation to any appreciable extent: they are interdependent. However, under favourable conditions action may trigger the search for the required knowledge and entail learning ('trial and error', 'learning by doing'). In addition, knowledge gained by learning may in some cases release action ('there is no harm in trying').

Existing knowledge is not always acted upon, however. It is not uncommon, for example, for knowledge developed in R&D departments to be shelved and to remain so (Wilson 1982). By the same token, action programmes that are not linked to new technological or institutional or organisational knowledge do not seem to have any penetration power.

Without such links they have a tendency to fade away without leaving too many traces behind (Ekstedt and Wirdenius 1995).

Successful renewal endeavours seem to unite action and learning. In the renowned ABB T50 project, for instance, the setting of specific targets, e.g. a 50 per cent reduction in order-to-delivery times, by senior managers coincided with the launch of massive development and training programmes within the scope of this radical renewal project. The knowledge potential of the permanent organisation (be it individual, group or organisational knowledge as well as institutional knowledge) joins with the action power of the temporary organisation. This knowledge potential inherent in many organisations will not be utilised for renewal unless catalysed by temporary action programmes.

Within the technical field, action taken includes, by necessity, the almost automatic replacement of old machinery by more sophisticated models. The need for adaptation and the changes precipitated by it are almost self-evident. In other spheres, a more drastic and all-encompassing approach may be required. In the case of institutional, organisational or individual change (requiring a mental reorientation), the launching of a specific and challenging renewal project may be the only available option. In addition, the introduction of alternative knowledge, developed in other environments, or comparisons with other organisational units or with competitors may release action. It is well known that external pressure, e.g. from customer demands, may be conducive to action.

The project cases illustrate different strategies of renewal. We argue that a crucial condition for renewal of and in an organisation is its implementation and utilisation of new knowledge. And the knowledge that is important is not just the individual knowledge of organisation members, but also the knowledge that is embedded in the organisation as a whole, and to a great extent this is of a non-individual nature. In a permanent organisation, it is the capacity for generating, diffusing, using, storing, retrieving and phasing out knowledge that counts. In a temporary organisation, it is the capacity of combining and using existing knowledge that is important.

In accordance with the propositions made in Chapters 5 and 6, we also maintain that there are four general spheres or levels of embedded knowledge and action, that are critical as targets for strategic action and vehicles for renewal (Ekstedt and Wirdenius 1994c). They are:

A   The real capital (physical facilities);
B   The formal and informal institutions and the rule systems;
C   The local work organisation (company culture and how resources are combined);
D   The individual organisation members.

Moreover, we argue that renewal initiatives involving all four spheres are more likely to produce the intended results. Also, renewal initiatives, directed towards some of these spheres of embedded knowledge and action, tend to produce stronger and more lasting effects than those focusing on other spheres. In addition, the sequencing and timing of renewal initiatives are of great importance. The spheres are also more or less accessible and easily influenced, and the available methods are more or less advanced. Work traditions and culture appear particularly to be difficult to change. Top management has only a limited or indirect influence in those spheres. However, through various organisational solutions (such as different cultural combinations) informal institutions of the belief system type can be influenced (Ekstedt *et al*. 1994). Combinations of cultural diversity might initiate a long-term renewal process, but it has to be done in such a way that the increased cultural friction favours creativity rather than conflict. Correspondingly, the sponsor of the temporary organisation could further creativity by recruiting team members representing diverse fields of knowledge.

Formal rules and restrictions are more easily influenced, and a change in behaviour could be effected if the new regulations are accompanied by threats about sanctions or promises about rewards. Forced behavioural changes will usually facilitate, but sometimes also obstruct, individuals' contribution to renewal. Initiatives directed towards one or both of the physical and the institutional spheres are more likely to have a lasting impact than those focusing on the individual sphere only. In the latter case, individual organisation members might expect the renewal effort to peter out.

We will now turn to a discussion of the use of unique temporary organisations (renewal projects) for the transformation of permanent and temporary organisations. This will be done in the light of findings from our case studies. Basic questions then are: What roles do action and knowledge formation play in the different cases? How do action and knowledge formation relate to each other in the projects? And what are the outcomes of the renewal projects? The discussion will be facilitated by a systematic classification of the cases.

Classification of the cases

The cases studied illustrate the action taken by senior managers to accomplish renewal of permanent and temporary organisations by means of a unique temporary organisation (a renewal project). Renewal efforts can take place within three different organisational contexts (flow-process, projectised and societal–interorganisational/projectised). These contexts appear to carry with them important contingencies for renewal, so the context dimension will be alluded to in what follows. Needless to say, the scope of the intended renewal action is important, so the approaches used will be classified into five groups according to the context and the scope of actions taken.

We start out by describing the renewal projects in terms of their overall character and in a synthesised form. Details of the renewal processes will be described in the next section. We have designed a simple notational system that appears to be useful for conveying information about the crucial aspects of renewal, and that notational system will be used in the following. We have deliberately tried to keep notation very simple with the result that some details may be lost. However, at this point the simplifications appear appropriate. In due course we will introduce some of the more complicated details. In total, five different types of renewal projects within the three organisational contexts can be discerned (in accordance with what was shown in Chapter 4):

I Flow-process

1   Senior managers in the permanent organisation (PO) initiate a total organisation renewal project by forming a unique temporary organisation [TO(u)] that is assigned the task of promoting and supporting the renewal of the whole organisation. The permanent and the unique temporary organisation interact in the change process as depicted below:

$$PO \Leftrightarrow TO(u)$$

2   Senior managers in the permanent organisation initiate a part-organisation renewal project by transforming a regular, recurring product development project [TO(d)] into a unique temporary organisation. The project is assigned the task of creating or renewing the particular product, as shown below:

$$PO \Leftrightarrow [TO(d) \Rightarrow TO(u)]$$

II Projectised

3   Senior managers in the permanent organisation initiate a total organisation renewal project by forming a unique temporary organisation, which is assigned the task of promoting and supporting the renewal of the whole organisation (permanent as well as temporary parts). This implies an interaction with the unique temporary organisation and also regular, recurring production projects [TO(p)]:

$$PO \Leftrightarrow TO(u) \text{ and } TO(u) \Leftrightarrow TO(p)$$

4   Senior managers in the permanent organisation initiate a part-organisation renewal project by transforming a regular, recurring production project into a unique temporary organisation, which is

assigned the task of renewing the particular production project (process and object):

$$PO \Leftrightarrow [TO(p) \Rightarrow TO(u)]$$

III Societal–interorganisational (projectised)

5   A group of interested POs initiates a societal renewal project by forming a unique temporary organisation, assigned the task of promoting and supporting the renewal of a societal organisation or object, as a kind of joint venture:

$$POs \Leftrightarrow TO(u)$$

All renewal cases studied have one thing in common. They are all based on intentions both as to *what to renew* (the target for renewal) and as to *how to renew* (the means applied for renewal). Thus, in the cases studied, change resulted from actions wittingly aimed at change in a particular direction (which is not the same as saying that outcome always, or even ever, is in accordance with intentions). In any case, this means that conscious actions and activities on the part of management are involved. By analysing whether such renewal activities are geared towards physical structures, institutions, the work organisation or individuals, we will give a general picture of how action and knowledge formation interact in renewal projects. The character of the 'marriage' provides information about actions taken and the qualities of knowledge formation. We will now focus on each of the five principal situations of radical renewal, analyse them in more detail and relate them to the cases that we have studied.

Renewal approaches

The five different types of renewal approaches outlined above will be used in the following as a systematising device. Using the description of the cases to be given below, we intend to illustrate how the transformation dilemma has been tackled. The descriptions are images of the transformations and illustrations of the trend towards neo-industrial organising. The images will be used in the next chapter for theorising about neo-industrial organising.

Group 1: Total organisation renewal in a flow-process context

In this group, top management in a permanent organisation with predominantly flow-process operations initiates a total organisation renewal project. A unique temporary organisation is created for that purpose, which results in a special interaction between the permanent and the unique temporary organisation designed for the renewal effort. Most of the time, the temporary organisation is at least partly overlapping in terms of membership with the permanent organisation. Using the notation as defined above, this results in: PO $\Rightarrow$ TO(u).

In total, 6 of the 25 cases belong to this first group: Swedish ABB Group, ABB Control, Sunds Defibrator, ABB ZWUS Signal, CSN and VL. In all these cases, the prime target of change is the work behaviour of all actors involved in the operations, with a view to achieving senior managerial expectations or visions of the future functioning of the organisation.

We will now briefly describe how in each of the cases management applied action in the various spheres of embedded knowledge and action. What were some of the most important features of the marriage? We use the four spheres introduced in previous chapters and alluded to here, i.e. A (real capital), B (institutions and rules), C (work organisation) and D (the individuals), to try to answer this question.

Swedish ABB Group

A   The former CEO carried out a radical decentralisation and debureaucratisation of the organisation, also involving geographical/ physical changes, which formed the basis of the T50 project.

B   Senior managers decided on a formal rule that throughput time should be drastically reduced (by 50 per cent) by a specified date. Thus, 'time' became a way of controlling as well as of evaluating efforts.

C   A central project group was set up, with one of the top managers of the ABB Group as the project manager and supported by highly qualified members from the various local ABB companies; a special T50 authorisation was introduced; a partner agreement was set up; a number of renewal tools such as benchmarking and goal-directed groups were recommended; and a variety of consultants were hired to support the renewal work.

D   Educational and training programmes were arranged for everyone in the organisation on 'Time thinking' and time planning, on customer focus and tools for continuous refinements. Managers were offered special courses on leadership (based on trust and confidence in the subordinate). Information and goodwill programmes were carried out not only internally but also externally, particularly to customers and suppliers.

ABB Control

A   Physical restructuring took place to prepare the organisation for goal-directed groups.

B   Formal rules about throughput times were issued.

C   The organisation was adapted to goal-directed groups, which in this case meant that blue-collar and white-collar workers and supervisors were assigned new roles; benchmarking was enforced; programmes for cooperating with customers and suppliers were introduced.

D Competencies were mapped in matrices, individual plans for competence development were drawn up and programmes for competence development for all were implemented (with a special stress on communication skills); managers were expected to carry out developmental dialogues with their subordinates.

Sunds Defibrator

A The workshop was physically rearranged and the machinery relocated.

B Formal rules for throughput times, stock turnover rates and cost levels were issued.

C Individual work was transformed into teamwork and supervisors were made project leaders of teams; norms were determined for leadership and the roles of production leaders and team members.

D Educational programmes about how to apply and use the so-called K-Concept (see Chapter 4) were instituted for everybody; special educational efforts were devoted to encouraging customer–supplier thinking and to running several machines; a learning centre was arranged; a daily news bulletin on the progress of the renewal project was distributed.

ABB ZWUS Signal

A Five divisions were created from the original ZWUS Signal Company and organised as independent companies.

B The Swedish project manager set specific operation targets for division managers as part of an effort to transform the company into an ABB company.

C Division managers were recruited from potentially competent people within the organisation. These people were given great authority and powers to act as prime motors of change; specially selected Swedish ABB consultants, headed by a chief project manager, acted as project managers for a number of subprojects; goal-directed groups were organised; a large number of employees were transferred from the independent companies to a temporary support unit.

D Division managers were given special management training and shop-floor employees took part in a short training course.

CSN

A An information system of a new generation type was developed and installed.

B   A detailed specification of requirements for the system was determined, and deadlines for its development and implementation were laid down.

C   A project team consisting of external consultants and highly qualified internal users of the system was formed; a top-level business leader was appointed as project manager.

D   Extensive training programmes for employees were carried out and combined with participation in the development work for the new system.

VL

A   No physical facilities were changed *per se*, but the formal organisation was transformed in several respects and in accordance with the renewal effort as a whole; a number of organisational units of a profit centre type were created.

B   Various programmes for how to carry out the planning were changed in line with a popular planning system developed by a group of consultants; the work division between politicians and civil servants was altered; the resource allocation system was changed.

C   The total change was carried out as part of the regular (transformed) organisation. There was no formal project group; the senior civil servant acted as project manager though he was supported by influential politicians.

D   Courses on how to measure output in health care as well as on how to use those measures were offered; managers at various levels were obliged to attend courses on leadership.

Discussion: group 1

In all of the cases renewal action was directed towards all four spheres of embedded knowledge and action, A, B, C and D, as is evident from Table 7.1. Judging from this set of cases, a total organisation renewal obviously requires a general approach with a view to influencing the whole stock of knowledge and action.

The approach is also sequential in most cases. First a change in the physical structure is carried out in order to make obsolete or break old work roles and behaviour patterns ('physically given action'), then formal rules for the renewal work are laid down and targets for action specified ('institutionally ruled action'). The project organisation needed to support the learning of new work roles and behaviours is then created. The most experienced and qualified people within the organisation are selected and brought together to form an effective support team ('organisationally conditioned action'). Finally, the new work behaviours are strengthened

Table 7.1 Distribution of total organisation renewal initiatives on different spheres of embedded knowledge and action within the flow-process organisations

	Renewal approach				
	A	B	C	D	*Prime target*
Group 1: flow – total					Work behaviour
Swedish ABB Group	×	×	×	×	of actors
ABB Control	×	×	×	×	concerned
Sunds Defibrator	×	×	×	×	
ABB ZWUS Signal	×	×	×	×	
CSN	×	×	×	×	
VL	×	×	×	×	

A, physical; B, institutional; C, organisational; D, individual.

by various forms of individual and group training for all actors concerned ('individually premeditated action').

When the physical restructuring is rather moderate, and is primarily done in the form of a reorganisation, as in VL for example, institutional initiatives play the central role in the change process. This also applies to the case of the Swedish ABB Group, where a radical reorganisation had taken place immediately before the T50 project was launched.

Physical structural transformations are an external threat and act as a strong coercion on actors to change their behaviour and learn new things. Structural changes can be expected to produce great effects providing senior managers can get them to be accepted and can extract commitment to adaptation from the actors; otherwise, major problems are to be expected. The same applies to institutional and rule system changes. It is not surprising, therefore, that these kinds of initiatives are usually accompanied by threats of sanctions or promises of rewards.

In isolation, changes in work organisation and efforts at influencing individual actors, through training for example, seem to have only a limited effect on actors' work behaviour. However, combined with the recruitment of staff with differing knowledge and experience their effect can be enhanced.

Generally, actors in these cases changed their behaviour in accordance with top management expectations. In the Swedish ABB Group, the reception of the renewal initiative varied considerably between subsidiary companies, but on the whole the corporate project goals seem to have been achieved. This is also true of the other ABB cases. In Sunds Defibrator and VL the change process was to some extent characterised by inertia and lack of action as a result of a change of CEO in the first case and difficulties in obtaining commitment from some local managers in the second case. The CSN project has been delayed by political decisions but has been developing as planned in other respects.

Group 2: part-organisation (product) renewal in a flow-process context

In this group, top management in the permanent organisation with a predominant flow-process operation turns a regular, recurring product development project into a renewal project, i.e. a unique temporary organisation. Using the notation as defined above, this results in a special kind of interaction between the permanent and the unique temporary organisation:

$$PO \Leftrightarrow [TO(d) \Rightarrow TO(u)]$$

Three out of our 25 cases fall into this group: Saab Military Aircraft 'JAS 39 Gripen', Volvo '850' and Saab Aircraft '2000'. In all cases, the prime target of change concerned the qualities of product or service, with a view to realising top management and customer expectations. However, in all cases top management came to define the project as more than just a regular product development project. The emphasis came to be on the future of the entire company even though product development concerns only parts of the total organisation. As with group 1, we will now go through each case along the same lines. The spheres of embedded knowledge and action are of primary concern.

Saab Military Aircraft 'JAS 39 Gripen'

A   No special activities related to the physical facilities were reported.

B   Saab's contract with the government (for developing the structure and handling of the system integration of the combined military aeroplane, JAS 39 Gripen) was essentially a fixed-priced deal; requirements of time, technique and finance were specified in detail; the requirements were such that there was a need to develop new materials and technical subsystems, which were still lacking at the time of signing the contract; the government, in the form of a government agency in charge of military equipment procurement (FMV), introduced a programme of 'earned value' in order to control and evaluate the progress of the project; Saab was forced to supply the earned value programme with data from the product development process as it unfolded.

C   A new role division between the company (Saab) and the governmental customer was introduced (the same was also true for suppliers and other governmental agencies). In this way, more responsibility was placed on the company; the governmental customer assumed responsibility for the technical groups through a team of subproject leaders under the main project leader; the selection of the management group and engineers was carried out very careful as the project was very much in the public eye; project management was strengthened and the project managers were trusted with technical and financial responsibilities; subcontractor purchasing of subsystems was increased; initially there was a lack of qualified engineers.

D   No special activities related to individual development were reported.

Volvo '850'

A   No special activities related to the physical facilities were reported.

B   A very detailed specification of demands on the new product with completely new capacities was established together with a plan specifying deadlines (that could be revised).

C   Product development was centralised; a project leader with special competences in technical, economical and planning matters was appointed; team members from all areas of specific competences were recruited to the project right from the start and, rather than selecting from the available people, a job specification was drawn up; the team remained the same from project to project so that all new experiences could be exploited; information about the project was distributed internally in the company, e.g. through the company newsletter; special attention was given to the question of how to exchange ideas and experiences continuously between the project organisation and the permanent organisation.

D   No special activities related to individual development were reported.

Saab '2000'

A   No special activities related to the physical facilities were reported.

B   The product was similar to the previous aeroplane (model 340) but was to be tailor made for each customer; certification of the product controlled the development work and the targets involved.

C   A small group of leaders for the project was chosen and the most skilled were assigned responsibility for special areas. They were also expected to ensure that know-how was transferred from project to project; many foreign subcontractors were used, creating some cultural friction of a problematic type; follow-up was monitored by means of a computerised control system (ARTEMIS).

D   No special activities related to individual development were reported.

Discussion: group 2

The renewal initiatives in the three product development cases had the product as their prime target of change as well as the vehicle for total organisational change. Actions were directed towards the institutional (rule based) and work organisational spheres, as illustrated in Table 7.2. Detailed specifications of requirements concerning the qualities of the new product governed the knowledge and action needed in the renewal work and thus the composition of the project team. The necessary competence was thus generally introduced into the project from the start (and continuously when the need arose) in the form of recruitment of qualified team members. Supplementary or strengthening training programmes are rare as are activities to change the physical facilities.

As the three projects here are classified as part-organisation projects, it should be pointed out that they are extraordinary efforts, requiring the allocation of great resources. Therefore, the products arising out of the projects are bound to have a great impact on all the activities of the organisations involved.

Commitment among project team members is generally very high for these projects since they are exceptional endeavours. However, unforeseeable technical problems in the Saab Military Aircraft JAS 39 Gripen project caused inertia. Much of the knowledge needed in this very complex project was not available at the start, nor was the amount of work necessary for generating it known beforehand. The Saab Aircraft 2000 project was affected by the JAS venture; competition for qualified staff ensued, which slowed down the development process. The Volvo project was a long-term endeavour that evidently fulfilled top management expectations.

Group 3: total organisation renewal in a projectised context

In the following cases, senior managers in the permanent organisation with projectised operations initiated a total organisation renewal project. A unique temporary organisation was created for that purpose, which resulted in a special interaction between the permanent and the unique temporary organisation, designed for the renewal effort, as well as between the unique temporary organisation and the project production

Table 7.2 Distribution of part-organisation renewal initiatives on different spheres of embedded knowledge and action within the flow-process organisations

	Renewal approach				
	A	B	C	D	Prime target
Group 2: flow – part					Product (via
Saab Military Aircraft					project team)
'JAS 39'		×	×		(Sphere D,
Volvo '850'		×	×		provided for by
Saab Aircraft '2000'		×	×		combinatorics)

A, physical; B, institutional; C, organisational; D, individual.

organisation. Using the notation defined above produces a two-sided result:

$$PO \Leftrightarrow TO(u) \text{ and } TO(u) \Leftrightarrow TO(p)$$

In total, 7 of the 25 cases fall into this group: Skanska Group, Diös Group, Diös Östra, Kullenberg, Ericsson, Digital Equipment and Young Klara. In all cases, the prime target of change was the work behaviour of all actors involved in the operations of the total organisation (permanent as well as project production organisation), with a view to realising top management expectations or visions of the future functioning of the organisation.

Skanska Group

A   No special activities related to the physical facilities were reported.
B   A formal rule about radical shortening of production time was issued, together with demands for improved product quality and a reduction in the costs of production; time was supposed to play a role as a control instrument.
C   Highly qualified central project leaders were appointed with the support of local representatives; a number of renewal tools were recommended: work model 3T (TotalTimeThinking), benchmarking, goal-directed groups, programmes for planning and production control, etc.; consultants were hired to support the renewal work; supporting structural/organisational changes were carried out at a macro level; a new work organisation with project engineers was initiated.
D   Educational programmes about work model 3T and other renewal tools were arranged for everybody. Managers and change leaders received particular effort; information programmes about 3T were introduced for subcontractors and suppliers.

Diös Group

A   No special activities related to the physical facilities were reported.
B   Goals for the coming year were made public and were given in profit terms; attempts were made to apply modern management techniques and to introduce a renewed business culture to an old family business with strong traditions.
C   The boards of the subsidiaries were modernised and professionalised; some functions at the corporate headquarters were decentralised; managers were exchanged; efforts to create a leadership team including the subsidiary managers were made; new accounting systems

for follow-up on projects and on the performance of the subsidiaries were introduced; consultants were hired to perform financial analysis and economic control; attempts were made to change the line of business for some of the subsidiaries and a new subsidiary was created.

D   Information was distributed to all employees about the critical situation of the corporation; local staff development programmes were introduced.

Diös Östra

A   No special activities related to the physical facilities were reported.

B   Targets for several years ahead were made public and given in profitability terms; efforts were made to change the traditional production-oriented company into a business-oriented company; concrete rules for forthcoming activities in the main lines of business were established in cooperation with all personnel.

C   Consultants were hired to analyse the market and to act as advisors in the renewal work; the CEO assumed the role of project leader for the renewal work, heading a team of influential leaders in the company; brainstorming sessions were held with the aim of developing solutions to the problems experienced; solutions were evaluated and the chosen solutions implemented.

D   Information about the serious situation of the company was given to everybody; follow-up meetings of the entire workforce were held at predetermined times to give information about the progress of the renewal project.

Kullenberg

A   No special activities related to the physical facilities were reported.

B   A new business philosophy was announced by the new CEO. One specific purpose for doing so was to restore confidence among potential customers and to counteract the poor reputation of the company in the marketplace.

C   Someone was recruited specifically to assist and support the renewal work; special planning sessions were held with senior managers and with the rest of the staff concerning the new business philosophy; an open house meeting was arranged every year for customers, suppliers and other interested parties; independent production groups were formed; researcher cooperation was initiated; managers held regular meetings to conduct strategic planning and business environment analyses in order to meet the challenge for 'continuous renewal'; all personnel were enrolled in the idea generation process in order to initiate local renewal projects; the top management group developed a new model for construction process control.

D   Educational programmes were implemented for all personnel; seminars about the new model for construction process control were arranged.

Ericsson

A   Prior to the project, the physical structure was changed from a traditional hardware production system to a customer-close software system; a transition from flow-process manufacturing to projectised service production took place. However, no special activities related to the physical facilities were reported during the project process.
B   The traditional hierarchical organisation was replaced by a network organisation; responsibility for individual learning and development of necessary knowledge was assigned to the local staff.
C   Aptitude tests were used in the selection of staff for the new work organisation; a self-directed group was organised and assigned the overall responsibility for production and customer relations.
D   Training sessions were given on group relations and in subjects related to work as required.

Digital Equipment

A   No special activities related to the physical facilities were reported.
B   Management by objectives was applied with strict control to ensure that agreed job objectives were fulfilled.
C   In personnel selection the focus was on educational level, problem-solving capacity and willingness to expend efforts on continuous learning; a multidimensional matrix organisation was set up to secure flexibility.
D   Extensive internal training in technical areas and customer relations was arranged with line staff as teachers; local staff were made responsible for the development and diffusion of knowledge; career changes were encouraged.

Young Klara

A   No special activities related to the physical facilities were reported.
B   The norm for theatrical performances, laid down by the director, was that the performances (the 'products') were to be innovative, the untested was to be tried and issues of current public interest were to be treated in an amusing fashion; they should arouse strong feelings in the audience and possibly involve the audience in the action; special rules as to how to produce a play were decided upon by the director.
C   The director of the theatre (who is also the art director) assumed the role of project leader in the renewal work with support from actors

as well as other staff members; usually all the actors participated in the productions so that the entire group could develop together; there was some turnover among actors, and this contributed to renewal; reference groups were organised with the task of giving feedback concerning the general quality of the performances.

D   A comprehensive programme of seminars was carried out with the entire group as preparation for a new production.

Discussion: group 3

The renewal approach in projectised organisations with recurring production projects is similar to the approach used in flow-process organisations. Thus, a prime initiative is to organise a project team of experienced people to act as promoters and supporters in the transformation process.

However, there are also differences related to the existence of a dominating temporary organisation. The permanent organisation is usually relatively small and intervenes only to a limited extent in the strongly decentralised activity of the project organisation, which is designed for flexible, quick and effective action. This probably explains why the cases do not present any examples of top management initiatives directed towards the physical facilities (Table 7.3).

Necessary physical restructurings, e.g. the procurement of new machinery, are initiated by the recurring projects and not by the renewal project organisation. In addition to organising a temporary renewal project team, senior managers try to facilitate the transformation process by changing the work and management organisation by creating centrally directed development groups, by seeking assistance from experts in organisational change processes, etc. Moreover, personnel development and training programmes are arranged in order to reinforce the new work behaviour.

In most cases the renewal initiatives were received favourably, triggering change activity. In the Skanska case, reactions varied between local units, but on the whole corporate goals seem to have been achieved. An exception is the Diös Construction Group case, where an old family culture withstood the change initiatives and the result was inertia. Kullenberg is a case of mixed experiences. At one level a radical change to a customer-oriented approach took place, whereas at another old and new company culture clashed and caused inertia. At Ericsson, the staff were transferred to projectised service production from a flow-process manufacturing situation. After reorganisation and participation in individual training sessions, they responded with commitment. The Digital Equipment approach, emphasising recruitment and training, is a long-term attempt to change work behaviour. In the Young Klara case, a high standard of professional attainment has been achieved through institutional rules, as well as by inspiring education and training initiatives.

Table 7.3 Distribution of total organisation renewal initiatives on different spheres of embedded knowledge and action within the projectised organisations

	Renewal approach				
	A	*B*	*C*	*D*	*Prime target*
Group 3: projectised – total					Work behaviour of actors
Skanska Group		×	×	×	concerned
Diös Group		×	×	×	(Sphere A is of
Diös Östra		×	×	×	recurring
Kullenberg		×	×	×	project
Ericsson		×	×	×	concern)
Digital Equipment		×	×	×	
Young Klara		×	×	×	

A, physical; B, institutional; C, organisational; D, individual.

Group 4: Part-organisation renewal in a projectised context

In the cases to follow, top management in the permanent organisation with predominantly projectised operations turns a regular, recurring production project into a radical renewal project, i.e. a unique temporary organisation. Using the notation as defined above, this results in a special kind of interaction between the permanent and the unique temporary organisation:

$$PO \Leftrightarrow [TO(p) \Rightarrow TO(u)]$$

This group contains six cases out of the 25: Royal Opera *'Lolita'*, Young Klara *'Money'*, Skanska 'Block Gångaren', Skanska 'Expressway Söder' and Kullenberg 'Södertälje Hospital'. In all cases, the prime target of change was the work behaviour of all actors involved in the project, with a view to realising top or local management expectations or visions of a future mode of running production projects and satisfying customer expectations about the product or service produced. However, top or local management came to define the production project as something more than a regular recurring production project, i.e. as a model project for the entire organisation.

Royal Opera 'Lolita'

A   Special stage and scenery designs were introduced.
B   The theme of the play chosen required a different, more realistic, acting performance.
C   An internationally renowned project team (comprising composer, art director, set designer and conductor) was put together; actors were recruited specifically for this play.

D   Actors were given extra training to cope with the difficult music arrangement.

Young Klara 'Money'

A   Special stage and scenery designs were introduced.
B   The theme of the play chosen required a new mode of role performance (commedia technique, talking and dancing at the same time).
C   A core project team (comprising the art director as project manager, producer, set designer, dramatist and cast) was organised; the performance was created jointly by the team in line with rules developed by the art director.
D   Special training sessions on the theme of the play were arranged for the actors both individually and as a group.

Skanska 'Block Gångaren'

A   The construction work was established in such a way that the renewal efforts would be facilitated.
B   A special incentive agreement was drawn up with customers.
C   Extra planning resources were allotted to the project; a staff member was appointed to be the lynchpin of the 3T effort.
D   The team participated in a special training programme on the 3T model.

Skanska 'Expressway Söder'

A   Construction work was established in such a way that the renewal efforts would be facilitated.
B   Targets regarding time, costs and quality were laid down; clear working objectives were established in terms of an activity plan.
C   Special resources for projecting, planning and production control were assigned to the project.
D   The team participated in a training programme on the 3T model.

Kullenberg 'Södertälje Hospital'

A   Construction work was established in such a way that the renewal efforts would be facilitated.
B   The project was described to all actors as a challenge and as an opportunity to realise a 'dream project'.
C   A project team was put together very early in the process (even before the quotation had been accepted) in order to discuss the overall plan; when the quotation was accepted, the project leader organised kick-

off meetings and problem-solving meetings with all leading actors; excursions were made to sites of similar projects; a plan for meetings was set up and all interested parties were invited; special meetings were set up to develop team spirit in the project management group and among other actors; special problem-solving meetings with the project team were organised in response to critical events; Supervisors were offered certain management tasks; when the project was regarded as complete all participants and their families were invited to a farewell party and a tour of the finished building.

D   The project team participated in the other educational and development programmes offered by the company.

Discussion: group 4

When a renewal effort is undertaken in an individual recurring project within a production organisation, the local project manager is at liberty to take initiatives within all four spheres (Table 7.4). These initiatives are taken to promote the notion that these production projects are far more important and should be given more weight than any other production project. In a sense, a feeling of uniqueness seems to be transmitted to the project members by various means, and this transmission takes place not only over the traditional life cycle of the project but also during the preproject and the post-project phases.

The physical structure is influenced by a change in, for example, the tangible work environment of the project in order to create favourable conditions for the development of a new work behaviour, which might contribute to a desirable outcome of the project. Rules for the realisation of the project are laid down with the aim of promoting behavioural changes

Table 7.4 Distribution of part-organisation renewal initiatives on different spheres of embedded knowledge and action within the projectised organisations

	Renewal approach				
	A	*B*	*C*	*D*	*Prime target*
Group 4: projectised – part					Work behaviour of actors
Royal Opera '*Lolita*'	×	×	×	×	concerned (and
Young Klara '*Money*'	×	×	×	×	product)
Skanska 'Block Gångaren'	×	×	×	×	
Skanska 'Expressway Söder'	×	×	×	×	
Kullenberg 'Södertälje Hospital'	×	×	×	×	

A, physical; B, institutional; C, organisational; D, individual.

by team members. The criteria for recruiting the project team are personal knowledge and experience, and the team is organised in such a way as to make most use of such attributes. In addition, training and information drives are carried out with a view to preparing the team for the new mode of working.

Work behaviour changes took place in all the production projects involved, and it seems that this has had an impact on the whole project organisation in the companies concerned, and indirectly also on the permanent organisation. However, in the case of the Royal Opera it is still too early to judge whether this project will have an effect on the future programme offered by the theatre. The Young Klara project, dealing with a new topic for the actors, required much preparation in terms of study and collection of information. The Skanska and Kullenberg cases were seen as models for future project work.

Group 5: societal–interorganisational renewal in a projectised context

In the following cases, senior managers in a number of permanent organisations, forming a consortium of interested organisations, initiate a singular societal renewal project. A unique temporary organisation is created for that purpose, which results in a special interaction between the permanent organisations and the unique temporary organisation designed for the renewal project. Using the notation defined above results in the following two-sided set-up, where the temporary organisation is similar to a joint venture:

$$POs \Leftrightarrow TO(u)$$

Altogether, 4 of the 25 cases belong to this group: 'Arlandastad', 'Uminova stad', 'Sophia Antipolis' and 'JAS 39 Gripen'. The first three concern efforts to create 'the modern city' and the fourth a total military defence system with the military aeroplane as a central ingredient. In all these cases, the prime target of change was the qualities of a product or service produced for a general societal level, with a view to realising the expectations or visions of the managers and the members of society.

'Arlandastad'

A   No special activities related to the physical facilities were reported. (An attractive location was chosen; see B.)

B   A conceptual paper outlining the principles of the layout of the city was published and this set out the principles to be used to control the project work. The paper included guidelines for architecture, streets, squares, parks and recreation areas, traffic, telecommunications and computer facilities as well as service facilities of various kinds. The purpose was said to be to create an attractive environment – externally as well as internally – for companies and their staff. The city was intended to attract companies that would benefit from being located close to Arlanda airport: IT related companies, general knowledge-intensive firms and service establishments.

C   The project leader initiated the project on his own by trying to get a number of organisational representatives interested in joining the project; an idea creation group with representatives from a variety of professional and know-how areas was formed; an intensive information campaign concerning the project was launched; networking was important; the project leader acted as a mouthpiece for the project and as its driving force; abundant information material, directed towards the network, was constructed to influence attitudes.

D   No special activities related to individual development were reported.

'Uminova stad'

A   No special activities related to the physical facilities were reported.

B   Rules for how to create a good external environment in the form of meeting places, recreation areas and parks were tentatively formulated; high-tech companies in biotechnology, electronics and the like were targeted, as well as housing companies.

C   The project was the initiative of a major construction company; it was viewed as a potentially interesting construction and development project; a steering group consisting of the planning officer of the town, its business secretary, representatives of the construction company and a financier was formed; an architectural competition was set up to develop a model for the research park.

D   No special activities related to individual development were reported.

'Sophia Antipolis'

A   No special activities related to the physical facilities were reported. (An attractive location was chosen; see B.)

B   Rules for exploiting the area were established, as were rules for the general architecture (no high-rise buildings but lots of glass in the facades), traffic, telecommunications, and so on. Environmentally, the burden or strain that the companies cause externally was given a definite limit. The aim was to create an external and internal environment that would attract companies as well as the 'workforce' in the areas of high technology, education, telecommunications and electronics. Companies, culture, education and a natural habitat combined to create the desirable environment.

C   The project was initiated by someone who saw the potential of the site to entice the increasing number of people who appreciate an attractive working environment and lifestyle. He generated acceptance for the ideas from international group of creative and knowledgeable individuals from the fields of science, culture and industry. The ideas were eventually developed by others with a long-term vision; this meant that responsibilities were shared by several people over time.

D   No special activities related to individual development were reported.

'JAS 39 Gripen'

A   No special activities related to the physical features were reported.

B   A specification was developed concerning the function, performance and price of the product (i.e. the whole defence system termed JAS 39 Gripen), and a time limit and a programme for continued reporting to the governmental customer on the progress of the product development work were put in place.

C   The cooperative groups set up in the first stage and involving the two principal partners (FMV and I G JAS) were dissolved and replaced by technique groups, tasked with following up the progress of the product development work, using the earned value technique and a stock of information.

D   No special activities related to individual development were reported.

Discussion: group 5

Singular societal renewal projects that are carried out as a joint venture between several organisations are strongly dependent for their success upon the knowledge and action potential of the project team. The selection of team members therefore appears to be crucial, as does the diversity of knowledge that is brought into the project. The essential driving force in the renewal work is the specification of requirements put before the team, which has to be complied with.

The physical and individual spheres are obviously of secondary importance in this type of project (Table 7.5).

As can be seen, these projects exhibit similarities with the product development projects discussed earlier (group 2), at least regarding the heavy action and knowledge demands on team members and the clear definition of the project task to be carried out.

The Arlandastad and Sophia Antipolis project teams contributed to the realisation of well-functioning societal 'products'. However, the Arlandastad team had to cope with the recent crisis on the real estate market, which delayed the project. The Uminova stad undertaking was characterised by inertia and lack of action as the project manager was unable to achieve agreement among the interested parties. The JAS 39 Gripen case had a committed project team who developed a well-functioning product. At one stage inertia occurred owing to unforeseeable problems with a new and unique technical system.

Table 7.5 Distribution of societal organisation renewal initiatives on different spheres of embedded knowledge and action within the interorganisational context

	Renewal approach				
	A	B	C	D	Prime target
Group 5: **interorganisational**					Product (via project team)
'Arlandastad'		×	×		(Sphere D
'Uminova stad'		×	×		provided for by
'Sophia Antipolis'		×	×		combinatorics)
'JAS 39'		×	×		

A, physical; B, institutional; C, organisational; D, individual.

Summarising renewal approaches

Table 7.6 shows how senior management renewal initiatives are distributed in the four spheres of embedded knowledge and action within the different organisational contexts. The prime objective of the initiatives is to induce new work behaviour by the actors involved or to create products with new qualities, by influencing the stock of knowledge within various spheres. Changes in the physical structure create new work roles and new action patterns. Institutional and rule changes can likewise force new behaviours. And organisational changes could also induce new work patterns, i.e. conditioned action. Efforts at developing individual knowledge can, under favourable conditions, reinforce the new work behaviour or evoke premeditated action.

The table also shows that the approach of top management differs between the various organisational contexts. Total organisational renewal of a flow-process organisation evidently requires a strong influence on all spheres. The same applies to a projectised organisation, except that in this case the opportunities for senior managers to utilise the power of physical restructuring are limited. In order to be effective, this type of production organisation must be flexible and act quickly, and must consider the physical requirements of each individual project independently. Furthermore, projectised operations are seldom particularly real capital intensive. Senior managers' ability to influence local activity is therefore more restricted than in a flow-process organisation.

In product renewal projects (part-organisational as well as societal–interorganisational), the knowledge and action potential of the project team (the combinatorics) is a crucial factor. In this case the challenge facing senior management is to bring together competence from many different fields to form a viable project team, notwithstanding the diverse professional backgrounds of the team members. The specifications of the final product – as defined by top management and often in consultation with the project team – will steer the renewal work.

Table 7.6 Distribution of renewal initiatives on different spheres of embedded knowledge and action within different organisational contexts – a summary

	Renewal approach				
	A	B	C	D	*Prime target*
Group 1: flow – total					Work behaviour
Swedish ABB Group	×	×	×	×	of actors
ABB Control	×	×	×	×	concerned
Sunds Defibrator	×	×	×	×	
ABB ZWUS Signal	×	×	×	×	
CSN	×	×	×	×	
VL	×	×	×	×	
Group 2: flow – part					Product (via
Saab Military Aircraft					project team)
'JAS 39'		×	×		(Sphere D,
Volvo '850'		×	×		provided for by
Saab Aircraft '2000'		×	×		combinatorics)
Group 3: projectised					Work behaviour
– total					of actors
Skanska Group		×	×	×	concerned
Diös Group		×	×	×	(Sphere A is of
Diös Östra		×	×	×	recurring
Kullenberg		×	×	×	project
Ericsson		×	×	×	concern)
Digital Equipment		×	×		
Young Klara		×	×		
Group 4: projectised					Work behaviour
– part					of actors
Royal Opera '*Lolita*'	×	×	×	×	concerned (and
Young Klara '*Money*'	×	×	×	×	product)
Skanska 'Block Gångaren'	×	×	×	×	
Skanska 'Expressway Söder'	×	×	×	×	
Kullenberg 'Södertälje Hospital'	×	×	×	×	
Group 5:					Product (via
interorganisational					project team)
'Arlandastad'		×	×		(Sphere D
'Uminova stad'		×	×		provided for by
'Sophia Antipolis'		×	×		combinatorics)
'JAS 39'		×	×		

A, physical; B, institutional; C, organisational; D, individual.

When the renewal initiative applies to an individual production project in projectised operations, action is directed towards all four spheres. The prime target for change in this case is the work behaviour of actors involved, with a view to enabling them to create a new procedure and a product of high standard.

The anatomy of renewal

Total organisation renewal projects (groups 1 and 3) differ from the other types of projects in several respects. They are all-embracing: the permanent organisation, represented by top management, forms a specially selected project group, while a temporary organisation supports and promotes the induction of a new work behaviour among all actors in the organisation (and possibly also external partners). And this change of behaviour is expected to occur without interfering with the regular operations. This kind of renewal project appears risky: changing a social system as complex as a large organisation is a delicate endeavour. It involves great uncertainty, not least because the mental change processes are long-term and irreversible. It is also hazardous because radical renewal of an organisation is a rare undertaking, which means that senior managers and the team members usually have no or little experience of such projects. They try to compensate for this by engaging external expert help, e.g. in the form of specialists in organisational change processes. Moreover, it is also a challenge because the task of defining the desired project outcome is difficult. It requires a clear and tempting vision of the future functioning of the organisation to be developed and communicated in a challenging way. Rhetorics are of prime importance in projects of this kind. In addition, the organisation has to function and produce at the same time as the transformation process proceeds.

Total organisation renewal projects – notwithstanding their need for delicate and difficult management action – are particularly important because they illustrate not only the need for, but also how to handle, the transformation dilemma.

Two types of renewal projects concern regular projects of a recurring type (groups 2 and 4, either production or product development projects), transformed into renewal projects by top management. The transformation act can be conceived of as illustrated in a parsimonious way in Figure 7.1. The two boxes on the right-hand side of the figure describe the context for recurring projects and the leftmost box the top management intervention. That intervention encompasses a variety of activities, as illustrated in the cases, including the creation of a special focus on the recurring project so that it serves its new status or function as a unique renewal project.

Projects in group 5 should be thought of as singular projects, originating from new ideas. They, as well as the projects in the other groups, are all

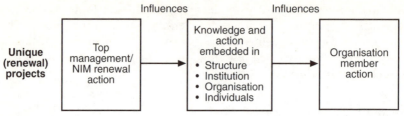

Figure 7.1 The anatomy of renewal.

renewal projects. Their progress and result are entirely determined by the knowledge and action potential of the project team.

In projects launched with a view to renewing the operations of entire organisations, top management action generally involves all spheres in the following sequence: physical structure, institutions/rules, work organisation and individuals ('playing field', 'rules of the game', 'team line-up' and 'individual player', according to the football metaphor discussed in Chapter 5). When, on the other hand, the projects have more specific objectives within the organisation, e.g. to renew a particular product or service, rules/specifications and team competence are the most crucial factors.

Thus, an ideal model of renewal of an entire organisation should integrate all the four spheres. In practice, however, it is not easy to coordinate these with respect to time and content. The capacity of senior management to influence and implement also varies greatly. It should be especially difficult to affect the institutional sphere. It is moulded by an interplay between external and internal conditions. It thus includes areas of power over which senior managers have only limited or indirect influence. Nor is there much scope for quickly changing traditions. It would be almost impossible to fundamentally change company culture, involving inherited ways of thinking and acting, at any particular point in time. It may perhaps be easier to influence rules and restrictions. It is well known that managers have ways of bringing pressure to bear on people, e.g. threats of transfer or dismissal, as well as incentives such as a pay rise.

By changing the structure (introducing new technology) or by introducing imperative targets (cost ceilings, time limits), management can force a change of behaviour on organisation members. This, in turn, will most likely lead to changed attitudes. What kind of attitudes will result is more difficult to foresee, however. To go the other way, i.e. to start out by changing attitudes using rhetorics in an attempt to bring about a new organisational culture and thus change behaviour, is probably even more problematic and uncertain.

Renewal endeavours that start out exclusively from the organisational or the individual sphere consequently have less chance of setting a deep mark than those that focus on one of the other two spheres. It is common for individuals to look upon change as a threat or as a bad thing. They therefore ignore the situation in the hope that it will go away and that things will revert to 'normal'. Pure organisation changes that have no connection with structure or institution have a tendency to end up this way. The formal shape of the organisation is changed but there is no change in the basic content of its operations.

Revisiting the transformation dilemma

A more realistic way to change organisational behaviour is thus to try to connect some of the spheres mentioned. This is especially true in a period of transformation from traditional industrial organisations to neo-industrial ones, when the dependency on technological change becomes a dilemma. In-built methods of handling development (R&D departments) have difficulty in coping with project organisation; the modern technology conquering the world (IT, biotech) is unpredictable when it comes to organisational influence. The old method of handling technological change no longer works very well. And in the search for new methods the institutional sphere becomes more important. Goal-directed groups (as in the ABB cases), for example, are an example of a combination of the institutional, organisational and individual spheres. The old work tradition of a tayloristic type is broken, and a new division of work is introduced, in which group members acquire new roles, which in turn creates demands for development of the individuals. Any attempt to directly affect the organisational culture – the inherited, tough way of thinking – is hardly possible in the short term. Via the structural sphere, however, e.g. by introduction of new technology, it is in many cases possible to introduce new rule systems and/or a new work tradition.

Thus, we have observed that one-sided efforts to develop individuals' knowledge (and thus their motivation) seem to be combined with initiatives focusing on physical and collective knowledge in order to bring about a radical renewal. We have also found that there are – or at least used to be – well-developed systems to renew capital-embedded knowledge. Methods of transferring, reusing and phasing out technology are well known. And, even if, for natural reasons, there are no unequivocal procedures to generate new capital-embedded knowledge, substantial resources are allocated precisely for this. The innovative process is institutionalised (e.g. in the form of R&D departments and public agencies) but still unpredictable.

Thus, the crucial problems are in our attitude to knowledge, inherent in the rules, roles and other organisational traditions of working life. First, awareness of the rules and roles that exist is often very diffuse. The underlying 'agenda' is often fixed without anyone even reflecting on it. In many activities, the working procedure is to a great extent tacit, and in some cases it can be difficult to articulate knowledge inherent in rules and roles at all. Second, methods of generating and phasing out institutionally and organisationally embedded knowledge are poorly developed. This is not strange considering the striving of institutions and organisations to preserve and transmit traditional knowledge, that is to create stability in the interplay between individuals. Renewal of this type of knowledge could endanger the existing order, whether or not it is effective in some other respect. The lack of 'second-order' knowledge (that is knowledge of the nature of the existing knowledge) is substantial, therefore, in many institutions and organisations. (Needless to say we are not aware of our own prejudices.)

With the transition to a supply system in which individuals increasingly are employed in service- and knowledge-intensive work, and where technology is getting a weaker – or at least different – connection with organisational design, the renewal problems discussed above become more and more important. People, combined with the knowledge that is embedded in the rules, roles and not least the traditions of the work organisation they carry, will come into focus. One might question whether the tough values of working life will be renewed more quickly if younger, more open-minded, more multicultural and more IT-experienced people have a greater influence in increasingly flattened organisations.

Summary

*   Successful renewal initiatives usually involve all spheres of embedded knowledge and action, but the spheres seem to be interdependent and more or less powerful as vehicles for organisational renewal, forming a kind of hierarchy, as shown in Table 7.7. Thus, they should be approached in sequence from the top downwards.

Table 7.7 Spheres of embedded knowledge and action in terms of power for renewal

		Ideal sequence of renewal action
Great power but unpredictable	Physical sphere	1
Great power, but difficult to affect	Institutional sphere	2
Modest power if applied solely	Organisational sphere	3
Modest power if applied solely	Individual sphere	4

- However, many formal and informal institutions and rules are particularly difficult to change, requiring long-term management influence (or perhaps the issuing of imperative rules).
- This makes the transformation dilemma more critical to handle concurrently with new technology (e.g. IT) becoming less powerful in determining organisation member action, i.e. in producing foreseeable renewal effects.

This chapter has outlined various approaches to the handling of the transformation dilemma. Some of the cases clearly illustrate the transformation of the organisation from flow-process to project-based operation, from a traditional industrial to a neo-industrial set-up. The Ericssson and ABB cases are typical examples of this.

The empirical observations give rise to a multitude of questions regarding essentials of renewal. However, we will leave that theme for now to devote the next chapter to a more abstract discussion of neo-industrial organising and managing. How and by whom will organisational renewal be handled in a project-intensive economy?

8 Neo-industrial managing

A crucial aspect of neo-industrial organising, although not necessarily the most crucial aspect, seems to concern how temporary and permanent entities or organisations are linked together. That aspect plays a prominent role in the present chapter, which describes the main reasoning being our thinking on neo-industrial organising and managing, especially the renewal aspects. The link is of descriptive as well as of normative importance at the managerial level. The following account is to be based on the empirical evidence at hand as well as on the argumentation put forward in the preceding chapters.

Our prime assertion is that temporary organisations have played an important role in the industrial system in the past, that they continue to do so and that their importance will grow in the future. This does not mean, however, that (supposedly) permanent organisations have had their day. On the contrary! They represent a long-term dimension in the economy and they are, furthermore, deeply rooted in the minds of virtually all actors related to industry. So all the signs are that they are here to stay even though notions of 'permanency' might change over time (paradoxically). The interface exposes a number of new or at least implicitly recognised problems, but also important opportunities. Apparently, there is a need to be explicit about that interaction if one wants to work towards solutions that might be of use in practice. How should combinations between the permanent and the temporary parts be arranged? A matrix organisation is not the solution to such an interaction or interface in our view, as will be discussed more fully below.

The key argument in the following discussion is that the two types of organisations have complementary as well as comparative advantages. As alluded to previously, the differences primarily concern the disposition for action and the capacity for learning, particularly from a renewal perspective. The organisational arrangement should utilise that fact, especially considering the renewal paradox frequently attached to temporary organisations. As mentioned in previous chapters, we have found that project organising generally creates systems that are flexible in some respects but rigid in others. In other words, such systems have difficulties in changing existing working patterns or in counteracting working patterns that are stabilised prematurely; these tend to recur from one project to another, especially when efficiency is promoted.

The concept of managing acquires a somewhat different meaning in a neo-industrial environment. Organising in itself is then a learning process as well as a management process. The common conception that management is primarily concerned with power relationships and with notions such as unity of command is difficult to house in a neo-industrial setting. The alternative appears to be a leadership that chiefly is entrepreneurial, the task being to handle the formation of the temporary organisations and to pay special attention to their relation to the permanent one. How can the permanent part be of support in setting up at the same time as it is an equally supportive driving force for the temporary? Organising in itself thus becomes a means to compete and win (temporarily) advantages in the market place through projects.

On the concurrent need for projects and permanent organisations

One way of combining the demands for stability and reliability with the concurrent demands for flexibility and focus on immediate action has been to introduce project elements into functionally orientated, stable organisations. This might be done by applying some kind of matrix idea or solution. As projects are in most cases multifunctional, they have to be supplied with a variety of functional expertise or competence, as well as to be treated as a unit. One possible advantage of a matrix organisation is that it lends itself to adaptation to the existing, usually functionally oriented, organisation structure with relatively simple means. The commonly stated disadvantage of the matrix organisation as a solution is that in this case projects will be taken less seriously. It is the functional, permanent organisation that dominates because it represents the stable dimension – and everyone knows that the day will come when the project is finished.

There are several reasons why the matrix organisation is not a good solution. Matrix organisations in a formalised and precise sense are very seldom used in a project context. This means that, even though this kind of a standard, catch-all solution has been around for a long time, it has not been able to establish itself as very useful when it comes to handling the permanency/temporary interface, except possibly in the construction industry (Bresnen 1990). Surely a matrix organisation might be a way to establish formal legitimacy for a project, but at the same time a matrix design establishes and institutionalises an adversary system (Galbraith 1977). Seeds of conflict are built in. However, very little adverse behaviour seems to be present in our cases. The interfaces have obviously been arranged in a more clever way in practice. A matrix organisation appears to be an inflexible construction that seems to become established on the terms of the permanent organisation and with all the rigidities inherent in such designs.

Another disadvantage of the matrix solution is that it implies that projects are intraorganisational, and that 'the host organisation' should have, and has, complete control over the different stages of the project process. Development along the line of 'virtual organisation' indicates that this is not the case. The type of cooperation in question – usually with a time limit – is *de facto* a temporary organisation with representation from a number of stakeholders, but without overall dominance by any one. In this case, it is obvious that matrix organisation cannot be a way of handling the above-mentioned concurrent demands.

But why are both temporary and permanent organisations needed? Some of the answers to this question have already appeared as part of the empirical illustrations used throughout this book. At this point it might be useful to refer to the differences between the various forms of organisations concerned. One should keep in mind that the differences are of mindset based on social construction rather than on factual matters. So what is permanent is a matter of how people conceive of something as permanent, and temporary is what is generally thought of as temporary. The same contention also applies to the difference between what is recurrent and what is unique. What is unique is in fact what is being described as unique. In a world in which people in general as well as most researchers are used to considering 'facts' rather than perceptions of 'social constructions' we might consider organisations as facts and pursue our discussion accordingly. Thus, the comparative advantages and disadvantages might be described in a summary way as follows.

Projects with recurrent tasks are effective in their function to perform the task (construction projects or recurring similar installation projects for different customers are typical examples), and they are usually very cost-efficient in getting the task done. In most cases, the members of these organisations are drawn from similar, earlier projects, so, unless something special happens, they settle into their roles quickly. The forms of coordination are also carefully acquired by lengthy practice, and require little extra in every new project. Typical of this group of projects is that they are perceived as recurrent. It could also be said that, through the recollection of each individual, a certain degree of transfer of knowledge between consecutive projects occurs. This knowledge is individually embedded, however, and has to be activated as part of a new project process, and this must be the responsibility of each individual. It is also worth mentioning that formal, individual-embedded learning is fairly modest in this type of organisation. The idea that a project is recurrent means that it may receive routine treatment. Individual reflection, which is a condition of individual learning on the job, is given little room. Any storing of possible collective experiences or any direct evaluation of previous projects exists as an exception rather than as a rule. Owing to the recurrent character of the projects, efficiency is emphasised only in a narrow sense. Cost-efficiency (i.e. reaching the goal stated or solving the problem in question utilising a minimum of resources) is the overriding issue for project members.

In conclusion, the transfer of learning from one project to the next of a similar type is modest. This is also true for consecutive projects of a recurrent type. To take once more an example from the construction industry, in general an architectural project is followed by a construction project. Sometimes, during the construction project, the builders uncover problems that should have been foreseen in the architectural project, but in general there are no mechanisms for distributing experiences between consecutive projects of the total effort in the construction industry. Evaluations over the whole chain are rarely performed. Moreover, evaluations that do occur may very well take on the nature of looking for scapegoats. And most people would make themselves targets for evaluations only if forced to. Another way to express the same thing is to say that prerequisites for organised learning simply do not exist.

Projects with markedly, genuinely unique tasks are characterised by great complexity, uncertainty and low internal cost-efficiency. Handling of the unique element in the project requires great openness, with sufficient room to search for solutions. The purposeful and straightforward passage from start to goal that characterises most recurrent projects is usually absent from this type of project. Ambiguities continue to play an important role over the entire lifespan of the project, implying reconsideration and replanning (see Gersick 1988). The frequent uncertainty as regards means–end chains demands a search for relevant new knowledge. But if unique projects are inefficient in terms of cost, they have a good chance of achieving external effectiveness, as so much effort has to be put into explaining the position and objective of the project in its environment. The uncertainty surrounding unique projects still implies that disagreement about goals, means or other aspects may very well remain after the project has been completed. It simply continues to be controversial in some respects. For precisely this reason – that one has to handle strong and important feelings of uncertainty – the conditions for individual learning are particularly good. The search for good, or at least reasonable, solutions triggers mechanisms of the 'curiosity arousal' type and similar reactions, and leads to a strong commitment on the part of those involved. In well-anchored renewal projects, with participants from both temporary and permanent parts of an organisation, this individual learning could well be transformed into collective knowledge.

Permanent organisations are more focused on routinised action than are projects. In most permanent organisations 'action' is probably not the primary focus, but the stress is rather on maintaining a 'going concern' in an almost static sense. However, permanent organisations are superior to the two types of projects discussed above when it comes to storing knowledge. The fact that the members of the organisation perceives it as permanent, creates a need not only to document experiences, but also to store these in such a way that the knowledge is retrievable. Both formal and informal information systems play an important part in embodying the prevalence of knowledge processes in permanent organisations.

The handling of concurrent demands for action and learning requires – as we see it – a kind of combination of permanence and temporality in the organising endeavour. Projects and permanent organisations have to be linked in suitable combinations or forms. And it is the search for such forms that dominates the reasoning that follows.

The essence of organising

It should be evident from the discussion above that action (to accomplish something or to get something done) and knowledge formation (to acquire or to collect, diffuse, utilise and discard experiences) are central elements in organised activity. *Action* and the organising of action have a different character in projects compared with permanent organisations. In projects, action is organised discontinuously. This implies that action is organised around a special task defined by content and by a temporal context, i.e. a starting and a finishing point are assigned to the task. This in itself creates a special attitude towards acting that differs from the one predominant in the permanent organisation. There, action is organised so as to be continuous, which implies that the action is routinised around tasks that remain virtually unchanged over time. Action that is repeated, e.g. in continuous production, thus tends to become routinised, and a routinised system is not apt to change. In fact, routinisation brings about difficulties when it comes to managing change. Projects with a time limit, on the other hand, can focus explicitly on change matters (even though such efforts are often also hampered by the fact that change is difficult to bring about in the fixed, routinised activities of an organisation).

Product development projects are organised in this way with a special task and with their own management and resource handling. Personnel and other resources are brought together in the project, and certain targets with specifications, time limits, etc. are applied to the work. The organising of action is thus closely related to the requirements and to the temporary nature of the project work. This is also true of a construction project, which is organised as a delimited task with its own management and other resources. The roles and relations within the project are well known from previous, similar projects, and action is organised in such a way as to ensure that the project goal is achieved, i.e. the construction task is finished on time. A production establishment that utilises some form of line production, however, has an entirely different way of organising action to the one used in the two types of projects mentioned. Action in this case is primarily based on recurring elements that can be continuously monitored and, as a matter of continuity, can also be controlled and compared with the nearest preceding elements. Performance in one time period can be compared with performance in previous time periods. Action is often firmly linked to the existing organisational conditions of work, and thus the routinisation is very strong.

For natural reasons, it is difficult to routinise strongly and bring about renewal simultaneously. The two types of action should therefore be considered separately: on the one hand, routinised, unchanged and continuous action with well-known and familiar tasks, performed by well-coordinated units and a staff that has been trained for those tasks and, on the other hand, targeted renewal tasks of a discontinuous nature and linked to immediate renewal goals.

Knowledge in an organised activity has to be brought in, generated and phased out, as well as maintained, utilised and diffused (a discussion on those phases is to be found in Ekstedt 1988). There is thus both a development and a utilisation aspect as far as knowledge is concerned. In the ideal situation, generation and phase-out are connected in such a way that old knowledge is phased out concurrently with the generation of new knowledge. Unlearning and learning are related to each other. One method to bring about this process is the introduction of new technology, so that when obsolete equipment is exchanged the knowledge that is stored in the organisation is changed at the same time. New routines have to be established at the same time as old routines are unlearned. Diffusion of knowledge can be achieved by the design of routines that are to be acted upon in the future. Quality control or store-handling systems are examples of this. However, there remains the problem that old knowledge stays on in the organisation, since unlearning is difficult and because the connection between the routines and the technology that initially brought in the routines is not made explicit. Unlearning is very seldom or never included in managers' normal responsibilities. Newly added knowledge often implies that the activity is becoming more complex because both old and new knowledge are housed simultaneously. This is particularly evident in the case of administrative changes, when some routines are changed without total abandonment of the old ones.

For this reason, among other things, it is hardly to be expected that an organisation will manage to utilise old and to develop new knowledge simultaneously. Similar to the action dimension, we can distinguish between two separate tasks for knowledge handling: on the one hand, the utilisation of old knowledge and, on the other, the development of new knowledge and phase-out of the old knowledge.

If the two central dimensions of our discussion this far, action and learning, are connected in a simple matrix (see Figure 8.1), a typology that we feel is quite useful appears.

The figure is intended to illustrate the line of reasoning to follow,

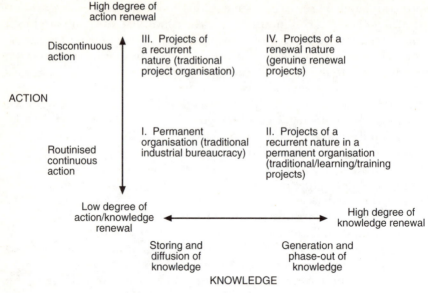

Figure 8.1 Combining type of action and knowledge process phases.

implying that action and knowledge in themselves involve both renewal elements and utilising aspects. Discontinuous, focused action (that supports renewal) can be juxtaposed to routinised and continuous action, for instance, and development of knowledge (generation and phase out) can be juxtaposed to diffusion and utilisation of established knowledge. In total, four different combinations or types of organisational classifications are conceivable.

Combination I, a low degree of knowledge renewal combined with routinised action, is the traditional industrial bureaucracy with routinised production flow process and with a relatively stable, fixed set-up of knowledge, to a great extent embedded in capital-intensive investments. This is the traditional, permanent, industrial organisation, where each day essentially is a repetition of the preceding day, and where most of what concerns both tasks and competence is a given in the situation. Routines and fixed norms can have their basis in the systems of the organisation, in its individuals or in the knowledge stored in individuals and in the physical resources. With some exaggeration one might assert that traditional organisation theory is preoccupied with industrial organisations of this type.

Combination II, a high degree of knowledge renewal but a low degree of action renewal, illustrates a situation in which knowledge is developed and changed but when corresponding changes in actions are not taken. These projects often support the dominating organisation in one way or another. Examples are traditional knowledge (or process and product) development projects or learning projects, which normally do not have immediate effects in the form of changes in routines or other aspects of organisation, even if new knowledge is produced. Such a situation may arise as a response to renewal demands directed towards the prevalent industrial bureaucracy. Efforts to develop knowledge, to learn and continuously make small changes is one way of trying to cope with demands for renewal. Often such endeavours are organised as learning or development projects in one form or the other, for example within the scope of the activity of some development departments. This implies organising with the principal aim of knowledge renewal or learning (cf. discussions by Senge 1990a, for example). A so-called 'learning organisation' may in fact fall into this category if the knowledge gained does not result in concrete action, or if the new knowledge is used to strengthen already established routines or to change them incrementally. Initiatives taken with the aim of knowledge development may be isolated phenomena, or the organisation may for some reason be incapable of exploiting the new knowledge. New knowledge is acquired, but there is no change in continuously organised routines, and the company thus falls into the trap of knowledge development without action.

Combination III, a low degree of knowledge renewal but a high degree of action, describes either isolated or recurrent action-oriented projects. Such projects include major installation projects at a customer site or other types of implementation projects that demand adjustment and flexibility on the part of the organisation carrying out the implementation. Such projects, if they are of type number III, do not lead to much knowledge renewal. Either difficulties arise in transferring the knowledge acquired to other projects or to the mother organisation or the organisation is simply unable to visualise/verbalise what the renewing element is. Every such project has to start more or less from scratch and go through the whole series of events every time. An extremely project-oriented activity, often based on a strong professional work division, with a weak permanent organisation, and without the capacity to link projects, could be of this type. Much traditional project theory and many traditional project management models are designed for this situation; in other words, they concentrate on the projects *per se* and overlook the fact that the projects are an integral part of their environment.

There are many fixed routines within projects of this type, but the difference from the permanent organisation is that the routines are mobilised in the presence of a certain limited and decomposable task, rather than within a permanent, existing organisation. Consequently, the routines and the routinisation become different, although very similar action patterns between different projects can be observed (see discussion in Engwall 1995; Lientz and Rea 1995). This is, in turn, one of the reasons why it is so difficult to develop genuinely new knowledge in a recurrent project. Those involved are guided above all by the collective experiences within the sector to which they belong, and it is not apparent to them that they need to pay attention to renewal questions; even if they do, they find it difficult to transfer their experiences to others.

Combination IV, with a high degree of both action and knowledge renewal, describes a genuine renewal situation, in that both what is done and the knowledge on which the action is based or leads to, in a sense, is new in relation to what the participants previously had to work with. Innovations and other breakthroughs of a pioneering kind (e.g. within a product development project) could be of this type if the result of the project is of not marginal but major importance. In other words, the central element of this situation is that knowledge is renewed at the same time as routines are abandoned and/or replaced by new routines.

The four combinations described above, and illustrated in Figure 8.1, also represent four different management contingencies. Completely unique management problems manifest themselves in combination IV (the genuine renewal) rather than combination I (traditional industrial bureaucracy). By this we mean that it is hardly productive from a managerial perspective to work in the same way in all different situations that might occur. Nor is it possible to organise work in a similar fashion. By analogy with discussions in previous chapters, organising models cannot be copied from experiences gained in traditional bureaucracies if the aim is to create new knowledge or new action patterns.

The renewal paradox in the neo-industrial organisation

The discussion above was aimed at describing the connection between project organising (temporary organisations) and traditional industrial organising (permanent organisations). The trend towards neo-industrial organisations implies that the project element of industrial activity is increasing. The permanent parts of companies (combination I in Figure 8.1 above) are diminishing in importance and in size to be replaced by projects that are organised in accordance with one of the other three combinations. The changes vary in character in different industries. In the case of traditional industrial companies, which previously delivered their products directly from the factory to the customer, the change could have the following implications; for each customer a project is organised with the team members responsible for the deliveries from the company and for ensuring that the products meet certain quality criteria. Thus, projects take precedence over production, as the project groups are acting as purchasers of the output of the permanent organisation. The workforce may also be employed principally in different projects rather than in a permanent organisation. Wärtsilä Diesel, many of the ABB companies and parts of Ericsson can be said to have passed through or started this development. The growth of outsourcing and the service sector has resulted in more companies having market relationships that are well suited for project organising. This applies to many areas of consultancy, which have expanded during recent decades, delivering relatively complex services to companies. In addition, companies less qualified from a knowledge-handling perspective, such as employment agents that lease temporary personnel to permanent companies, can have an outspoken project-like character.

Product development, which by tradition is a project organised field, can also be accorded increased importance by a more distinct focusing on the development task and the transfer of developed products or technical solutions to other parts of the company. This can, for example, enable several similar product development projects to be organised in parallel, as in the Danish company Oticon (Eskerod 1997). Alternatively, a project could also have responsibility for the production and updating or changing of the product, as occurred in Canon and Saab Aircraft, and to some extent also in Volvo. Projects can also be used as a form of collaboration between different companies, when the task to be performed cannot easily be handled by one company. Many major development projects are of this type, e.g. the development of the new military aeroplane JAS 39 Gripen in Sweden. Another example is the development of a new business park in the north of Stockholm, Arlandastad. To the changes mentioned above should be added the sectors of industry that are already project organised, such as the building construction sector, architects, construction consultants, technical experts and advertising agencies.

The neo-industrial organisation, characterised by increased project application and a shrinking permanent organisation, is facing a new type of renewal problem and novel management problems in comparison with those existing in more traditionally organised companies. As alluded to previously, that renewal problem can be formulated as a paradox. A company in which a significant part of the activity is organised as projects can in principle reorganise its activity each time a new project is undertaken. It should then be relatively easy to take in lessons learned and emerging new conditions that could influence future organising, and by this make it possible to undergo continuous renewal and updating of the activity. Despite this, it is well known from traditionally organised activities that this is not the case (Ekstedt *et al.* 1992). Instead, projects tend to be repeated, i.e. projects are organised in the same way as before, and thus the possibilities of flexibility and renewal offered by the project form in theory are not exploited. In terms of the earlier reasoning, the projects are organised as in combination III in Figure 8.1 above. It may well be that this renewal paradox is on the increase with the increasing use of projects because of the standardisation efforts that are currently under way (Eskerod and Östergren 1998). This phenomenon is paradoxical in that the most flexible form of organisation does not seem to lead to fundamental renewal.

Several explanations for the widespread phenomenon denoted the renewal paradox in project-organised activity are conceivable. One is the lack of built-in renewal institutions in R&D departments in traditional industrial companies. A closely related explanation has to do with the changed role of technology. In process industries, for instance, a great deal of knowledge is stored in the real capital, i.e. machinery, and special staff are continuously engaged in improving the processes. At the same time, the real capital functions as a stabilising factor and thus has an uncertainty-reducing effect. The organisation is built up around the factory and its equipment. In project-organised activity, this platform is lacking, and technology has a more independent role. It is not uncommon for it to be replaced by mental stability in the form of fixed work traditions. In the construction sector, for example, the professional way of thinking has a strong influence. Ideas questioning the traditional role division and logistics are counteracted. The flexibility in time and space of the project organisation is thus stabilised by more or less explicit rules on how to do the work. These can constitute an almost invisible obstacle to renewal, thus leading to the paradox (Ekstedt and Wirdenius 1992).

In the neo-industrial organisation the renewal problem is closely related to this paradox, and the main problem or challenge for management in this type of organisation is how to bring about and maintain renewal. In the following section we will concentrate the discussion on this issue, and more precisely try to answer the question of the task of management in the neo-industrial organisation in general, and the solution of the renewal problems in particular.

Refined managerial roles in the neo-industrial organisation

The challenge for management in the neo-industrial setting is to act in a system consisting of both temporary projects (of different types) and components of a permanent type. Some tasks are better organised in a permanent setting, a permanent organisation, whereas others are better suited for temporary organising. Thus, in the following, we will argue that there is a need for a new type of managerial role – with a new set of tasks – which we here name neo-industrial management (NIM). We will try to define the main characteristics of management tasks in permanent organisations (POs) and temporary organisations (TOs) in order to relate them in various ways to NIM. This proposed role distribution (or distribution of required skills and aptitudes) should be observed by leaders of permanent parts and of projects, as well as by general management.

POs are exemplified by traditional industrial organisations, the chief advantages of which are the ability to organise their activity in a rational way and to exploit economies of scale. This type of organisation is characterised by traditional production tasks. The tasks are best organised in line with traditional management methods and principles of organisation, and routinised action is important. To accomplish what is expected, and to be efficient while doing just that, implies that it is principally established knowledge that is exploited within the PO.

Change – to the extent that it is takes place at all – is incremental, which means that change efforts involve not a total questioning of the established activity, but rather some marginal refinement of the current procedures. The management of a PO has thus to handle production and production systems in an efficient way. In the neo-industrial environment the PO has no particularly extensive strategic contacts with the world around besides those concerning direct production questions. The managerial tasks in the PO is summarised in Table 8.1.

If a managerial task in the PO is to handle long series and productivity, the TO has to answer for the direct, unique type of action. It is in the TO that the substantiated, special wishes of the customer are realised. In order to manage these wishes, a number of advanced demands are made on the TO. These demands can vary considerably between different TOs, e.g. between recurring projects and unique development projects.

TOs usually act based on a description of what is to be accomplished. In recurring projects, such as construction projects, the description can be detailed. In development and renewal projects the objective is often diffuse, and – as occurred in several of the projects that we have studied – may change during the course of the project. The organisation of the project work is usually not part of the contract, which implies that the project management and the project team have to be able to work on their own. In addition, in recurring projects the demand for quick action is often quite pronounced.

Flexibility is something of a cliché when used to characterise a TO. It can describe sensitivity towards the customer or management, but it can also be about the ability to foresee and solve problems that arise. Flexibility thus involves both communication skills and problem-solving capacities. The ability to cooperate is a closely related quality, which is also valued. All these qualities are valuable skills for people who work in TOs, and particularly for project leaders. The project leader is at the same time superior, interpreter of contracts and broker between customers and the PO and the NIM. Table 8.2 summarises the management tasks that should be refined in TOs.

Table 8.1 Managerial tasks in the permanent organisation

- The permanent organisation organises and performs production tasks
- The permanent organisation seeks to attain economic efficiency through economies of scale and long series and through the learning curve

Which among other things is due to
- Capacity to manage and control the activity in an efficient way
- Capacity to utilise established knowledge
- Capacity to carry through incremental change ('everyday learning' and 'everyday improvements')

Table 8.2 Management tasks in the temporary organisation

• The TO guarantees that the demands of the customer are fulfilled in practice
• The TO guarantees that time and cost schedules are pursued, i.e. fulfils the assignment of the NIM

Which among other things is due to
• Capacity to act independently, with concentration, promptly and in a flexible way
• Capacity to anticipate problems and solve unforeseen problems
• Capacity to carry on a dialogue with the customer and the PO with a sensitive ear
• The capacity of the project management to convey the content of the dialogue to the other team members
• Capacity to cooperate with different actors, and to adapt to different environments and conditions
• Capacity to develop new knowledge and to phase out old knowledge

In practice, these two organisational forms, PO and TO, are as different from each other as the two sets of different managerial tasks indicate. In general, management of the traditional, permanent industrial organisation has developed in accordance with a bureaucratic tradition. Stability seems to foster bureaucracy. Project management, on the other hand, has developed under different, more flexible, conditions. However, in recent years, even the project management form of leading has become more formalised as a result of various standardisation efforts, although as a rule flexibility is a key word that characterises TOs. Thus, it is fair to say that the two sets of tasks still diverge, although the management role in economic systems involving both permanent and temporary components is very seldom problematised and discussed. Drawing upon the multitude of experiences in the cases we have been studying, we are in a position to suggest the need for and the existence of a new role. It is this new role that forms the basis for neo-industrial management (NIM), which we will discuss next.

NIM's strengths reside in combining the permanent and temporary parts in a clever way. From the former, NIM derives long-term commitment and business confidence. This is reflected in the image of the organisation, usually expressed by a brand name, and is important for the signing of contracts and for business transactions: the customer must feel confident that the NIM is capable of delivering goods or services that meet a certain, predetermined standard. From the latter comes confidence in the NIM's potential to create and run projects within the scope of given economic conditions. The buyer looks for a very particular bargain – a low and predefined price is important, but so are quality and delivery time. Also the owner – if there is an obvious owner – must have confidence in the NIM. For companies quoted on the stock exchange the NIM's long-term capacity to generate new projects is of vital importance.

Confidence in the NIM is thus based on the kind of capabilities attached to the organisation. Which capability is most important of course varies depending on the area of activity. In the case of large scale, capital-intensive production, the most important factor is the ability to arrange long-term financing. In other cases, it may be crucial to ensure sufficient financial stability to fund risky projects. However, NIM is not just about the management of financial and real capital, but more about the management human capital. The NIM must have the capacity to promote collective as well as individual competence formation. This could mean generating new knowledge, that is contributing to the innovation process, but it could also mean the ability to combine knowledge and resources at the creation of projects. Particularly important is the NIM's capacity to transfer knowledge to future projects and to the PO. Project plans should be checked, managers appointed, contracts signed and followed up. NIMs that succeed in getting their capabilities noticed also have the qualities to make an impression on the market. What has been said can be summed up as in Table 8.3.

So far we have discussed a refined work division between TOs and POs, and furthermore expressed what kind of tasks the NIM – the comprehensive general management of the neo-industrial organisation – should have. By way of conclusion we ask ourselves what tools are at its disposal to perform its leadership.

Table 8.3 The neo-industrial management (NIM) role

- Define and create fields of action for the activity
- Get the PO and the TO to collaborate, function as a whole and strive towards the same goals
- The NIM name (trademark) and image guarantee trustworthiness when creating contractual relations
- Confidence in being able to deliver goods and services of a certain standard
- Confidence in being able to form good projects (as to price, quality and time)
- Confidence in being able to generate new projects (with long-term return to owners)

Which among other things is due to
- Capacity for financing long-term investments (capital-intensive production) and risky projects
- Capacity to design effective projects, i.e. combine resources with adequate knowledge content
- Capacity to be seen and gain a position on the market
- Capacity to utilise knowledge from projects carried out
- Capacity to generate new useful knowledge: innovation power
- Capacity to evaluate project plans and to suck up knowledge from the world around
- Capacity to select the right management for different types of projects and the PO and to sign and follow up contracts

---

The traditional CEO and the project manager in the shadow of NIM

In a sense, NIM is working in a polarised environment. On the one hand is the traditional PO with its bureaucratic management and, on the other, the TOs with their transitory quality and independent and flexible project management. The relations between these organisations and the NIM can be illustrated as in Figure 8.2.

The NIM thus has three principal tasks. The first is to define the aim and direction of the total set of activities. Good knowledge of the market, technology and available resources is then necessary. The second task is to create collaboration and effective work division between the PO and the TOs. This requires good knowledge of the potential of different organisation units, as well as the ability to stimulate communication between the PO and the TOs. Moreover, this implies that the NIM must understand the 'languages' of the two types of organisations, and act as an interpreter between the units. The third task is the future-oriented activity: to further development and competence formation. Knowledge that is generated in the TO and in permanent parts has to be exploited and transformed to future activity. In order to avoid ending up in a renewal paradox knowledge from different traditions has to be combined.

But what are the prospects for NIM being able to perform well and to cope with its tasks? What powerful means are at its disposal? It is, of course, obvious that the NIM cannot possibly exercise a direct and detailed control. This would require other methods. The steering has to be more indirect. We envisage four different ways in which to proceed. First, the NIM always has the opportunity to create new projects, either regular production projects or renewal projects directed towards its own domain. The direction and aim of the activity and the way of working will be affected by this. Second, it is the NIM that appoints leaders and potential leaders

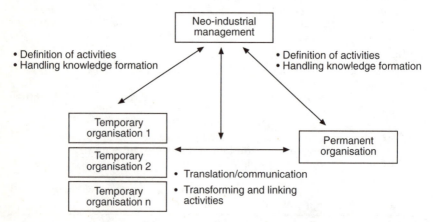

Figure 8.2 Main relations in the neo-industrial organisation

in the PO and in the TOs. A deliberate choice of project managers presents great opportunities for continuous influence on and control of the economic activity. This can be an effective way for the NIM to keep the renewal work alive. Third, the NIM can follow up both temporary and permanent activity by recurrent and independent evaluations. With these as a basis, there is a great opportunity for the NIM to design future projects in such a way that ingrained modes of thinking are avoided. Fourth, the NIM can profit from its advantage in being able to understand the language of both the PO and TO. As a boundary walker, the NIM has a great opportunity to spread and establish ideas about the activity.

Neo-industrial management and the renewal paradox

Neo-industrial management has the capacity to neutralise or avoid the renewal paradox that may face a projectised company of a neo-industrial type, perhaps with detrimental effects for the economy as a whole. By this we mean the situation where short-term flexibility could conceal a fundamental inertia. Recurring projects are certainly very flexible, but only within certain terms of reference. The strictly formal and informal institutions in which some project-organised activities have to operate leave little room for profound renewal, i.e. renewal that challenges ingrained methods of working, roles and rules. In other words, what kind of management has the power to assume the neo-industrial managerial challenge – a challenge that consists in finding ways to design projects that will catalyse real renewal activity when needed, and then making it possible for parts of the permanent organisation to transfer the results to future activity?

The words 'when needed' in the sentence above actually conceal an important antithesis to the renewal paradox, which is that too much reflection could have an adverse effect on efficiency. In other words, concentrating too much on renewal efforts tends to lead to overspending on the projects. However, we found no evidence of the renewal paradox antithesis. In a competitive environment, the marketplace probably cures any company of that kind of 'disease'. So, judging from the case studies and our previous experience of projectised industries, the renewal paradox is an overriding concern.

But there are also other dangers and pitfalls to attend to. Traditional PO managers have great difficulty working in a projectised environment. A hierarchical structure adapts poorly to projects that emerge and exist alongside the flow-process production. Project-organised activity involves much independent work, work that is often transformed or even changed entirely as the project work proceeds. Managers in the hierarchical structure – especially middle managers – often seem to become an impediment to the project group. Their managerial ideas about continuous direction and efforts aimed at monitoring all activities have a tendency to reinforce traditional, practised action. In addition, many project members find it difficult to adopt project thinking, especially if they are working in staff or line functions concurrently with their project assignments. Project leaders could also have concomitant staff functions.

When traditional industrial organisations start to make more use of projects, they usually find that they lack project management experience and training. Conflicts of interest between the different roles results in uncertainty. New thinking arising from the projects is slow to have an effect on the organisation. Numerous product development projects, for example, have generated ideas that have been rejected by the PO management. One startling example is the report that senior managers in the pharmaceutical company Astra on several occasions tried to stop the development of the now internationally best-selling gastric ulcer drug Losec (Östholm *et al.* 1996). And industrial history is replete with similar examples.

It is probably easier for PO managers to absorb the gradual improvement in operations initiated by permanent development departments. The tendency for certainty and stability often gains priority over initiatives directed towards innovations and new thinking. There are many indications that managers in traditional POs have difficulty in coping with this variant of the renewal paradox. They may perhaps even find it hard to perceive the problem. However, this is not true of managers engaged in project-organised activity.

In the construction industry, for example, the problem of disseminating experiences and knowledge from one project to another is well known. It can be the case that advanced knowledge is present in the organisation without being used. A much discussed case is the poisonous sealing material Rhoca-Gil, used in the construction of the railway tunnels through the Halland Ridge in southern Sweden. The main contractor knew of the hazardous qualities of the material, but the project management responsible for the construction site had not taken it in. This is not an uncommon state of affairs.

The emphasis on action by project management can eclipse general knowledge formation. The problem is thus primarily a structural one. Many senior managers are aware of this and try to do something about it. Various methods to improve the diffusion of knowledge have been tested. In some companies knowledge and experiences gained are documented in a systematic way. The problem is then to get project managers, especially the managers of new projects, to seek out and utilise this information. In addition, some companies have established special support functions for renewal, linked to top management, such as Kullenberg Construction Stockholm, although they still find it difficult to create general interest in trying new approaches in the project work (Wirdenius 1991).

There are also other kinds of locking-in problems with project-organised activity. Customers' demand for flexibility requires a high level of sensitivity in the project group. However, if the relationship with the customer is too close, they may start to get their own ideas, with the result that opportunities to develop project activity are restricted. However, there might be other products and customers involved in the future. An organisation that is incapable of breeding new ideas about future projects, and thus neglects long-term knowledge formation, can create concern among its owners. The price of its shares on the stock market may tumble, and freedom of action may be curtailed.

The traditional way of recruiting senior managers in project-organised activity probably also contributes to the present state of affairs of long-term and strategic thinking being slow to gain general acceptance. New managers are often selected from successful project leaders. It is often difficult for them to appreciate that the role of the head of a group or company is quite different from running a successful project. In this role, the ability to manage temporary operations and at the same time apply strategic thinking – in order to bring about long-term knowledge formation – is put to the test.

We can thus observe that both PO and TO managers find it difficult to handle more fundamental renewal in activities requiring permanent and temporary organisations to exist side by side. A new form of leadership is therefore needed, one capable of handling the renewal paradox in neo-industrial organisations, a leadership that is stuck neither in the flow-production culture nor in the recurring project culture but which understands the languages of both cultures. In other words, a leadership that does not fall into the same rut as PO and TO managers is to be preferred. Isolated development departments and introvert professionalism have to be replaced by something more dynamic. Of course, as always, it is easier to say what not to do than what should be done. The question is 'what can NIM do that traditional PO and TO managers cannot do?'.

The experiences of our 25 renewal case studies can give some guidance. In several cases, senior managers did in fact adopt a NIM-like attitude (or guise). Indeed, this observation is in line with the empirical observation that, among 22 CEOs of the largest Swedish companies (Jönsson 1995), every one of them as part of their career had been responsible for at least one major renewal project. In many cases, they attributed their rise to the position of CEO to that project experience.

Traditional, well-institutionalised renewal work has been replaced or supplemented by renewal projects. These projects aim to change the mode of working in the permanent or temporary organisation and/or to renew the products being produced. In many cases, the managers of renewal projects are given complete authority to change both the physical structure and the rule system that regulates the activity. These changes are then being supported by training programmes and transformations of the work organisation. It has also proved to be important for senior managers to have a vision of the road ahead and to consider the project in progress as a part of a total ongoing effort rather than as something that is isolated (see also Lundin and Söderholm 1997). Experience shows that organisational changes for their own sake, without a link to technology (new processes or products) or to institutional conditions (new roles and rules), have a tendency to come to nothing.

The renewal paradox and combinatorics

NIM can try to neutralise the renewal paradox by implementing a renewal project. But such a project can also be an indicator of another current problem, i.e. a transformation dilemma. Renewal projects can also be a way to handle the transformation from a traditional flow-production organisation with hierarchical structures to an organisation with a major component of projectised activity; this is in fact the way to realise the transition from traditional industrial to neo-industrial organisation (Midler 1995). To resolve the paradox something else is needed, namely a project design that both does away with ingrained roles and rules and facilitates the diffusion of knowledge developed within projects to the rest of the organisation. These are the two major challenges involved.

As far as the first challenge is concerned, namely the design of projects that could catalyse fundamental renewal activity, there is reason to refer specifically to the discussion on knowledge formation in Chapter 6. We argued that temporary organisations can be built on combinations of people from either the same culture or a diversity of cultures. In the short term, the homogenising strategy is more likely to contribute to efficiency and refinements of working routines, but this strategy will also increase group cohesion and resistance to new ideas. To avoid the renewal paradox it is probably better to implement the pluralistic integration strategy. We argued that there are three principal reasons why controlled cultural friction in pluralistic projects could contribute to renewal. First, a broader selection of experiences and competences facilitates the renewal search process. Second, the possibilities of combinations are increased. Knowledge developed in one context can be combined with knowledge developed in another context. Third, confrontation with other cultures can increase awareness of one's own culture.

There is much that points towards the need for a new leadership that has the capacity to carry through a pluralistic integration strategy, i.e. NIM. Traditional project leaders usually find it difficult to conceive of projects with members from a completely different professional culture. They themselves are, as a rule, moulded by long experience of the organisation culture in which they operate. They have been accustomed to functioning together with colleagues with a minimum of communication. If people with a different competence enter the group, much of the ordinary and trivial must be put into words. Leadership suddenly becomes more complicated. But at the same time, the enforced articulation can contribute to a deeper level of thinking, or at least to second thoughts, and thus to a climate more conducive to development. For traditional PO managers, the difficulty of implementing a pluralistic integration strategy is even greater, if possible. On the whole, they may find it hard to perceive differences between different project cultures. They may also have difficulty in participating in the diffusion of knowledge between projects, because of their lack of a language to communicate with members of other projects.

In the NIM, the ability to understand different professional cultures is combined with the opportunity to keep out of the daily project work as well as out of current activities of a permanent type. There has to be room for interpretation of the world around and the long-term course of events. The NIM thus plays a crucial role in the formation of projects in connection with the purchase of services and production, with deliveries and with the evaluation of the various activities. The remaining activity is managed mainly by the traditional TOs and POs. The creation of pluralistically integrated projects with the potential to become productive requires experience and the ability to interpret broad references. The design of future projects must to a great extent be based on independent and carefully designed evaluations of projects carried out.

The renewal paradox and knowledge/action transfer

Evaluations are, furthermore, of vital importance when it comes to the diffusion of knowledge, which is the second neo-industrial challenge. Projects that are innovative are of little use if the results or new ideas they generate are not disseminated within the organisation. Again, for this task, the NIM should be better suited than either the PO or TO managers. As the facilitator of contracts with the customer, the NIM is an independent authority in relation to the PO and the TO. The NIM thus has the ability to rise above the traditional antagonism between office and shop floor. The NIM designs future projects in response to previous results and evaluations of different kinds. Projects can be evaluated through follow-up sessions with key actors, but the results of development endeavours, formal investigations and customer inquiries can also form the basis of new projects. Moreover, the NIM has the power to organise a permanent central support function for renewal, as well as to conclude agreements with subcontractors. In all these situations, the NIM has an opportunity to benefit from experiences and knowledge gained in all parts of the organisation.

However, mutual knowledge transfer can also be promoted in other ways. Earlier in this chapter we discussed different combinations of types of action and phases of the knowledge process (see Figure 8.1), and the various kinds of organisations formed by this. Based on this simplified categorisation, a model for knowledge transfer can be outlined. The categories used were as follows:

I   Traditional industrial bureaucracies (POs) characterised by a low degree of action and knowledge renewal.
II Learning projects of a recurrent nature supporting the PO, and aiming at individual process or product development. Characterised by a low degree of action renewal and a high degree of knowledge renewal.
III Recurrent projects in project-organised operations and characterised by a high degree of action renewal and a low degree of knowledge renewal.
IV Projects of a renewal nature and characterised by a high degree of both action and knowledge renewal.

In traditional and other bureaucracies (I), learning projects (II) are often used with a view to promoting renewal. The participants often find these projects very stimulating while they are in progress, but on returning to routinised activity in the PO they usually find it difficult to utilise the knowledge acquired. After a while, things revert to normal. A principal reason for learning projects having such a limited effect is their weak linkage to action and its renewal. The renewal paradox of the neo-industrial organisation is best illustrated by category III, i.e. recurrent projects in a projectised environment, where new experiences and new knowledge have difficulty influencing activity. How are regular production projects to achieve a higher degree of knowledge renewal? Is it possible to find combinations that promote knowledge transfer and exchange?

The Skanska total organisation renewal project 3T (category IV) could be a starting point for the development of a dynamic model for a project-intensive environment (Figure 8.3). The central renewal project team was in this case composed of a set of very experienced individuals working in close cooperation with corporate senior management (NIM). They came from different permanent activities as well as from the construction project activities. In the course of the renewal project, new staff replaced those who were appointed to leading positions in other parts of the corporation. In contrast to the learning projects described above, the renewal action was an integral part of the development of knowledge. Those with experience from the 3T project management team were to put the ideas developed into practice. It is, of course, very important that the renewal project causes action, but it is also essential that people working in the production projects have confidence in those who sponsor the renewal project, or at least feel that there are elements of realism in the suggested changes. It is not surprising, therefore, that long experience of project management, communication skills and rhetorics proved to be crucial competencies here.

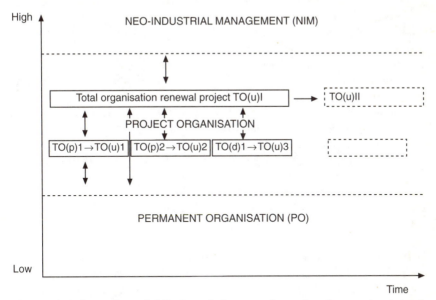

Figure 8.3 A dynamic model for knowledge transfer and exchange via renewal projects. TO(u), unique renewal project; TO(p), recurring production project; TO(d), recurring development project.

An idealised dynamic model for knowledge transfer and exchange in neo-industrial economic activity thus includes renewal projects (IV) that are deeply rooted in permanent activity as well as in the production projects, i.e. the radical renewal cannot be carried through by special 'renewal departments' (such as R&D or training departments). An exchange of staff between project and renewal activity, as occurred in Digital for example, is not enough. Renewal carried out by genuine renewal projects has great advantages. First, new knowledge can be generated without ties to the ingrained rules and roles that often develop in recurrent production and, second, a project of this type can be separated from daily activity and have its own targets, adapted for independent evaluation. The success of renewal projects of this kind is contingent upon NIM-type management that is independent of the PO and the TOs and their limitations, and endowed with the power to force through such projects and to further transfer and exchange knowledge.

Finally, as indicated in the first section of this chapter, neo-industrial organisations already exist. We have tried to produce something of a conceptual model of the content of the major management challenges in neo-industrial organisations and, thus, show how to view projects in this context.

Organising

This last remark leads us to a discussion of the term 'organising' (as opposed to organisation). As illustrated in the discussion on managerial tasks and roles, the traditional notions of management in permanent and temporary organisations are deeply rooted in the managers themselves as well as in the various environments within which the managers act. Managers are faced with a set of stable expectations about their role. The role expectations are, in general, self-reinforcing in the sense that there is an almost natural tendency to adhere to them. Attempts to adopt an appropriate NIM role are met with resistance in terms of external or internal pressure on the actors. In addition, our empirical cases seem to show that managers are sometimes forced to fall back into traditional PO or TO management behaviours.

This is one reason why it is more appropriate to talk about organising. The NIM role has to be reinforced occasionally so that those involved do not revert to traditional methods. Just as no one form of organisation is the ideal solution, NIM tasks will never be stable and unvarying. Adaptations will always be needed. 'The only thing that is stable is change' is a phrase often used in public debates on where business life is going, but most participants in debates seem unable to extract the correct stance to that insight. 'Organising' is it!

This completes our present discussion of the micro level of neo-industrial management. The final chapter will treat the neo-industrial development in a macro-oriented way.

9 Neo-industrial organising – implications and prospects

The account has up until now dealt with renewal of the economic activity in different individual organisations. We have intended to demonstrate that increased use of projects in the economy influences conditions for renewal, especially those related to knowledge formation in organisations. It appears to be much more difficult to apply traditional methods of improving knowledge processes (e.g. 'learning organisation' approaches) in temporary than in permanent organisations. Quite simply, other methods are needed to influence projectised organisations. Among other things, we have argued in favour of using combinatorics of knowledge in a conscious way as a method to bring about fundamental renewal. Directly and indirectly, we have been addressing the inherent problems of the renewal paradox in a projectised environment. In this concluding chapter, we turn to the meso level of analysis/synthesis over and above the individual organisation, be it permanent or temporary. An impressive range of issues are involved here, so it is necessary to extract a few of the most important ones. To be more specific, we want to revisit the transformation dilemma problem and to describe the likely effects of increasing project work on individuals' working lives. Finally, we will adopt a stance on projectisation, inspired by critical theory, as a preliminary to debates on projectisation and new research. Questions that are tentatively answered in this final chapter are as follows:

- What are the implications of the transformation dilemma for the institutions surrounding organisations?
- In the labour market, will the contractual relations between company and individual be affected?
- Will personal work satisfaction, identity and participation be impaired in a projectised economy?
- Will the labour market become segmented and precarious for individuals?
- How are the size and power relations of organisations influenced by the current projectisation?
- Is it possible to draw any conclusions on the future structure of companies and organisations?

- What are the most urgent research issues connected with project-isation?

In the following we will deal first with the labour or labour-market related questions.

Will terms of employment be affected in a projectised economy?

In the popular debate, flexibility, projects and short-term employment are discussed together. We will try to be a bit more sophisticated by distinguishing between different forms of economic activity, on the one hand, and contractual relations of the individual on the other. Which form of employment applies in different types of organisations? There is currently much talk about the demand for increased flexibility in the economy. At the same time, however, there are many interpretations of the term flexibility. Our empirical findings regarding the way to organise economic activity seem to tell us that, in a consumer/buyer-driven economy, temporary organisational solutions more often than previously satisfy the resulting demand for flexibility. Such solutions are also being used increasingly to solve problems within organisations. But what are the implications of project-organised activity for the employment relationship between the organisation and the individual? And, if the organisation is a temporary entity, what is the employment situation for the individual?

There is no clear-cut answer to this question. There are evidently some people who are permanently employed in project-organised activity. For example, in the Swedish construction industry, workers are now employed not just for a particular project, but by the construction company through a special legal arrangement. At the same time, of course, some people are engaged only temporarily for the duration of a project and at the associated direct market-related pay. In general, consultants operate under this type of arrangement. It is very likely, however, that there are several other forms of flexibility in operation. A variety of temporary engagements rewarded by flexible market-led pay should be possible in connection with project-based solutions. Wage and salary rates are likely to be affected as well, but those concerns are outwith the scope of our discussion, as it depends so much on factors outside the concrete economic activity. (This last point raises questions about the future of trade unions.) Instead, in accordance with our previous discussion, we focus on the relationship between the organisational form of economic activity (flow-process operations or projectised operations) and the contractual implications for individuals (permanent or temporary engagement) (see Table 9.1).

Permanent employment is normal for organisations whose activity is mainly organised as flow-process operations, and this is typical among industrial organisations. From now on we will call the organisations that

Table 9.1 Relationship between the organisational form of industrial activity and the contract between the company and the individual

Permanent employment	Temporary employment
Flow-process operations	
A *Industrial companies and public services* • Stationary real capital, assembly line production, multilevel managerial decisions, bureaucracy • Strong PO and weak TOs • Limited negotiation and search costs and great monitoring costs	B *Manpower-leasing* • Firms that lease out and hire staff for current activity during periods of staff shortage in client companies • Short-term employment (examples include secretarial /office/specialist service agencies) • Putting out systems • PO with broker function to reduce search costs of client companies
Projectised operations	
C *Commisioned companies* • Recurring projects operations (for example, construction companies, technical/organisation /management/IT consulting firms • Weak PO with broker function and strong TOs • High negotiation costs and limited monitoring costs	D *Professionals/practitioners* • Individuals who are recruited to projects in A and C, or who create projects ('free agents') (for example, freelance writers/ journalists/artists/craftsmen/ longshoremen/self-employed consultants) • No PO • High costs involved in establishing a name for themselves and keeping up to date

fit into quadrant A the *industrial companies*, even though a large part of public service production, for example, also belongs to this group. The production of standardised products or the same level of service in long series lays the foundation for stable relations between actors. The relations are essentially stable for a long period of time, and time-consuming negotiations can be avoided. In heavy industry, stability is further strengthened by immobile machinery that is built to function for many years to come. A hierarchical decision system keeps transaction costs down for intraorganisational search processes and negotiations. However, this system is marred by very high monitoring costs. Decision makers build up many levels (or layers) between themselves and those who perform the economic activities. Special functions for supervision and control are built into the system. And even if the economic activity in general is perceived as permanent, a preparedness for handling changes in the surrounding environment has to be built into the organisation. In addition, there is likely to be a considerable support staff.

Knowledge is mostly embedded in these organisations in two ways. In industry, real capital plays a crucial part. New machinery and new technology usually mean more advanced activity. However, organisation-embedded knowledge is also important. In time, large, long-lived and tradition-bound organisations develop their own unique culture. Old factories and their modern successors often become small societies within society.

The organisations and the institutions of the labour market have been strongly influenced by the traditional industry, since this has dominated economic life for a very long time, essentially from the very beginning of industrialisation. It appears that the public sector, in particular, has adopted its ideas and ideals, which has led to large-scale organising, among other things. But the relations between the parties of the labour market have also been institutionalised, which manifests itself, for example, in current labour legislation. The relationship between employers and employees is seen as a more or less permanent and constant struggle, and accordingly it is possible to describe the relationship in detail.

In these organisations, even renewal work is made permanent and transferred to supporting suborganisations, such as R&D, rationalisation and training departments. However, as we have seen, these conditions have come to be challenged recently. There is a transformation dilemma in the making at the company level. Large permanent organisations are made the objects of radical renewal initiatives, e.g. ABB in the T50 project. Large hierarchical organisations obviously find it increasingly difficult to engage their members in the problems of their customers, which is perhaps not surprising given the number of levels generally to be found within them. Senior managers may respond by, for example, implementing customer focusing programmes or radical reorganisation ventures. In many companies, parts of the activity have also been externalised. Among our cases, Saab's aeroplane production is the most pronounced example of this. Components are purchased from international specialist companies. In addition, a major part of the support functions have come to be outsourced to project-organised consulting companies. This traditional industrial company, in which almost all activity was once under one roof, has been transformed into a coordinating organisation that puts together, designs and develops production systems combined with services. In other words, it has become a neo-industrial organisation, run by the NIM. Such an organisation can change its form continuously; subcontractors are replaced and projects are added and finished/ abandoned. For the buyer, these changes are undetectable, since the products and services are sold under the trademark of the host organisation (because this inspires confidence).

It is also quite common for traditional industrial organisations themselves to run projects. Project organisation is particularly common in connection with development work that occupies a large part of the staff in technologically advanced companies, such as Ericsson. Individuals from different parts of the hierarchy can participate in projects, as can, interestingly, people from other companies, such as subcontractors, customers or independent consulting companies. It is also the case that flow-process organisations lease their staff to other companies during periods of weak demand for their own product. In a company manufacturing aluminium boats, for example, the most essential resource is welders who can perform complicated aluminium welding. Such a company could, when working below capacity, lease the skilled welders to other companies. The combination of flow-process organisation and permanent employment is thus challenged in many quarters.

The combination of flow-process operations and temporary employment is less common, but again seems to be gaining ground. We call those organisations that qualify for a place in quadrant B *manpower-leasing companies*. Historically, the so-called 'putting out' system was widespread within the textile sector, for example. Ericsson also once had a large homeworking department linked to its factory in Stockholm. Employees, mostly women, worked at home on certain parts in the manufacturing chain. During periods of high demand for the products, many employees received plenty of work; during quiet periods a few people received a small amount of work. Opportunities for homeworking have again increased as a result of modern IT. Geographic distances are seen as no obstacle to participation in a centrally controlled production process.

Another trend is even more obvious. More and more companies are being formed to lease staff to other companies. These firms perform a broker function that is particularly useful in a projectised economy in which combinatorics is judged to be important. Customers rid themselves of the high costs of recruiting staff for tasks that are of only short duration. The personnel hired are paid only when working, and that is the limit of the recruiting company's obligation. When no work is available, no compensation is paid. However, there is some variation in how staff are compensated by the leasing company: they can be paid either for the time worked or for the task accomplished, or both.

Manpower-leasing companies have until recently been mostly concerned with rather routine activities, such as secretarial and office work. However, their spheres of activity seem to be becoming broader as well as more advanced. Personnel with more education and training are being hired. It is not uncommon for financial and bookkeeping functions to be offered. This organisational form requires a short period of acclimatisation, though, and the work tasks consequently have to be rather standardised. The knowledge required has to be institutionalised so as to be readily adaptable to different environments. The person hired must of course be able to start work straight away and without instruction, although the introduction is often facilitated by the fact that the same people are often re-engaged at the same company. In some cases, companies seem to mix pure consulting assignments with personnel leasing.

The scale of this activity seems to vary between different countries. In Sweden, only a few per cent of the labour force fall into this group, whereas in The Netherlands the corresponding figure is about 10 per cent (according to the Dutch employers' union statistics). It is difficult to determine the size of this group when activities are mixed and also include consulting assignments. However, the need for a short period of acclimatisation limits the potential of this form of employment. A high demand for problem-solving capacity and a good knowledge of the products or services requires project activity rather than mere manpower-leasing.

The current trend is probably towards a combination of projectised operations and permanent employment. For the sake of simplicity, we call the organisations in quadrant C *commissioned companies* or *consulting companies* as they can be of two general types. The relative decrease in the number of people employed in traditional industry in the industrialised world usually coincides with a parallel increase of the industry-related service sector. These services are chiefly offered by companies that utilise projects to manage their economic activity. IT, management and technical consultancies are examples of specialist companies that carry out assignments within their specialist field in large companies. It is hardly the case, however, that the consulting sector is replacing the industrial sector, quite the opposite. An advanced industrial activity that produces unique solutions is often supplemented by an advanced consulting activity.

The project-organised way of working is, as we know, far from new. Construction companies have worked in this way naturally and by tradition. Italy's current textile industry is based on many small, flexible companies producing short runs of customer-adapted products that are so specific that they can be viewed as unique projects. When Piore and Sabel speak about a Second Industrial Divide, with the growth of 'flexible specialisation', they could be describing a transition from the A to the C quadrant; from long series of standardised production to specially designed, short series. In the Italian Prato system, the search process between the small, family, manufacturing businesses and the market in the form of department stores and fashion houses is handled by special brokers, impanatores. It is variants of this new organisational form that is spreading to many parts of the economy. The demand for customer-adapted, in some cases unique and advanced, solutions speaks in favour of this type of organisation. The permanent parts of these companies perform external as well as internal broker functions. These are the ones that build up a net of contacts with customers, and the ones that sign contracts with customers. It is also the permanent organisation that chooses and forms the project group. But the assignment itself is carried out by the group. The cost of monitoring is minimised as it is in the interest of the project members to meet the aims of the assignment because, naturally, they want to be engaged in future projects.

Consulting companies working for large industrial companies may come to depend on these assignments. It can be in the interest of the large company to lease the staff of the consulting company instead of buying their own solution. Supervision is easier, and the organisation-embedded knowledge of the large company can be increased. For the consulting company that survives on a particular and attractive competence, such a development may be fatal. Depletion of organisation-embedded knowledge could undermine the activity or business concept of the organisation. Although it retains broker-like functions, there is a risk that a knowledge-intensive company will be transformed into a manpower-leasing company, with only general institution-embedded knowledge remaining. In order to keep its independence, a consulting company needs to have a clear business concept that can be defended by a manifest knowledge advantage.

How then do these relations influence the terms of employment? Both consultancies and industrial organisations are interested in signing long-term contracts with individuals with desirable knowledge. The attraction can consist of strongly specialised and unique knowledge that the individual has acquired and that is part of the knowledge embedded in the company. A particular and attractive skill suggests that the individual is able to manage project work. Many consultancy companies have taken great pains to develop special methods for working and for solving problems. It can be both costly and time-consuming to replace staff who are already part of this unique company culture. However, at the same time it must be remembered that consultancies rely on an influx of commissions. Whereas manufacturing companies can postpone an order when they have too much work, consultancies cannot stock up orders, although they may be able to increase training and internal development projects when assignments are thin on the ground. In summary, one can say that the activity in quadrant C is characterised by a striving after permanent employment arrangements, but that it lacks the stability found in traditional industrial activity.

In the combination of projectised operations and temporary employment you will find *professionals or practitioners*. Accordingly, this is our designation of quadrant D. What characterises projectised activity is the limited period within which the project must take place. To have a reasonable chance of contributing to a project, participants require good introductory knowledge, but this is not sufficient. The individual must also be known to keep up with the competition in the market. Reputation usually comes from the demonstration of an extraordinary ability in some respect. To attain a marketable knowledge often requires high search costs in the form of extensive studies or training in the 'hard school of life'. Of course, the rewards may be great and may include fame. For writers, freelance professionals within different domains or individual entre-preneurs the lack of a permanent affiliation to a highly regulated organisation is a highly valued freedom.

This lack of affiliation to any organisation also has a downside of course. Each individual must conduct all his or her own negotiations in a market that in many respects is short of rules and lacks clear roles. It is not uncommon, therefore, for individuals in this exposed situation to try to strengthen their position by seeking the support of professional organisations. How will this unstable quadrant develop? There is evidence to suggest that it will expand, despite the difficulties of individuals asserting themselves on the market. The rapidly developing media sector, with new ways for individuals to be seen and known, seems to be highly attractive to young people. Schools of drama and other artistic education have waiting lists of prospective students. A degree of security afforded by study allowances and other grants, together with a hard alternative labour market, reduces the sacrifices associated with this type of work.

Will work participation and work identity be impaired in a projectised economy?

According to the discussion in the previous chapter, neo-industrial management (NIM) is administering an economic activity that increasingly is carried out by subcontractors and project groups. The need for monitoring functions is decreasing at the same time as the demand for capacity to design, carry out and follow up contracts is increasing. The tasks of managers, particularly those associated with the NIM role, are becoming more strategic and forward-looking, with development, competence formation, marketing and drawing from the outside world high on the agenda. In this knowledge-intensive environment, the need for hierarchical control is reduced, while at the same time the influence of the employees over their daily work increases. However, there is nothing in this development to indicate that general managers in senior positions will relinquish power when it comes to defining and creating fields of action for the economic activity. In fact, quite the opposite may happen. In many lines of business, large corporations are tending to become still larger, with fewer real decision makers. This is particularly evident in branches of industry with high marketing and development costs, such as the pharmaceutical industry.

NIM places a high value on the creation of a brand name for its products. This identity-building activity hopefully 'infects' those who work with these products so that they view NIM tasks as important. Even in more traditional industrial organisations, production staff are becoming more involved with the outside world, participating in the activity from order to delivery, for example through the medium of autonomous/goal-directed groups. It is also the case that companies are using more and more components that are made in another flow-process organisation with permanent staff. Production as well as specialised development work is thus externalised. The large industrial enterprise is consequently replaced by a coordinating organisation. The result for those who work in subcontractor companies throughout the world is that the product becomes anonymous; it is sold in someone else's name – often in the name of a foreign organisation. For many subcontractor companies, often in developing countries, the situation is much as it was once in traditional industrial companies. A strict hierarchical decision order prevails, the organisation members find it difficult to identify with a distant, anonymous management, and their influence over the activity remains extremely limited.

Different conditions of relations and commitment thus apply to those who are active within quadrant A. Many find it difficult to identify with the company; others with more difficult tasks may find it easier. Exerting influence is easier for those employed in keeping production systems together than for those who work for as replaceable subcontractors. The latter group will find it difficult to change an organisation structure in which certain rules and roles are stabilised or even written in cement. When we discussed our cases (Chapter 7), one of the main findings was that the force of change must be very strong to affect the institutions of the work organisation. Strong pressure from the market or from new technical solutions is needed.

In quadrant B, employees' identification with and participation in the leasing as well as the client company activity is bound to be low. They have a brief and limited interface with the people working there. The relation with the leasing company usually takes the form of an instruction that the individual must comply with. Consequently, an increase in the number of people employed in quadrant B is likely to have a negative effect on the ability of individuals to affect their work; this, in turn, can have a detrimental effect on job satisfaction. This statement is, however, contradicted by the fact that 'temps' sometimes claim that it is interesting to work in different environments and thus get to know many people. However, such relationships are probably very superficial compared with those that can develop in projectised organisations.

In the projectised organisations in quadrant C, relations between individuals are usually of shorter duration than in industrial companies, but they can be more profound. The organisation members design, develop and run projects together. They are jointly participating in the creation of something new. Moreover, in many projects the sense of belonging is strengthened by the actors' professional fellowship and team spirit, as in the construction sector. It is also the norm for some project members to collaborate in the next project. One example of this is construction gangs, which represent an institutionalised form of bringing about discipline and continuity in the formation of project groups. Typical of project work is a high level of participation in the activity. The participants are usually very committed to what they are doing; the work is about solving the task at hand and achieving joint goals. In longer-term projects it is easy for individuals to identify with the project itself, but also with the product. A builder may point at a house and say with pride: 'I participated in the building of that house!'

In project-organised activity, there may be a great physical as well as mental distance between those who work in the projects and those who work in the permanent parts. The project members meet their customers more often and deal with them more closely than does the central management. An IT consultant spends almost all his time with the customers. A consultant who becomes highly sought after can even leave the consultancy to become an individual professional or practitioner (free agent) , i.e. move into quadrant D. It is in the light of these facts that we should view the ambitions of the permanent management of such a company to create a joint company culture. They have to offer 'the loose-living human capital' an attractive fellowship. Good pay is not enough. If the permanent parts of the organisation can exhibit strong fellowship and identity, then this should be seen as a way of disassociating it from the temporary parts. The difficult task facing senior or general management (NIM) then becomes the creation of a fellowship for both those who work in the flow-process production and those who work in the projects, and an even more difficult task is to develop a feeling of solidarity within the whole organisation.

The professionals in quadrant D are characterised by their low inclination to become affiliated to an organisation, preferring to create their own identity. When they take part in projects arranged by some organisation it is because they want to participate and have a real influence over their own work situation. For the professional, personal integrity is important. If he maintains this and his professional attraction there is of course no need for him to commit himself to an organisation. He will continue to be in demand in the future.

In Table 9.2 we tentatively summarise how identification with the organisation and participation in the work design of employees differ between four idealised types of work organisation.

Will the labour market become segmented and precarious in a projectised economy?

We have so far shown that the mode of production, as well as the contractual relations between organisation and employee differ quite dramatically between different parts of the labour market. We are, of course, aware of the fact that our model, with only four formalised organisational types, is a simplification to say the least. The dividing line between different types can often be blurred, and a typology based on an

Table 9.2 Employee identification with the organisation and participation in work design in different types of organisations

	Identification with		Participation in work design	
	Permanent part	Temporary part	Permanent part	Temporary part
Industrial companies	Strong	Weak	Weak–strong	Strong–weak
Manpower-leasing companies	Weak	Absent	Weak	Absent
Commissioned companies	Weak	Strong	Weak	Strong
Professionals	Lacking	Weak	Lacking	Strong-weak

extended set of variables could of course be devised. However, we believe that the model remains a good starting point, as it encompasses both the way of working for the employee and his position on the labour market. In this section we bring a *dynamic force* to the model by asking ourselves what would happen if the share of the labour force employed in temporary organisations, compared with permanent ones, increased dramatically. In other words, what would happen to the labour market if economic activity became more projectised? Would changes in the different organisational types in terms of size and influence occur if more and more people were engaged in temporary activity? Do such dynamics indicate that some parts of the potential labour force will be marginalised?

If we examine the entire model as it is depicted in Table 9.1, we can conclude that there are marked flows from quadrant A to the others, although the flows are probably of different strength. Quadrant B will reach its size limit. The companies operating in this quadrant have difficulty in penetrating into knowledge-intensive activity. In Sweden, considering international comparisons, it seems that this ceiling is still far from being reached. In addition, it may be in the interest of the leasing companies to have a large 'stable' of individuals at their disposal, thus increasing competition among the individuals on their books, enabling pay to be decreased. The current difficulty in breaking into the labour market, especially for young people, means that the barrier to entry is lower for quadrant B than for the other quadrants. This ensures that manpower-leasing companies have a large supply of potential staff.

In quadrant C, demands on those who are recruited are usually great in terms of knowledge and cooperation. Furthermore, companies in this quadrant are primarily seeking individuals with sound experience of project work which, with the current educational system in most countries, is an impossible requirement for school leavers. However, it is the relation between quadrants A and C that has recently been affected by developments in industry: as we have seen, a combination of consulting and personnel-leasing companies may come to the fore. The permanent parts of consulting companies – and perhaps also of manpower-leasing companies – combine and experiment with various forms of employment, and with commissions and personnel leasing.

In a projectised economy, it may become generally more difficult to gain a foothold in the labour market. Project organisation demands actors with experience: both specialised knowledge and the ability to work in groups. However, insight into an organisation's particular mode of working may also be a requirement, making the barriers to employment in the consultancy companies of quadrant C very high. Becoming part of the permanent 'picked troops' that form the top management (NIM) of neo-industrial organisations is even more difficult since it requires both project knowledge and an aptitude for strategic work. We have already noted that in ABB individuals were promoted to senior managers only after they had proved their worth as project managers.

The competence required in the neo-industrial organisation may contribute to the creation of a 'reserve army' of staff who are able to enter the labour market only where the barriers are low. In our model, those without experience and permanent connections have access to quadrant B and possibly quadrant D. Quadrant B acts as a buffer of variations in economic activity. In times of prosperity or high economic activities, many can find a good occupation, whereas only a few can obtain work in the opposite situation. As we have noted, it is in the interest of these companies to have a large group of people to choose from. It is possible that some people might try to get along in quadrant D as practitioners/freelances, with short assignments. This quadrant includes artists, but also those working on commissions, such as professionals in the construction or IT sector. In sparsely populated areas, people commonly have many and varied occupations, earning their living from a large number of different assignments. Survival in quadrant D is, of course, facilitated in societies with a social security safety net. Activity in quadrant D can also be seen as a platform for innovations and renewal. New ideas are tested on a small scale. If they work, they can form the basis for new companies, which eventually can grow strong. Highly qualified free agents could also contribute to renewal in organisations already established.

This reasoning results in an approximate division of the labour market into different segments. In the middle is a core group, consisting of the staff of permanent, contract-signing parts of the neo-industrial organisation, i.e. the NIM. Around this nucleus is an inner ring containing the project-employed in quadrant C and those who work as industrial subcontractors in quadrant A. The next ring is composed of those who gain temporary employment in quadrants B and D. The outermost ring comprises the unemployed, those who have not managed to breach the barriers of working life. Adopting a military metaphor, we could divide the neo-industrial labour market into 'commanding force', 'supporting troops', 'mercenary troops' and 'reserve army' (Figure 9.1).

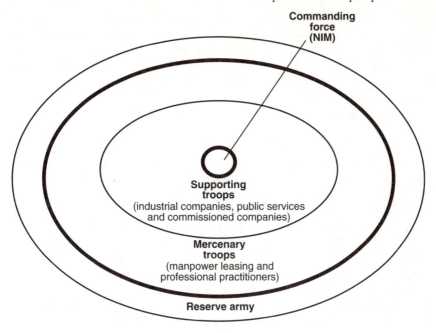

Figure 9.1   Segmentation of the labour market.

Labour force movements

A segmented or polarised labour market is far from new in the industrial economies. A new element in the neo-industrial, projectised economy is the higher barriers between being entirely outside and being part of the labour market. The barriers are due to the high level of knowledge required for project work. A particular dilemma is that project work is to a great extent based on experiential knowledge, a type of knowledge that is difficult to acquire for those who are completely new to the field. As long as the education system continues to neglect this area, and fails to encourage students to gain work experience in realistic project situations, young people will find it difficult to break into the work market. Adapting the education system to the neo-industrial mode of organising would therefore contribute to a lowering of the barriers.

However, an economic system increasingly characterised by a high prevalence of projects could reasonably be expected to have at its disposal a set of people who have been employed in projects that have been completed. Essentially, these individuals are waiting for their next project assignment, and in fact this group constitutes a prerequisite for new projects and for the functioning of a projectised economy. Evidently, there is a need for a human resource broker able to facilitate the combinatorics involved in getting new projects off the ground. In other words, there is a need for an employment agency of a different type. The ability to match available and suitable manpower with existing projects is not the sole task. Initiating and defining projects for the available personnel is an equally credible role. This example serves to illustrate a principal point of our reasoning, namely that traditional institutions of the industrialised society might be forced to make radical changes when they adapt to projectisation.

We have already suggested that the barriers to entry for quadrants B and D (manpower-leasing companies and professionals) are lower than for quadrants A and D (industrial and commissioned companies). Work in these quadrants can be a step on the road to a more stable working life. In some respects, activity in these quadrants appears to be insecure and less attractive. In quadrant B, activity is usually very routinised and simple, but at the same time it is a way for individuals to gain experience of working life, albeit superficial. It is also important for individuals to become known in other parts of working life. People who make a favourable impression on the company to which they have been leased may be permanently recruited. That this situation does in fact occur is evident from the fact that the manpower-leasing companies are introducing more and more long-term employment benefits. Some companies, such as Proffice, in fact speak openly of recruitment as a field of activity. There are also indications that all manpower-leasing companies are not equal. A diversifying and intensifying of competence development is taking place. Personnel in some companies may come to mix routine work in other companies with specific assignments and even outright projects.

Trying to approach more stable terms of employment via quadrant D is probably a rather uncertain approach, but at the same time more challenging than via quadrant B. For strong and creative individuals this can be a route into working life – or more likely – a route back to working life. People who already have strong contacts in the workplace are better qualified to create their own projects or to become engaged in other projects than those with little work experience. This applies to construction workers, for example, who quickly find work when there is construction activity. For those with ambitions to make a name for themselves in some sphere of activity, working as a freelance on a project basis can be seen as a possibility. The attraction of this route is increased by the threat of unemployment otherwise. However, a basic income guaranteed by society may be a prerequisite of daring to go this way.

Efforts to handle the transformation dilemma

The transformation dilemma has its origin in the fact that the organisations and institutions of the industrial society have problems adapting to the new demand patterns (more individualistic ones) and new production conditions (primarily IT) that have developed in recent years. Earlier in the book we dealt chiefly with those problems that concern the renewal capacity of the organisations. We have also touched upon how our examples seem to elucidate the way in which the transformation dilemma has been attacked at the micro level. However, although the transformation dilemma makes itself felt at the local level, it is in fact a matter for the level over and above the local.

The last few years have seen an upsurge of educational efforts concerning temporary organisations, primarily project management. The increase in demand and the increase in efforts to promote such educational ventures seem to correspond with changes in the membership of professional organisations, which have undergone dramatic increases in recent years. Although private institutions (read consultants) appear to be leading the way, traditional universities are also now offering some relevant courses. Courses in project management also seem to be a very popular part of corporate efforts to promote efficiency through continuing staff education. Outside pure educational arenas, PMI and IPMA are also offering certifications in project management. PMI is well known for its certification of project management professionals and, although various competing ventures have been launched, the PMI way has become dominant.

Educational ventures, as well as certification, are currently streamlining the predominant view of what project management is about. The role of the project manager is aligned according to a standard model fostered in the educational material of the major educational suppliers. The dangers in this are evident, since education becomes a portal to the renewal paradox, whereby standardised behaviours are not questioned. At the least it appears that well-intentioned educational efforts might have detrimental effects on practical renewal work. Independent research could be viewed as providing warning signals and a wide range of perspectives on projects. The fact is, however, that research on temporary ventures is uncommon. As mentioned in Chapter 3, organisational theorists very seldom, if ever, study temporary entities from the specific viewpoint of their very temporariness. One obvious reason for this is that research funding seems to come from traditional organisational sources (i.e. research on industry is financed by industry), which not unnaturally prefer to avoid (or at last not promote) matters not related to traditional permanent organisations.

Summarising this discussion of how the transformation dilemma might be treated at levels beyond the micro level, we suggest variety in research and educational efforts in order to make the micro level better able to handle the transformation dilemma. Variability rather than standardisation seems to be more appropriate.

Global renommée and local presence

In this chapter, we have discussed how individuals in the labour market might be affected by increasing projectisation, and we have also alluded to the transformation dilemma. But at the meso level, other questions are important, such as: how will the size and power relations of companies and organisations be influenced? There is, of course, no simple and clear-cut answer to this question, although some fixed points emerge from the previous discussions. What will happen to the institutions that surround and act in the organisations is still more difficult to foresee. What will happen when existing rules and roles become obsolete and are questioned? How will politicians, union leaders, voters, etc. react?

In Chapter 8, we discussed which tasks managers have or should have in various types of organisations. We distinguished between management in permanent organisations, temporary organisations and neo-industrial organisations. These are not three unequivocally different organisations but different ways of organising economic activity. Neo-industrial organising implies the coexistence of permanent and temporary organisations. It can be assumed that NIM primarily develops from the permanent activity of some major organisation, e.g. an organisations such ABB, which was formerly run in a flow-process manner as well as project-organised companies such as Skanska. However, NIM could also have its basis in investment companies that administer ownership. In this chapter we have partly changed perspective and scrutinised organisations from the individual's viewpoint, i.e. how individuals are tied to them. We believe that a flow from traditional industrial companies and other bureaucracies towards commissioned companies, manpower-leasing companies and professionals can be observed. The flow towards commissioned companies is clearly empirically verified. In the extension of this discussion, a segmented labour market concealing various types of organisations is thus conceivable. At the heart are to be found those organisations that house the NIM. Next to them are the commissioned companies and product suppliers. Further out and in looser forms the manpower-leasing companies and the professionals are to be found. These forms could be characterised as some kind of imaginary organisations.

Ultimately, the NIM organisation obtains its strength from the confidence of its customers in the brand name at its disposal. That is what supplies the power and the financial scope to move in many directions. Customers sign agreements and even pay in advance. Subcontractors sign complex contracts. Advanced development projects, e.g. in collaboration with renowned universities, could be started. Well-founded project plans could be presented when bidding for large projects. The permanent organisation around the NIM need not be large. Neither is it necessary for the NIM to be particularly visible. What is important is that its trademark is seen in TV commercials, at airports, on the Internet or worn by well-known sportspeople. The name must come to be associated with successful projects. The NIM, e.g. in the form of the executive office of a corporation, is located with advantage in international financial centres, such as New York, London, Frankfurt, Zurich or Tokyo. For some organisations it is also important to be near to political centres, although this can be risky in the case of organisations with a global status. They do not want a clear national identity. Their aim is to become extra-national.

This is the global side of the neo-industrial organisation; it can have an influence over a very extensive and widespread activity. This influence is quite different from that exercised by the traditional industrial company, where the monitoring of production is directly subordinate to senior management. Here the influence is indirect, through the use of subcontractors and the creation of project groups. Evaluation is market led; inferior subcontractors are screened out if they fall down on the job, and project managers who do not comply with agreements they have entered into will hardly be entrusted with another assignment. Moreover, the NIM can appoint separate specialists on evaluation and audit in order to obtain a better analysis of how the contracted groups work and build up their competence before future commitments.

This shifting of the transaction costs of economic activity from monitoring to negotiation makes it possible to build up very large organisational spheres. These spheres are much looser in composition than the traditional industrial companies, however, and they can quickly change in size according to the supply of projects. Depending on their fields of action, the spheres can be more or less sensitive to economic fluctuations. This, in turn, has effects on other types of organisations. Commissioned companies and product suppliers expand in times of prosperity and downsize in times of recession. It is also conceivable that the state of the market affects the flows between the different types of companies. In times of prosperity, manpower-leasing companies have difficulty in keeping the staff, who receive offers of permanent employment after working for a short time in the client company. Thus, the manpower-leasing companies may come to function as a bridge between unemployment and employment. They might certainly resist the transition by increasing the proportion of remuneration in the form of a fixed salary. In times of depression, these companies can take out insurance in the form of building up a large pool of available staff.

Neo-industrial organising has also a local aspect. Economic activity, i.e. the production and the exchange of services, takes place where production establishments and people are to be found. The increasing service content of almost every activity creates a need for closeness. The work of the companies is carried out in direct interaction with customers wherever they are located. This means, among other things, that commissioned companies tend to establish local, predominantly independent, branches in smaller cities. International companies, such as Digital, Skanska, Cap Gemini and Ernest & Young have been established in many small and medium-sized Swedish cities. There they participate in projects together with industrial companies, municipalities and county councils.

Neo-industrial organising and the traditional institutions

The institutions of the labour market, i.e. its formal and informal rules and roles, have been moulded by a society dominated by traditional industrial companies. In countries such as Sweden, Finland and The Netherlands, the relation between very large companies and a relatively homogeneous and strong trade union movement have made particularly distinct imprints. A transition towards other forms of organising leads to a questioning of the existing system. Already, in relation to companies of the manpower-leasing type, institutional uncertainty is increasing. Working hours are regulated in an indistinct way. Employees have difficulty influencing their work situation because they are not employed where they work and their place of work also changes constantly. It is also conceivable that the employer, i.e. the manpower-leasing company, has little interest in investing in personnel development as long as there exists a large reserve of people from which to draw. If pure leasing of manpower is the leading business concept, the broker function becomes the central one. However, if the manpower-leasing companies broaden their activity, for which some evidence is becoming apparent, it is also in their interest to deepen their relations with their staff, and to prepare them for other and more advanced work tasks.

Organisations of the commissioned companies type (quadrant C) are a still greater threat to the current welfare institutions. In these companies, work is goal and problem directed rather than rule directed. Fulfilling the goals according to a given agreement is the central endeavour; how this is accomplished is more open. A detailed regulation of the relations between the actors is perceived as a hindrance. Projects become the natural way of working, which implies that both spatial and time-based relations between the actors in the market will be manifested in a great number of different arrangements. The work is performed in a great many different ways, in a great number of different constellations and at a great number of places: at home, in the car, with the customer or at a central office. In addition, the rate of working can vary substantially. Some periods in a project are characterised by low activity, whereas in others the work can last almost the whole day and night. In many projects, influence and responsibility are to a great extent delegated irrespective of the kind of formal rule system in place. This state of affairs is in itself hardly a threat to the welfare state: the problem is that many of the present rules bear upon the wrong realities. It takes an institutional development to solve it.

The activity of professional practitioners is, if possible, becoming even more alienated from the traditional industrial model with its institutions. In this case, even the worth of wage/salary work is open to question. Professionals act on their own competence or personality when they carry out activities. The dividing line between work and leisure becomes blurred. Indeed, income from their efforts may even be of secondary importance. The essential thing might be to find fulfilment, to have the opportunity to express one's feelings and to find forms for sharing these with others. The relation between employer and employee is either of an indistinct and occasional nature or absent altogether. As a consequence, the system now regulating these relations is operating in the dark.

But it is not likely to be from the professional circle or from the manpower-leasing companies that the development of the institutions of neo-industrial organising will originate. It will in all probability start from the main economic activity to be found in the relation between the NIM, on the one hand, and the commissioned companies and subcontractors on the other. But how should such rules be formulated to meet the needs of the almost extra-national character of the NIM and also the local connections of the commissioned companies and subcontractors? And who should do this? Which arenas have the capability of covering this spectrum? This is quite another story, however.

A final word of caution

Throughout this book we have striven to form a coherent picture of what we have observed is going on in industry today and how that development can be alleviated and supported in various ways. In essence, we have defined our role as to describe micro details of the current development and to foretell the neo-industrial change at the meso level rather than asking critical questions about that development. In doing so, we realise that our effort may be seen as something that is legitimising and prescribing a social movement that perhaps should be scrutinised with a critical eye instead. The scholarly tasks should also encompass a critical examination. For that reason we want to end the book with a short critical discussion, critical in the sense that the development foreseen may well take a different direction as well as in the sense that there are aspects of this development that will have a major effect on the current power distribution in society and related developments that are not discussed here. This scrutiny will be rudimentary though, meaning that it is an indication of where research should go in the future.

So, is this projectisation taking place? Is there an emerging neo-industrial economy? It should be noted that all the cases we have studied could be described as belonging to the traditional, industrialised part of the world, i.e. generally speaking the Western hemisphere. It might well be that emerging economic giants such as mainland China will change the economic and industrial map of the world considerably at the same time as the functioning of the Chinese economy will make its imprints on the rest of the world, and that influence might have very little to do with the present Western way of thinking of and handling industry. A new set of prototypes may come into vogue. In other words, abundance of examples is no guarantee that the phenomenon will have a dominant role and prevail in the very long term. People are likely to change their ideas and their prescriptions for how to organise society.

Turning to projectisation *per se*, one might argue that in the traditional industrial society the relationship between employers and employees was a significant one for societal development. It also tended to be a very stable one, often turning into some kind of power balance setting the agenda for much societal debate. Projectisation seems to bring with it considerably less stable relationships. Unionisation is currently declining in Sweden as well as in most of the rest of the Western world, and central organisations, labour as well as employers, seem to be losing membership and influence. In a society in which temporariness is playing an increasingly important role, the labour market battles seem to be developing a new strand; it is more of a micro type and less of a general public affair. There no longer seem to be any clear-cut counterparts, or they are becoming anonymous, leaving room for irresolution or vacillation. In this neo-industrial uncertainty in the labour market, new solutions to new as well as old problems are likely to appear. However, our bases for making any statements on that macro level are fairly weak.

All in all, there is considerable room for research on the role of projects and temporary organisations. As indicated in this final section as well as in the rest of the book, it seems that boundary-spanning activities between permanent and temporary organisations are the most crucial when it comes to understanding and handling the transformation that we have labelled neo-industrial organising.

Bibliography

ABB (1994) *50×T50: 50 exempel från olika delar av svenska ABB* (50×T50: 50 *Examples from Various Parts of The Swedish ABB*, in Swedish). Asea Brown Boveri AB, Koncernstab, Information, Västerås, Sweden.

Anderson, Å. E. and Sahlin, N.-E. (1993) 'Framtidens vetenskap' (Science for the future), *Framtider*, 3: 4.

Aoyama, Y. and Castells, M. (1994) 'Path towards the information society: employment structure in the G 7 countries', *International Labour Review*, 133: 1.

Argyris, C. and Schön, D. A. (1978) *Organizational Learning*, Reading, MA: Addison-Wesley.

Bates, R. H. (1989) *Beyond the Miracle of Market*, Cambridge, MA: Cambridge University Press.

Bell, D. (1976) *The Coming of Post-Industrial Society: A Venture in Social Forecasting*, New York: Basic Colophon.

Beniger, J. R. (1986) *The Control Revolution: Technological and Economic Origins of the Information Society*, Cambridge, MA: Harward University Press.

Berger, P. L. and Luckmann, T. (1966) *The Social Construction of Reality : A Treatise in the Sociology of Knowledge*, London: Penguin.

Berry, J. (1983) 'Acculturation: A comparative analysis of alternative forms'. In Samuda, R. J. and Woods, S. L. (eds) *Perspectives in Immigrant and Minority Education*, pp. 66–77, Lanham, MD: University Press of America.

Blomquist, T. and Packendorff, J. (1998) *Ekonomisk styrning för förändring* (*Management Control for Change*, in Swedish), Umeå: Umeå Business School.

Boman, H. (1992) *Förändringen: En berättelse om svenska ABB och T50* (*The Change: A Story about The Swedish ABB and T50*, in Swedish), Stockholm: Affärsvärlden.

Bower, G. H. and Hildegard, E. R. (1981) *Theories of Learning*, Englewood Cliffs, NJ: Prentice-Hall.

Boyle, C., Wheale, P. and Sturgess, B. (1984) *People, Science, and Technology. A Guide to Advanced Industrial Society*, Brighton: Wheatsheaf Books.

Boznak, R. G. (1996) 'Management of projects: a giant step beyond project management', *PMI Network*, X(1): 27–30.

Bresnen, M. (1990) *Organising Construction*, London: Routledge.

Broström, A. (ed.) (1991) *Arbetsorganisation och produktivitet* (*Work Organisation and Productivity*, in Swedish) *Expertrapport nr 5 till Produktivitetsdelegationen*, Stockholm: Allmänna förlaget.

Brytting, T., De Geer, H. and Silfverberg, G. (1993) *Moral i verksamhet* (*Ethics at Work*, in Swedish), Stockholm: Natur och Kultur.

Bröchner, J., Ekstedt, E., Lundin, R. A. and Wirdenius, H. (1991) *Att bygga med kunskap. Förnyelseförmåga i byggsektorn* (*Constructing with Knowledge. Renewal capacity in the Construction Industry*, in Swedish), Stockholm: Byggforskningsrådets förlag.

Burns, T. and Stalker, G. (1961) *The Management of Innovation*, London: Tavistock.

Casey, T. W., Anhua, D., Ekstedt, E., Yijing, L., Rojot, J. and Wirdenius, H. (1996) 'Enterprise, its management and culture: a comparative reflection in a transnational context'. In Nish, C., Redding, G. and Sek-hong, N. (eds) *Work and Society, Labour and Human Resources in East Asia*, Hong Kong: Hong Kong University Press.

Castells, M. (1996) *The Rise of the Network Society*, Malden, MA: Blackwell.

Clegg, S. R. (1990) *Modern Organizations. Organization Studies in the Postmodern World*, London: Sage.

Coase, R. H. (1988) *The Firm, the Market, and the Law*, Chicago: University of Chicago Press.

Cohen, M. D. and Sproull, L. S. (eds) (1996) *Organizational Learning*, Thousand Oaks, CA: Sage.

Cyert, R. M. and March, J. G. (1963) *A Behavioral Theory of the Firm*, Englewood Cliffs, NJ: Prentice-Hall.

Czarniawska, B. and Joerges, B. (1996) 'Travels of ideas'. In Czarniawska, B. and Sevón, G. (eds) *Translating Organizational Change*, pp. 13–48, Berlin: de Gruyter.

Czarniawska, B. and Sevón, G. (1996) *Translating Organizational Change*, Berlin: de Gruyter.

David, P. (1990) 'The dynamo and the computer. A historical perspective on the modern productivity paradox', *American Economic Review*, 80: 4.

Davidow, W. H. and Malone, M. S. (1992) *The Virtual Corporation*, New York: Harper Business.

De Geer, H. and Ekstedt, E. (1991) 'Digital Equipment, att organisera, leda och förnya kunskapsföretag' (Digital Equipment, organising, leading and renewing knowledge intensive firms, in Swedish). In Broström, A. (ed.) *Arbetsorganisation och produktivitet, Expertrapport nr 5 till Produktivitetsdelegationen*, Stockholm: Allmänna förlaget.

Dinsmore, P. (1996) 'Up & down the organization', *PM Network*, X(3): 9–11.

Drucker, P. F. (1969) *The Age of Discontinuity*, New York: Harper & Row.

Eccles, R. G., Nohria, N. and Berkley, J. D. (1992) *Beyond the Hype: Rediscovering the Essence of Management*, Boston, MA: Harvard Business School.

Ekstedt, E. (1988) *Humankapital i brytningstid, Kunskapsuppbyggnad och förnyelse i företag* (*Human Capital in a Period of Rapid Transition – Knowledge Formation and Renewal of Companies*, in Swedish), Stockholm: Allmänna förlaget.

Ekstedt, E. (1991) 'Ericsson i Östersund – att utnyttja kompetensreserven' (Ericsson in Östersund – To utilise the potential of competence, in Swedish). In Broström, A. (ed.) *Arbetsorganisation och produktivitet. Expertrapport nr 5 till Produktivitetsdelegationen*, pp. 79–107, Stockholm: Allmänna förlaget.

Ekstedt, E. (1996) *Cultural Friction – Energy for Renewal of Neo-Industrial Organizations* (working paper), Uppsala: University of Uppsala.

Ekstedt, E. and Henning, R. (1997) 'Western management in Poland and the Baltic States – a study of practical integration'. In Owsinski, J. and Stepniak, A. (eds) *The Nordic- Baltic Europe: Integration Risks, Barriers & Opportunities*, pp. 223–56, Warsaw, Sopot: The Interfaces Institute.

Ekstedt, E. and Söderholm, A. (1998) 'Neo-industrial organizing: linking projects and permanent organization'. In *Proceedings of the Third International Research Network on Organizing by Projects (IRNOP III): The Nature and Role of Projects in the Next 20 years: Research Issues and Problems*, Calgary, 6–8 July 1998.

Ekstedt, E. and Wirdenius, H. (1992) 'Kompetensutveckling i projektorganiserade företag – rollförändringar i byggprocessen' (Competence development in project organised companies – role changes in the construction process, in Swedish). In Marking, C. (ed.) *Kompetens i Arbete*, Kompetensutredningen, Stockholm: Publica.

Ekstedt, E. and Wirdenius, H. (1993) *Knowledge Transfer and Mental Change: Applying Project Management in the Reconstruction of a Polish–Swedish Engineering Company*, pp. 324–29, Moscow: Internet Proceedings.

Ekstedt, E. and Wirdenius, H. (1994a) *Beyond PMBOK for Renewal Projects*, Proceedings of the Project Management Institute Conference, Vancouver.

Ekstedt, E. and Wirdenius, H. (1994b) *Communication of Renewal Projects: Comparing a National Professional Service Organization and an International Manufacturing Company*(working paper), Stockholm: FAInstitute.

Ekstedt, E. and Wirdenius, H. (1994c) *Renewal and the Embeddedness of Knowledge: Towards a Comprehensive View of the Development of Knowledge in Organizations* (working paper), Stockholm: FAInstitute.

Ekstedt, E. and Wirdenius, H. (1995) 'Renewal projects: sender target and receiver competence in ABB "T50" and Skanska "3T"', *Scandinavian Journal of Management*, 11: 409–21.

Ekstedt, E. and Wirdenius, H. (1996) 'Struktur, Institution och Individ: Kunskapens bindning och organisationers förnyelse' (Structure, institution and individual: Knowledge embeddedness and organisational renewal, in Swedish). In Ekvall, G. (ed.) *Navigatör och inspiratör*, Stockholm: Studentlitteratur.

Ekstedt, E., Lundin, R. A. and Wirdenius, H. (1992) 'Conceptions and renewal in construction companies', *European Management Journal*, 10: 202–9.

Ekstedt, E., Lundin, R. A., Söderholm, A. and Wirdenius, H. (1993) *Project Organization in the Squeeze between Short-run Flexibility and Long-run Inertia*, Proceedings of Project Management Institute Conference, San Diego. pp. 586–90.

Ekstedt, E., Henning, R., Andersson, R., Elvander, N., Forsgren, M., Malmberg, A. and Norgren, L. (1994) *Kulturell friktion: Konfliktkälla och förnyelsekraft i en integrerad ekonomi (Cultural Friction. Source of Conflict and Renewal Force in an Integrated Economy*, in Swedish), Stockholm: SNS.

Ekvall, G. (1990) *Idéer, organisationsklimat och ledningsfilosofi (Ideas, Organizational Climate and Leadership Philosophy*, in Swedish), Stockholm: Norstedts.

Eliasson, G. (1992) *Arbetet – dess betydelse, dess innehåll dess kvalitet och dess ersättning (Work – Its Significance, Contents, Quality and Pay*, in Swedish), Stockholm: Almqvist & Wiksell.

Elvander, N. and Elvander-Seim, A. (1995) *Gränslös samverkan. Fackets svar på företagens internationalisering (Unbounded Cooperation. Labour Union Response to the Internationalisation of Enterprises*, in Swedish), Stockholm: SNS.

Eneroth, B. (1990) *Att handla på känn (To Act by Instinct*, in Swedish), Stockholm: Natur och kultur.

Engwall, M. (1995) *Jakten på det effektiva projektet (Hunting for the Effective Project*, in Swedish), Stockholm: Nerenius & Santérus.

Eriksson, J. (1997) *Drivkrafter bakom projekt. Förekomsten av projekt ur ett institutionellt och populationsekologiskt perspektiv* (*Driving Forces behind Projects. The Prevalence of Projects from an Institutional and Population Ecology Perspective*, in Swedish), unpublished MBA thesis, University of Umeå.

Eskerod, P. (1997) *Nye perspektiver på fordeling af menneskelige ressourcer i et projektorganiseret multiprojekt-miljø* (*New Perspectives on Allocation of Human Resources in a Multiproject Context Managed by Projects*, in Danish), diss, Handelshøjskole Syd, Sønderborg.

Eskerod, P. and Östergren, K. (1998) 'Bureaucratizing projects? – on the standardization trend'. In Hartman, F., Jergeas, G. and Thomas, J. (eds) *IRNOP III Proceedings – The Nature and Role of Projects in the Next 20 Years: Research Issues and Problems*, Calgary: University of Calgary.

Ester, P., Halman, L. and de Moor, R. (eds) (1994) *The Individualizing Society. Value Change in Europe and North America*, Tilburg: Tilburg University Press.

Eurich, N.P., (1985) *Corporate Classrooms*, Princeton, NJ: Princeton University Press.

Ferlie, E. and McNulty, T. (1997) '"Going to market": changing patterns in the organization and character of process research,'*Scandinavian Journal of Management*, 13: 367–387.

Finkelstein, J. (1986) *The Third Industrial Revolution – Questions and Implications for Historians*, Proceedings of the World Conference in Economic History, Bern.

Forsman, A. (1984) *Det nya tjänstesamhället*. Stockholm: Gidlunds.

Foucault, M. (1987) *Övervakning och straff – fängelsets födelse* (*Supervision and Punishment – the Birth of Prisons*, Swedish translation from the French original), Lund: Studentlitteratur.

Freeman, C., Clark, J. and Luc, S. (1983) *Unemployment and Technical Innovation. A Study of Long Waves and Economic development*, London: Frances Pinter.

Fukuyama, F. (1995) *Trust – The Social Virtues and the Creation of Prosperity*, London: Hamish Hamilton.

Furåker, B. (1995) 'Tjänstesamhälle eller postindustriellt samhälle – Några begrepp och teoretiska perspektiv' (Service society or post-industrial society – some concepts and theoretical perspectives, in Swedish). In Svensson, L. G. and Orban, P. (eds) *Människan i Tjänstesamhället* (*The Human Being in the Service Society*, in Swedish), Lund: Studentlitteratur.

Galbraith, J. R. (1977) *Organization Design*, Reading, MA: Addison Wesley.

Gareis, R. (1990) *Handbook of Management by Projects*, Vienna: Manz.

Gershuny, J. and Miles, I. (1983) *The New Service Economy. The Transformation of Employment in Industrial Societies*, London: Frances Pinter.

Gersick, C. (1988) 'Time and transitions in work teams', *Academy of Management Journal*, 31: 9–41.

Giddens, A. (1976) *New rules of Sociological Method*, London: Hutchinson.

Giddens, A. (1984) *The Constitution of Society. Outline of the Theory of Structure*, Berkeley, CA: University of California Press.

Gioia, D. A. and Poole, P. P. (1984) 'Scripts in organizational behavior', *Academy of Management Review*, 9: 449–59.

Glaser, B. G. and Strauss, A. L. (1967) *The Discovery of Grounded Theory. Strategies for Qualitative Research*, Chicago: Aldine Publishing Company.

Grabher, G. (1989) *Against De-Industralisation. A Strategy for Old Industrial Areas*, Berlin: Proceedings Wissenshaftzentrum Berlin.

Granovetter, M. (1973) 'The strength of weak ties', *American Journal of Sociology*, 78: 1360–80.

Hampden Turner, C. (1990) *Corporate Culture – from Vicious to Virtuous Circles*, London: Hutchinson.

Handy, C (1989) *The Age of Unreason*, London: Business Books Limited.

Harré, R. and Gillett, G. (1994) *The Discursive Mind*, Thousand Oaks, CA: Sage.

Hart, H. and Berger, A. (1994) *Using Time to Generate Corporate Renewal: Experiences from the T50-Programme in Asea Brown Boveri, Sweden*, Proceedings of the 4th International Production Management Conference on Managment and New Production Systems, London.

Hedberg, B., Nyström, P. and Starbuck, W. (1976) 'Camping on seesaws: Prescriptions for a self-designing organization', *Administrative Science Quarterly*, 21: 41–65.

Hedberg, B., Dahlgren, G., Hansson, J. and Olve, N.-G. (1997) *Virtual Organizations and Beyond – Discover Imaginary Systems*, Chichester: Wiley.

Helvey, T. C. (1971) *The Age of Information – An Interdisciplinary Survey of Cybernetics*, Englewood Cliffs, NJ: Prentice-Hall.

Henning, R. and Norgren, L. (1992) 'Formerna för teknikutvecklingens internationalisering' (The forms for technological development and internationalisation, in Swedish), *Ekonomisk Debatt* 2.

Hirshman, A.O., (1970) *Exit, Voice and Loyalty. Resposes to Decline in Firms, Organizations, and States*, Cambridge MA: Harward University Press.

Hofstede, G. (1980, 1993) *Culture's Consequenses. International Differences in Work-Related Values*, Beverly Hills, CA: Sage.

Holm, U. (1994) *Internationalization of Second Degree* (dissertation), Uppsala: Acta Universitatis Upsaliensis.

Huemer, L. (1998) *Trust in Business Relations. Economic Logic or Social Interaction*, Umeå: Boréa.

Hägg, I. and Johansson, J. (1982) *Företag i nätverk. Ny syn på konkurrenkraft* (*Companies in Networks. A New Perspective on Competitive Strength*, in Swedish), Stockholm: SNS.

Illeris, S. (1996) *The Service Economy – A Geographical Approach*, Chichester: Wiley.

Ingelhart, R. (1990) *Cultural Shift in Advanced Industrial Society*, Princeton, NJ: Princeton University Press.

Jameson, F. (1985) 'Postmodernism and consumer society'. In Foster, I. H. (ed.) *Postmodern Culture*, London: Pluto Press.

Jansson, D. (1992) *Spelet kring investeringskalkyler: Om den strategiska användningen av det för-givet-tagna* (*The Game Around Investment Calculations: on the Strategic Use of the Taken-for-Granted*, in Swedish), Stockholm: Norstedts.

Jarillo, J. C. (1993) *Strategic Networks. Creating the Borderless Organization*, Oxford: Butterworth Heinemann.

Jepperson, R. L. (1991) 'Institutions, institutional effects, and institutionalism'. In W. W. Powell and P. J. DiMaggio (eds) *The New Institutionalism in Organizational Analysis*, pp. 143-63, Chicago: University of Chicago Press.

Johansson, J. and Mattson, L.-G. (1987) 'Interorganizational relations in industrial systems: a network approach compared with the transaction-cost approach', *International Studies of Management and Organization*, 17(1): 34–48.

Jönsson, S. (1995) *Goda utsikter: Svenskt Management i perspektiv* (*Good Prospects: Swedish Management in Perspective*, in Swedish), Stockholm: Nerenius & Santérus.

Jörberg, L. (1982) *Konjunktur, struktur och internationellt beroende – Industriella kriser i svensk ekonomi* (*Trade Conditions, Structure and International Dependence – Industrial Crises in the Swedish Economy*, in Swedish), Lund: Economic History Department.

Kanter, R. M. (1989) *When Giants Learn to Dance*, London: Simon & Schuster.

Krosse, H. A. J., Paauwe, J. and Williams, A. R. T. (eds) (1996) *Shared Frontiers of Learning*, Delft: Eburon.

Kuhn, T. S. (1970) *The Structure of Scientific Revolutions*, Chicago: University of Chicago Press.

Kungliga Teatern (1986) *Innan ridån går upp* (*Before the Curtain Rises*, in Swedish), Stockholm: Royal Opera.

Laine-Sveiby, K. (1991) *Företag i kulturmöten* (*Corporations in Cultural Meetings*, dissertation, in Swedish), University of Stockholm.

Lant, T. K. and Mezias, S. J. (1990) 'Managing discontinuous change: a simulation study of organizational learning and entrepreneurship', *Strategic Management Journal*, 11: 147–80.

Lasch, C. (1978) *The Culture of Narcissism*, New York: Norton.

Lawrence, P. R. and Lorsch, J. W. (1967) *Organization and Environment. Managing Differentiation and Integration*, Boston: Harvard University Press.

Lewis, R. (1973) *The New Service Society*, London: Longman.

Lientz, B. P.and Rea, K. P. (1995) *Project Management for the 21st Century*, San Diego: Academic Press.

Lindbergh, L. and Sandström, C. (1994) *Produktutveckling som projekt: En studie av Saab 2000 och Volvo 850* (*Product Development as a Project: A Study of the Saab 2000 and Volvo 850*, working paper, in Swedish), Umeå: Umeå Business School, Umeå University.

Lorentzoni, G. (1981) *From Vertical Integration to Vertical Disintegration*, Bologna: University of Bologna.

Louis, M. R. (1981) 'A cultural perspective on organizations: the need for and consequences of viewing organizations as culture-bearing milieux', *Human Systems Management*, 2: 246–58.

Louise database (1996) Örebro: Statistics Sweden.

Lundgren, K. (1998) *Life-Long Learning. The Key to Europe's Economic Revival*, Stockholm: National Institute for Working Life.

Lundgren, K. and Wirberg, S. (1997) *IT-Rapporten. Om kunskapsbaserad ekonomi, sysselsättning och förändrade kompetenskrav* (*About Knowledge-based Economy, Employment and Changed Requirements for Competence*, in Swedish), Stockholm: National Institute for Working Life.

Lundin, R. A. and Midler C. (eds) (1998) *Projects as Arenas for Renewal and Learning Processes*, Norwell, MA: Kluwer Academic Publishers.

Lundin, R. A. and Söderholm, A. (1993) *Renewal of Complex Organizations: A Project Approach*, pp. 60–5. Moscow: Internet Proceedings.

Lundin, R. A. and Söderholm, A. (1994) 'Management for renewal – culture moulded by imaginization', presented at the IFSAM Conference 'Linking Management Scholars Worldswide' in Dallas, Texas, 17–19 August 1994, Summary in 'Proceedings', pp. 116–17.

Lundin, R. A. and Söderholm, A. (1995) 'A theory of the temporary organization', *Scandinavian Journal of Management*, 11: 437–55.

Lundin, R. A. and Söderholm, A. (1997) *Ledning för förnyelse i landsting: Strategiska projekt i komplexa organisationer* (*Management for Renewal in Health Care Organizations: Strategic Projects in Complex Organizations*, in Swedish), Stockholm: Nerenius & Santérus.

Lundin, R. A. and Wirdenius, H. (1989) *Företagsförnyelse och kulturskifte: Erfarenheter från Diös-koncernen* (*Enterprise Renewal and Culture Shift: Experiences from the Diös Group*, in Swedish), Stockholm: Norstedts.

Lundin, R. A. and Wirdenius, H. (1990) 'Interactive research', *Scandinavian Journal of Management*, 6(2): 12–142.

Lundin, R. A. and Wirdenius, H. (1995) *Opera and Theater Projects as Arenas and Vehicles for Change and Learning* (working paper), Umeå: Umeå Business School, Umeå University.

Lundin, R. A., Söderholm, A. and Wirdenius, H. (1992) *Att bygga den moderna kunskapsstaden* (*To Build the Modern Knowledge-Based City*, working paper, in Swedish), Umeå: Umeå Business School, Umeå University.

Lundin, R. A., Müllern, T., Söderholm, A. Wirdenius, H. and Östergren, K. (1995) *En analys av de projektadministrativa förutsättningarna för JAS-projektets genomförande: En slutrapport till RRV från Sveolin AB* (*An Analysis of the Project Management Bases for the Realization of the JAS Project: A Final Report to the National Auditing Board from Sveolin AB*, in Swedish), Umeå: Sveolin AB.

Lyttkens, L. (1981) *Människors möten* (*People's Meetings*, in Swedish), Lund: Doxa.

Machlup, F. (1962) *The Production and Distribution of Knowledge in the United States*, Princeton, NJ: Princeton University Press.

March, J. G. (1988) *Decisions and Organizations*, Oxford: Basil Blackwell.

March, J. G. (1995) 'The future, disposable organizations and the rigidities of imagination', *Organization*, 2: 427–40.

March, J. G. and Olsen, J. P. (1989) *Rediscovering Institutions. The organizational Basis of Politics*, New York: The Free Press.

Martin, J. and Butler, D. (1981) *Viewdata and the Information Society*, Englewood Cliffs, NJ: Prentice-Hall.

Mead, G. H. (1934) *Mind, Self and Society. From the Standpoint of a Social Behaviorist*, Chicago: University of Chicago.

Midler, C. (1995) '"Projectification" of the firm: The Renault case', *Scandinavian Journal of Management*, 11: 363–75.

Miner, A. S. and Mezias, S. J. (1996) 'Ugly duckling no more: Pasts and futures of organizational learning research', *Organization Science*, 7(1): 88–99.

Myhrholm, M. and Ullström, J. (1997) *Strukturell sysselsättningsomvandling i Sverige och i G7-länderna 1920–1990* (*Structural change in Occupations in Sweden and in the G7 Countries 1920–90*, working paper), University of Uppsala.

Naisbitt, J. (1982) *Megatrends. Ten New Directions Transforming our Lives*, New York: Warner Books.

Nish, I., Redding, G. and Ng Sek-hong (eds) (1996) *Work and Society: Labour and Human Resources in East Asia*, Hong Kong: Hong Kong University Press.

Nonaka, I. and Takeuchi, H. (1995) *The Knowledge-Creating Company – How Japanese companies Create the Dynamics of Innovation*, Oxford: Oxford University Press.

Norén, L (1995) *Tolkande företagsekonomisk forskning* (*Interpretative Research in Business Administration*, in Swedish), Lund: Studentlitteratur.

Norgren, L. (1989) *Kunskapsöverföring från universitet till företag. En studie av universitetsforskningens betydelse för de svenska läkemedelsföretagens produktlanseringar 1945–1984* (*The Transfer of Knowledge from University to Company. A Study of the Importance of University Research for the Introduction of New Products in the Swedish Pharmaceutical Industry, 1945–1984*). Stockholm: Allmänna Förlaget.

North, D. C. (1990) *Institutions, Institutional Growth and Economic Performance*, Cambridge, UK, Cambridge University Press.

Orlikowski, W. (1992) 'The duality of technology: rethinking the concept of technology in organizations', *Organization Science*, 3: 398–427.

Orlikowski, W. and Robey, D. (1991) 'Information technology and structuring of organizations', *Information Systems Research*, 2: 143–69.

Østerberg, D. (1986) *Metasocialogisk essä* (*Meta-sociological Essay*, in Swedish), Gothenburg: Korpen.

Östholm, I., Eliasson, G., Reinius, U. and Sandberg, N-E. (1996) *Nya skapelser. Losec-entreprenörens recept* (*New Creations. The ordinations from the Entrepreneurs of Losec*, in Swedish), Smedjebacken: Fischer & Co.

Peters, T. J. and Waterman, R. H. Jr (1982) *In Search of Excellence*, New York: Harper & Row.

Pfeffer, J. and Salancik, G. R. (1978) *The External Control of Organizations. A Resource Dependence Perspective*, New York: Harper & Row.

Piore, M. and Sabel, C. (1984) *The Second Industrial Divide*, New York: Basic Books.

Philips, Å. (1988) *Eldsjälar* (*Souls of Fire*), Stockholm: EFI.

Pmbok guide (1996) *A Guide to the Project Management Book of Knowledge*, Upper Darby, PA: PMI.

Polanyi, M. (1958) *Personal Knowledge*, London: Routledge & Keagan Paul.

Pondy, L. R., Frost, P. J., Morgan, G. and Dandridge, T. C. (eds) (1983) *Organizational Symbolism*, Greenwich, CT: JAI Press.

Powell, W. W. (1990) 'Neither market nor hierarchy: network forms of organization', in Staw, B.M. and Cummings, L. L. (eds), *Research in Organizational Behavior,* Vol. 12, pp. 295–336, Greenwich, CT: JAI Press.

Powell, W. W. and DiMaggio, P. J. (1991) *The New Institutionalism in Organizational Analysis*. Chicago: The University of Chicago Press.

Pugh, D. and Hinings, C. R. (1976) *Organizationl Structure: Extensions and Replications: the Aston Programme II*, Farnborough, UK: Saxon House.

Putnam, R. D. (1993) *Making Democracy Work: Civic Traditions in Modern Italy*, Princeton, NJ: Princeton University Press.

Rolf, B. (1991) *Profession, tradition och tyst kunskap* (*Profession, Tradition, and Tacit Knowledge*, in Swedish), Nora: Nya Doxa.

Rolf, B., Ekstedt, E. and Barnett, R. (1993) *Kvalitet och kunskapsprocess i högre utbildning* (*Quality and Knowledge Processes in Higher Education*, in Swedish), Nora: Nya Doxa.

Rosenberg, N. (1994) *Exploring the Black Box. Technology, Economics and History*, Cambridge, MA: Cambridge University Press.

Røvik, K.-A. (1996) 'Deinstitutionalization and the logic of fashion', in Czarniawska, B. and Sevón, G. (eds) *Translating Organizational Change*, Berlin: Walter de Gruyter.

Schein, E. (1996) 'Culture: The missing concept in organization studies', *Administrative Science Quarterly*, 40: 229–40.

Schumpeter, J. A. (1966/1943) *Capitalism, Socialism and Democracy*, London: Allen & Unwin.

Schön, D. A. (1983) *The Reflective Practitioner: How Professionals Think in Action*, London: Temple Smith.

Scott, W. R. (1995) *Institutions and Organizations*, Thousand Oaks, CA: Sage.

Scott, W. R., Meyer, J. W. and Associates (1994) *Institutional Environments and Organizations. Structural Complexity and Individualism,* Thousand Oaks, CA: Sage.

Selznick, P. (1957) *Leadership in Administration,* New York: Harper & Row.

Senge, P. M. (1990a), *The Fifth Discipline: The Art and Practice of the Learning Organization,* New York: Doubledaykap.

Senge, P. M. (1990b) 'The leader's new work: building learning organizations'. *Sloan Management Review,* 32(1): 7–23.

Shani, A. B. and Stjernberg, T. (1994) 'Integration of change in organizations: alternative learning and transformation mechanisms'. In Pasmore, W. A. and Woodman R. W. (eds) *Research in Organizational Change and Development,* Greenwich, CO: JAI Press.

Simon, H. (1947) *Administrative Behavior: A Study of Decision-making Processes in Administrative Organization,* New York: Macmillan.

Singelman, J. (1978) *From Agriculture to Services,* London: Sage.

Sjöstrand, S.-E. (ed.) (1993) *Institutional Change. Theory and Empirical Findings,* New York: Sharpe.

Skog, E. (1996) *Diversity: Så satsar amerikanska företag på mångfald* (*Diversity. How American Companies Embrace Multiplicity,* in Swedish), Stockholm: IVA.

Smircich, L. (1983) 'Concepts of culture and organizational analysis', *Administrative Science Quarterly,* 28: 339–58.

Snehota, I. (1990) *Notes on a Theory of Business Enterprise,* Uppsala: Uppsala Universitet.

Sparby, M. (ed.) (1986) *Unga Klara: Barnteater som konst* (*Child and Youth as Art,* in Swedish), Stockholm-Hedemora: Gidlunds.

Steen, R. (1991) ABB distribution. in Eklund, K. (ed.) *Arbetsorganisation och produktivitet* (*Work Organization and Productivity,* in Swedish). Expert Report Number 5 to the Productivity Delegation, Stockholm.

Storper, M. and Salais, R. (1997) *Worlds of Production. The Action Framework of the Economy,* Cambridge, MA: Harvard University Press.

Sundin, E. (1996) 'Kulturell mix bakom Astra-framgång' ('Cultural mix behind the astra success', in Swedish), *Headhunter,* 13: 1–4.

Sveiby, K.-E. (1997) *The New Organizational Wealth: Managing and Measuring Knowledge Based Assets,* San Fransisco: Berret–Koeler.

Sveiby, K.-E. and Risling, A. (1986) *Kunskapsföretaget – seklets viktigaste ledarutmaning* (*The Knowledge-Intensive Company – The Most Important Challenge for Management of this Century,* in Swedish), Malmö: Liber.

Swierczek, F. and Hirsch, G. (1994) 'Joint ventures in Asia and Multicultural Management', *European Management Journal,* 12, 2:197–209.

Touraine, A. (1971) *The Post-Industrial Society,* New York: Random House.

Turner, B. A. (1971) *Exploring the Industrial Subculture,* London: Macmillan.

Tyre, M. J. and Orlikowski, W. J. (1994) 'Windows of Opportunity: Temporal Patterns of Technological Adaptation in Organizations', *Organization Science,* 5, 1: 98–118.

von Wright, G. H. (1967) 'The logic of action. A sketch'. In N. Rescher (ed.) *The Logic of Decision and Action,* pp. 121–46, Pittsburgh: University of Pittsburgh Press.

Weber, M. (1968) *Economy and Society: An Interpretative Sociology,* Vol. 3, New York: Bedminister Press (first published 1924).

Weick, K. E. (1969) *The Social psychology of Organizing*, Reading, MA: Addison-Wesley.

Wikman, A., Andersson, A. and Bastin, M. (1998) *Nya relationer i arbetslivet. (New Relations in Working Life*.). Örebro and Solna: Statistics Sweden and National Institute of Working Life.

Wikström, S., Elg, U. and Johansson, U. (1989) *Den dolda förnyelsen. En granskning av konsumentföretagens och konsumtionens omvandling* (The hidden renewal. Scrutinizing change of consumer companies and consumption), Kristianstad SNS förlag.

Williamson, O. E. (1983) *Markets and Hierarchies, Analyses and Antitrust Implications*, New York: The Free Press.

Wilson, T. L. (1982) *Patterns of Successful Project Unshelving in Industrial Business Development* (PhD thesis). Cleveland, OH: Case-Western Reserve University.

Winch, P. (1958) *The Idea of Social Science*, London: Routledge.

Wirdenius, H. (1991) *Ledning mot förnyelse: Erfarenheter från byggbranschen (Management towards Renewal: Experiences from the Construction Industry*, in Swedish, Stockholm: Building Research Council.

Wirdenius, H. (1992) *Transcribed Interview with H. Peralta and A. Peinado, Côte d'Azur Development, Nice, 1 October 1992*, Stockholm: FAInstitute.

Wirdenius, H. (1994) *Corporate Renewal Projects: ABB T50 vs. Skanska 3T* (working paper), Stockholm: FAInstitute.

Yle-Anttila, P. (1997) *ICT-O Benchmarking. Benchmarking the Diffusion and Benefits of New Information and Communication Technologies (ICT) and Organisational Arrangements (O)* (working paper), Helsinki: ETLA

Zuboff, S. (1988) *In the Age of the Smart Machine – The Future of Work and Power*, New York: Basic Books.

Index